How to die happy

by

Martin O'Toole

Written and edited by Martin O'Toole
Cover design: Josh Kimnell
Illustrations: Josh Kimnell
Layout: Josh Kimnell & Martin O'Toole
Proofreader: Becky Ashwell

Published by
Lawrence Goes Rogue (Publishing) Ltd
First edition printing, February 2023

Visit:
howtodiehappybook.com
howtodiehappypodcast.com

Follow:
@martinotoole
@howtodiehappy_podcast

Paperback ISBN: 978-1-7393155-0-4
E-book ISBN: 978-1-7393155-1-1
Audiobook ISBN: 978-1-7393155-2-8

With Gratitude

This book would not exist were it not for the support and input from a cherished few and, the divine creativity of many.

In curating the wise words and philosophies of many great human thinkers, I've made every effort to credit all people quoted under fair use. Please get in touch if anyone has been miscredited or if a correction is required. Future editions will be updated accordingly.

Huge thanks to Terae for your candid feedback — lovingly and succinctly delivered as always. This book is better because you told me the truth.

Love to James for introducing me to the healing potency of the super-intelligent Ayahuasca and Huachuma plants. You strapped my awakening to a rocket.

Thanks to Jules for your unwavering support and endless patience. And thank you for the constant reminders to live by my own advice.

Gratitude to all the listeners, guests, and contributors to the *How To Die Happy* podcast. Earth School is a better place with you in attendance.

And finally, here's to you, the heroes who dare to self-inquire, posing the question of all questions: "Who am I?" You are beautiful expressions of loving awareness. May your journey to know thyself be blessed with many fruitful lessons. Peace and love to you all.

For Jules

Thank you for your unending support
of my transformation as a writer, guiding
me to become a better man, and showing
me facets of love I did not know existed.

I see and honour you
with all my heart and soul.

This Book

Many excellent books already tackle specific facets of mindfulness, mental health, and personal and spiritual development. They collectively pave the way for readers to create a new and happy life. As the title suggests, this book rises to the challenge of answering one of life's great mysteries — in one volume. As you read on, you will learn that there is no singular panacea for finding everlasting happiness. Depending on your conditioning and past experiences, a great deal of work may be required.

Sustainable contentment cannot be hacked. Hence, you and I must explore distraction, death, and the crucial role of impermanence in a vibrant and contented life. We shall study the anatomy of happiness. We'll introduce and discuss concepts and methods that lay the foundations for your personal growth journey.

A Sidenote About Samsara

Throughout this book, I refer to the game of life as "Samsara", the Buddhist name for the phenomenon of existence, otherwise referred to as "the wheel of suffering".

Samsara is the endless cycle of birth, death, and rebirth, peppered with a healthy smidgen of adversity. Regardless of our willingness, as living participants in this game, you and I are Samsaric citizens. So how should we live in this place to enjoy all it offers, accepting our pain while mastering our suffering?

Table of Contents

The Paradoxical Pursuit of Happiness

It's a pleasure to introduce *How To Die Happy*, by Martin O'Toole. He isn't an internationally renowned qi gong teacher or spiritual master (that's me), so I don't know what he's doing writing a book about happiness in the first place. I'm happy — read my book! Of course, I try the wit and cheeky charm of Mr O'Toole; but such treasure can only be found within this book's pages.

It's not common for a recovered addict with a former life of suffering to share wisdom and insights on the elusive and often paradoxical concept of happiness. You see, Martin was not a student of mine. Or maybe, in the greater sense, he is. The student has surpassed the teacher. Wait — hold on a second. He is both unqualified *and* qualified to write this book. Maybe, therefore, I'm unqualified to write this foreword? Paradox mirrors the same contradiction in the very nature of the pursuit of happiness. But, as Martin demonstrates in this book, it is through embracing the oddities and contradictions that we can find true joy and contentment.

Mr O'Toole has masterfully woven together the teachings of ancient wisdom keepers whom I call upon often — Lao Tzu, the Buddha, and Confucius, to name a few. This madman has found a way to weave such wisdom into a tapestry of interconnected insight and understanding. The result is a charming and witty guide to attaining happiness that is both heartfelt and funny. Plus, there are pictures — he calls them "diagrams". "To find happiness, you'll need a map", I like to say.

With his straightforward and easy-to-follow *Anatomy of Happy*, Martin has distilled a selection of lessons and teachings of the great masters into a single, accessible guide for all of us to follow. Whether a seasoned practitioner or a curious beginner, *How To Die Happy* will provide you with the tools and understanding you need to cultivate lasting joy and happiness in your life.

So sit back, relax, and allow this guide to take you on a transformative journey. Your happiness awaits.

With cheeky, O'Toole-inspired gratitude,

— Lee Holden, founder of Holden Qi Gong, international meditation and qi gong instructor, author, and TV personality.

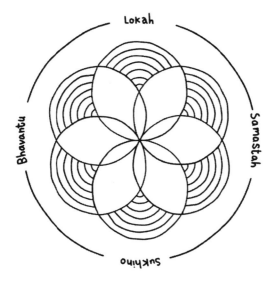

Lokah

Samastah

Sukhino

Bhavantu

How to Die Happy

Writing this book, I was acutely aware I must tread carefully around several particularly sticky territories, expressing views that might challenge 21st-century conventional and materialist thinking. I kept returning to the same thing: all I can do is speak my truth, borne from my personal experience of curating and working with psychological, psychedelic, physical, and spiritual wisdom, some of which dates back thousands of years. Some might find the ancient and religious nature of said teachings challenging. Such knowledge has been forgotten or distorted by man's inherent need to brand Universal wisdom with ego, thus warping its purity and rendering it less accessible. Men did the warping because men created our religious systems of control.

Ultimately, *How To Die Happy* is a guide to understanding the anatomy of happiness, written by someone who never thought he could be happy (that's me). Whatever your beliefs, this book is stuffed with practical insights and a process anyone can follow to find a meaningful daily practice that produces a natural state of joy. Achieving such a pseudo-Nirvanic state calls for self-inquiry, work and sacrifice, but it will be your most meaningful endeavour in this lifetime.

It's funny to write about death and happiness — the latter being a prize actively pursued by the majority; the former, we go out of our way to ignore. And what is happiness anyway? Why on earth should we expect such a thing? Is it even attainable in these days of distraction and despair? There's a cosmic joke in all of this, the irony of which is certainly not lost on me. Having spent decades living in a constant state of abject fear and the suffering naturally accrued through the pursuit of success, I was gifted a second chance. Coming full circle was made possible through a process of voluntarily dying before it was my time to die. There were many fantastic byproducts of this beautifully messy metamorphosis. One bonus being that I now fully embrace the transformative power of life in the present moment.

The third potentially prickly territory involves critical observation of certain aspects of our modern-day consumerist way of life. I assert that what we in the developed world believe to be "reality" adversely affects the growth potential of our individual and collective psyches. So, to do a deep-dive exploration into the many facets of the anatomy of happiness, we must also consider life's superficiality, with the hope of transforming one's mood and mindset.

Amidst sharing the ancient and contemporary wisdom of others is a collection of personal stories animating some of the philosophical and theological theories shared while illustrating our potential for change. You'll find much relatable, some perhaps fantastical. Either way, I hope it entertains, and that this book sheds light on happiness and your healthy pursuit of this most sought-after prize.

In Part One, we'll point a bright beam at the taboo of all taboos, namely death and *dying*. Whether or not you believe death to be the end is broadly irrelevant as long as together, we can conclude that life is worth living and loving. Given the inevitable fact that all our lives will cease, we may wish to spend more time engineering a life story less likely to result in regret. Some people believe you cannot plan for death. This book aims to bury such ideas while unearthing the blueprints to dying well, hidden right under our noses, in how we choose to live. Hence, Part Two discusses *doing*, and Part Three, *being*. The anatomy of happiness is accessible to everyone, and as with all things, it boils down to choice.

Are you drowning in a sea of self-suffering? Do you feel uninspired by life on the hamster wheel? Perhaps you think there's more to living, yet you cannot see the wood through the trees. Or have you already begun the work of personal development — pushed through that impossible break, and are headed towards the open ocean? Do you seek possibilities that will redefine your life's journey? Wherever this book finds you, consider this an invitation to re-evaluate two of the least appreciated yet powerful tools at your disposal: choice and free will. These gifts define our journeys. Their tremendous power can change everything you think you know, enabling you to write a new life story less focused on the final pages than on the enthralling chapters that precede.

While I utilise examples of my life story, this book is about you, and humanity's boundless potential. To explore our shared relationship with life, happiness and death, I must first tell you how I came to be a self-taught expert in the art of suffering.

Part One

Dying

CHAPTER ONE

A Life of Ten Men

The secret of life is to "die before you die" — and find that there is no death.

— Eckhart Tolle

I would often begin my stories by saying, "I've lived the life of ten men!" because cataloguing my co-created stories of self-suffering seemed to entertain and make me more attractive. Although, when one is addicted to drama, one does accrue a tale or two, destructive and perverse as they may often turn out to be. While making light of the spilt milk under burnt bridges across the landscape of my life, mental illness lurked and loomed despite my best efforts to discourage it. Thus, pursuing a life of diversion, I would steer into the winds of change to prevent any chance of a pause. Introspection wasn't welcome in my camp in those days. I lacked empathy to the point of sociopathy, mistreating many in search of intimacy, validation, distraction, and success. A life of friction gave me purpose, and I became adept at sidestepping responsibility, having convinced myself that blame ordinarily lay elsewhere. Unconscious through it all, I worked, fucked, drank, and snorted, treating body and mind with heinous disdain. The more bitter the events, the more belligerent I was in their wake, hell-bent on swimming against high and low tide. It took over four decades, two divorces, three mental breakdowns, countless physical injuries, and one near-suicide to question whether this was living. I know, right? Where were the signs?

I played many roles during the first 43 years of this lifetime: an abused child, an altar boy, a bully, a thief, and an entertainer. A drug dealer, a punch-bag, a vigilante, a good son, a founder, a friend, and a philanderer. A high-functioning alcoholic, a rubbish husband, a bad son, a bully, a suicidal self-harmer, and an occasional good brother. I was a narcissist, a lousy friend, a selfish business partner, a cheat, a lover, a liar, and a terrible brother. I was a rescuer, a fighter, an expert gaslighter — the list goes on and on.

Restless, I wore many coats with zero interest in keeping warm. What I did to others returned to me, and vice versa, following the law of karma. I was attracting what I saw in myself, and it was all incredibly exhausting. I darted between dramas like a maladjusted pinball with purpose. Though I had no idea back then, it was to explore the myriad ways I could suffer. This catastrophic catalogue was indicative of a person who could not love.

We all suffer, and perhaps some of the above reminded you of a facet of your own experience. It's in our nature to enjoy misery just as much as we find it difficult to forgive, let go of fear, be open to love, or effectively communicate. Complaining, blaming, and sidestepping responsibility are commonplace behaviours of the wounded inner child. Playing the victim is often comparatively simpler than observing and learning from the lessons infused in our challenging life events. In truth, we are co-responsible for most of what happens to us — especially if we repeat the same cycles without change.

So what brings about a personal pivot? I'd suddenly reached a point where I could no longer stand my own bullshit. I was sick of hearing the voice in my head complaining about the myriad issues I'd undeniably designed. Though we cannot control events, we can influence and transform what happens next. Hence, I replaced "Why is this happening to me?" with "What might this teach me?"

As simple as the idea was, this profound mental re-jig did

wonders for my view of life and my understanding of its symbiosis with death.

I'm not a scientist, doctor, counsellor, guru, academic, or life coach. Nor am I a death coach, though such a title would bring any business card to life. I'm just another expression of consciousness having a human experience. I've said, done, thought, and encountered much the same as you, and you have doubtless suffered significant hardships in comparison. Of course, our stories share some structural similarities, including the existence of the ego and perhaps even that of The Hero's Journey. We all share a beginning, a middle, and an end, and it's the latter two that this book is designed to address.

Before my unexpected upgrade, "Martin v1.0" had a relatively successful career, status, and stuff. Despite all the darkness, my high-functioning ability deceived me and everyone else about how unhappy I really was. And when the rampage was finally over, my awkward awakening began. With the newfound gift of self-realisation, I observed that every moment of suffering and beautiful lesson along the way had been invited through the front door and offered cocktails and cocaine.

So at a point on the path, I learned to separate from my ego. I removed the mask and forced us both to look beneath, and we sat together in the searing fire of silence. That's how I discovered the anatomy of happiness, which I look forward to explaining in more detail. Rising from that death, seeing life's illusion through new eyes, we can experience the gift of a new life inside a life. Thus, with ten fabled lives before me, having discarded my suffering, I found love, vulnerability, an open heart, and an open mind. The former sings as I contemplate my metamorphosis, since now I feel grateful to be alive every moment of every day. To have lived even one whole life is quite a thing. To live and die in the same lifetime is quite another. To share that story is the greatest gift I have to offer. Please take whatever resonates and leave the rest. My main wish is to plant a seed. And that together, at least in these pages, we begin a germination process of new thinking.

We can choose to reinvent ourselves at any time, and since we're all teachers and learners, the learning never ends. As Carl Jung once said: "Life really does begin at forty. Up until then, you are just doing research". Wherever this book finds you, I hope it helps.

So if you're ready to learn how to die before you die, hop aboard the *Happy Express*. As you might expect, the route begins in a less cheerful, more challenging place. Fear not, though, friend. When you reach this book's end, you'll have all you need to fully understand and embody long-lasting happiness. The rest is up to you.

CHAPTER TWO

Deathbed Regrets

Yesterday was heavy;
put it down.

— Unknown

Despite the taboo topic, I've become fascinated with the art of dying well. Is denying the inevitable healthy when such behaviour creates unwelcome surprises later down the line? Why do so many of us discount discussions of death?

We all have a story, rarely are they fairy tales. As we plough through life's box of chocolates, it's not uncommon for us to say (or not say) and do (or not do) things that we later regret. Tarnishing said tale. However, if we motor on, never assessing or addressing regretful moments, do we not carry this burden for years? In such cases, are we unconsciously retaining dis-ease? It's a hefty weight, after all. Some of us spend our whole lives bearing shame and regret. Cumbersome, compounded emotions clouding our hearts and minds, we take these dark passengers to the very end of the road.

So, there you are — in the latter stages of life — still living in the past or an unattainable future. Even then, you're incapable of forgiveness. Even then, you cannot let go or express your true feelings. Suffice it to ask: is this what you want for yourself? To spend the last years of your life unhappy, unable to be present, all thanks to the train of regrets chug-chugging through your failing, fearful mind?

Like you, my life to date was not without incident. Though,

by no means do I claim uniqueness; I'm just another Samsaric citizen doing the rounds. As is traditional, I bore the shame and regret of my thoughts and actions for decades, and the weight of my co-created drama nearly drove me to suicide. Holding on to such neuroses created quite a mess. However, at a point in time, I suddenly didn't like what I saw. A distinct lump of internal work followed my observation of this inventory.

In recent years, I've been blessed with lessons of sobriety, self-love, forgiveness, acceptance, awareness, gratitude, and presence. Through my tempestuous transformation, I learned that to live a life within a life had already been a gift, but two was an outright miracle. One might say that I died. This "ego death" experience drove me to review and reinvent. Upon realising I knew very little, I became a scholar in the art of living well. And I'll continue such practice until my Earth School graduation.

So now, perhaps somewhat surprisingly, if you told me I only had five minutes left to live, I'd wave my goodbyes and then spend my last few minutes contemplating how unequivocally grateful I am for the gifts I've received during my stay.

Seeing life through a new lens, I'm keen to promote others' open audit of shame and regret, so they might see how incredible life without such baggage can be. Do you long to let go of grudges that you might rebuild bridges? Do you wish you'd said: "I love you" more? That you could better express your truth with family and friends? Or are you deferring such inconsequential concerns until you've achieved this goal or that milestone? Or perhaps until Hell freezes over?

What if you suddenly ran out of time?

Grab a pen and spend a few minutes imagining that you have five minutes left to live — not in the future, but right now at this point in your life. *Five minutes left.* Consider your end-of-life regrets. Close your eyes if it helps (you're dying, after all). Take a little time to breathe into these reflections consciously. When you've thought of your list, as an exercise, write it down. I've left the following page blank for you.

My top ten end-of-life regrets

Feel like sharing?
Tag @martinotoole and @howtodiehappy_podcast #howtodiehappy

In the final years, folks often lament the lives they didn't live. A few concepts circulate surrounding this idea. In *The Top Five Regrets of the Dying*, Bronnie Ware introduces common deathbed regrets gleaned during her stint working as a palliative care worker. Her anecdotes are interesting, not least because they feel entirely likely.

Digging into the subject further, I found more themes surrounding deathbed regrets, which I've posed as statements as follows:

1. I wish I had taken better care of my body.
2. I wish I'd dared to live more truthfully.
3. I wish I'd had the courage to express my feelings.
4. I should've said "I love you" more.
5. I wish I'd let go of grudges.
6. I wish I'd left work at work and made more time for family.
7. I wish I'd stayed in touch with friends.
8. I wish I'd been the better person in conflicts.
9. I wish I'd realised that happiness was a choice much sooner.
10. I wish I'd pursued my dreams.

Heartbreaking if true, right?

While unable to find much research on deathbed regrets, I did find a 2005 American paper titled *What We Regret Most... And Why* by Neal J. Roese and Amy Summerville. The report collates and analyses several studies surrounding the regret phenomenon. Nine of these papers were published between 1989 and 2003 and contain some highly insightful metadata. That said, one wonders whether attitudes might have changed since.

The research required participants to review their lives and consider what three (from a list of eight) aspects they would change if they could reset the clock. Other studies asked what parts of life they would alter, while another inquired about people's most significant regrets. Subjects varied vastly across these studies, from adults of different ages and occupations to undergraduates, adult women, a collection of people from a vehicle licensing database. There was even a representative sample of elderly residents of Lafayette, Indiana.

Uncovering regrets of action ("I wish I hadn't said this") and inaction ("I wish I had done that"), the studies demonstrated interesting results. Perhaps most intriguing is that as this era's subjects grew older, inevitable reality set in as their choices became naturally curbed: "A new romance or new career are open possibilities for the young but somewhat more difficult for the elderly", says one study (Wrosch and Heckhausen, 2002).

Apparently, older individuals rarely regretted focusing on personal actions during this era. As their life opportunities faded, so did their most painful regrets. Instead, "neutered" regrets emphasising other people's actions replaced these feelings. So these studies proved a correlation between advancing age, diminishing opportunity, and gradual regret reduction. People feel there's no point in regretting something they no longer have the power to change. Though for how many years might we hold on to regret before such acceptance? This seems more relevant to regrets of things one has not done rather than for something one could change at any point in life, even in one's dying days.

While not specific, there were clear categories for Americans' biggest regrets as follows:

Education 32%
Career 22%

Romance 15%
Parenting 10%
Self 5.47%
Leisure 2.55%
Finance 2.52%
Family 2.25%
Health 1.47%
Friends 1.44%
Spirituality 1.33%
Community 0.95%

These figures might well be said to demonstrate the participants' weighted focus on the material. It's telling, for example, that the more considerable regrets relate to education and career. Both are presumably connected to regrets over lacking financial freedom and the trappings that come with further education and subsequent career choices. Fundamentally, the question remains: are we focused on aspects of living most likely to provide true happiness? If not, we have a chance to change our course.

The paper summarises: "Based on these previous demonstrations, we suggest that the domains in life that contain people's biggest regrets are marked by the greatest opportunity for corrective action". Indeed, this makes perfect sense. It is not surprising that people regret career and education decisions in adulthood (with time left to change their course). I suspect, however, that such thoughts change entirely when one begins to realise their mortality. At this point, one surely cares less about education and a successful career — about the stuff one has or has not accrued. I imagine that when one reaches life's latter stages, we consider its true beauty, love, experience, family, and friends. Living in peace, free from hatred or resentment towards one another. I'm a hippie like that.

Whether we carry regret right to the end is broadly irrelevant. Far from being present, burdening one's mind with irreversible past events is unhealthy. Moreover, it might cultivate unnecessary sickness and an untimely end. Consider this chapter an opportunity to candidly observe the thoughts and feelings you suppress or indefinitely postpone. In contemplating them now, you give yourself a little breathing room and a chance to change — before time deprives you of this luxury altogether. By observing our hopes and fears, we connect the prospect of a good death with that of a life well-lived.

CHAPTER THREE

Death the Destroyer

**Everybody wants to go
to Heaven, but nobody
wants to die.**

— **Albert King**

There are a few inimitable truths in life, but perhaps none such has had more philosophy, faith, guesswork, or clichés attached than the subject of death. Yet here I am, throwing more thinking into the pot. Where to start? With the obvious, of course: death is a truth that many of us choose to ignore.

There are lots of ways to die, but if we skip the actual events leading up to one's demise, there are apparently just four causes behind an irreversible loss of brain stem function. These are: starvation of oxygen, high bodily temperature, or chemical toxin, and physical damage.

According to the Bioethics Research Lab, 120 people die each minute worldwide. That's 7,425 every hour, 178,000 daily, and 65 million people every year, all getting their wings. That's some churn! And yet we're still surprised every time someone dies. My point may appear glib, but rest assured it is not my intention to belittle our natural predilection towards fearing death and the grieving process. I'm merely highlighting that with a mental reframe, we might be less surprised by the inevitable, thus beginning to do ourselves a tremendous emotional service.

There are so many opportunities to pop our clogs that perhaps it isn't any wonder that folks fear what's around the corner. But at what point does our inherent fear of death practically obstruct the *being alive* bit that's arguably the whole point of existence? Come to think of it, how many more countless life opportunities do we miss or avoid altogether out of fear? And if we live without truly embracing the prospect of death, are we ceasing the full potential of each moment of each day? No, we're not.

Your parents are going to die if they haven't already. Your brothers and sisters too — along with your cat, the dog, grandparents, best friends, children, ex-boyfriends, ex-wives, your favourite person at work, the kid who bullied you at school, your MacBook, your car, the list goes on. Every one of those things will either hurtle, pootle, or in some cases, crawl very slowly towards a finite point of change. In material terms, all of this will end. Does considering such a reality resonate or trigger fear and despair? If the latter, then why? The question may be unwelcome, but such probing is necessary to set the scene. It's time to ask ourselves why, for so many of us, talking about death is deemed so inappropriate — so irreverent — when dying is a fundamental part of life.

For our society to evolve, perhaps one of the critical issues we must tackle is our nonsensical association with death. It's positively backwards. Contrary to generations of conditioning, there is no catastrophe or tragedy in death, nor is it avoidable. Messy? Sometimes. Inconvenient? Yup. Postponable? On occasion. However, we do ourselves no favours by seeing death as a frightening and unwelcome enemy. And to get to the bottom of the curious cognitive dissonance we possess around the inevitability of our impending end, we first ought to contemplate why (in Western society, at least) we struggle so much to embrace our finite nature.

Big, Bad Death

Death comes in all shapes, sizes, and genders. In many cultures, life's end has been personified in mythology, usually taking on somewhat fearful characteristics. For instance, the European Grim Reaper wanders around in a particularly menacing hooded cloak, collecting dead souls and pointing them towards the underworld with his long, bony fingers. At the same time, the Irish Banshee assumes a female form, shrieking in the night to announce someone's passing. Hel, the Nordic character, warns of impending death by wandering through town with a broom (of all things). Upstaging the old Norse cleaning lady is India's King Yama, who romps around atop a giant buffalo, lassoing lost souls and directing them to their stop. There are more of these fables — many more. For centuries, these tales of entities have become folklore and the subject of bedtime stories that are 100 per cent guaranteed to prevent any sleep whatsoever. Let alone Hollywood and the mainstream media's share of voice on the topic, jacked into the collective's amygdalae as they undoubtedly are. In a great many cultures, death is a most unwelcome event. Is it any wonder we fear life's final transitional phase, given its projection as a terrifying horror show?

The Enemy

Medicine has also changed the game. A society that once experienced higher death rates in children and shorter average lifespans has evolved into a healthier bunch of humans — in some ways, at least. Our life expectancy is now the longest it's ever been — up to the age of 85 if you occupy a developed country. So perhaps as we avoid more illnesses, living longer in a safer place, death is less likely to feature on our radar.

Medicine's intervention in the process of dying runs much deeper, though, now taking a proactive hold of a person's final days. No longer are we freely allowed to die in the peace of our own homes. Our dignity is often trampled as we're forcefully migrated to a more sanitised setting, usually to make someone other than ourselves more comfortable about our impending end. In the hospital, we're plugged in, transfused, infused, observed, discussed, and "made comfortable" as the pharmaceuticals flow, dulling our senses and awareness. Still no peace for us, as the constant electronic "beep" of the EKG monitor or some such machinery reminds us of our new and unfortunate situation. In many such cases, we're seen more as a failing meat suit than as a frightened (perhaps terrified) human on our last legs. In this day and age, while dying is as much an ordeal for one's mental health as the body, death must be vanquished or postponed at all costs.

In the developed world, there are rules to follow in dying. And so off we're taken — to whichever clinical setting is deemed appropriate. One has to wonder: how do all these additional factors affect our subconscious when considering the process of dying?

Terrified as we are of death, when our cards are marked by terminal illness, we're hell-bent on prolonging life through medical or pharmaceutical intervention. For decades we've been encouraged to attempt to cheat death — by weeks or even months — using such treatments. But in instances where the medicine makes us more sick and less present, who benefits from this approach? Instead of mindfully preparing for our end, we might spend our last months and weeks more exhausted and sicker than we would be were our bodies not pumped full of synthetic drugs. These words are by no means intended as insensitive. Nor are they designed to offend our incredible palliative healthcare workers, some of which I spoke to in researching this book. Compassionate caregivers that they are, terminal healthcare professionals have the unique experience of working with the dying and dead. With such incomprehensible levels of empathy, I do not question their motives and instead praise their selfless service. I merely seek to question the levels of clinical and pharmaceutical intervention for so many during their dying days.

Undoubtedly, one author, in particular, offers remarkable insights surrounding Western medicine's treatment of the dying. Elizabeth Kübler-Ross, MD, wrote the bestselling *On Death & Dying* (first published in 1969). It's a guide to help medical professionals and clergy better consider the dying's needs, feelings, and wishes. In considering the medical-political complex's intervention in palliative care, Kübler-Ross asks: "Are we becoming less human or more human?" Facing the distinct possibility of dehumanising the dying, she encourages the medical profession to exercise as much humanity as possible during treatment of the terminally ill.

Kübler-Ross suggests that since the unconscious mind finds the concept of natural death inconceivable, we perceive that someone or something will end our life. "Therefore, death itself is associated with a 'bad act', a frightening happening", she says. What a fearful bunch we have become. But then fear plays such a gargantuan part in the human psyche, doesn't it? Especially when it comes to fear of the unknown.

So if societal conditioning discourages our acceptance of mortality, how on earth can any of us be expected to venture further in our thinking? If death isn't even on the radar, then surely an afterlife gets little to no airtime? Furthermore, how does all that inherent fear affect our mental health and our lives from day to day?

Instead of investing incalculable resources into keeping us alive that little longer, we would do well to spend time developing infrastructure that encourages healthy and open dialogue around this subject. We must reframe the subject of death in an entirely more mindful and healthy way. This, in turn, would have positive and long-lasting ramifications on how we live.

Conditioning our Children

Fear is like a virus, and whether we know we have it or not, it is all too easy to spread. Exercising a woeful lack of self-awareness, most of us will pass our fears to our children. If asked to explain death to a child, we might do so with a whitewash prediction of how the deceased's departure was to "A place better than this". Or by telling them that "God" took the recently demised, much like some omnipotent kidnapper in the night. Apparently, "God's will" can be brutal like that. We also often keep children away from the dying or dead — forbidden to visit clinics or sit by the bedside of their dying relatives. Likewise, kids are often excluded from funerals or end-of-life celebrations. From what do we believe we are protecting these children other than the truth? It's possible that, during their formative years, we are teaching them to have a fearful or unrealistic relationship with death. Therefore, we're more likely amplifying our own denial and lack of acceptance.

Speaking of funerals, what about the bizarre way we treat dead bodies? We dress them, put make-up on them, and embalm them to make them look alive and last longer. And we often spend a lump of money doing this, placing the corpse in a huge polished box with a range of metallic handles on offer, depending on your budget. It may be a surprise to learn that some families even give undertakers underwear to put on their dead relatives. So attached to material form are we that we wish to extend the illusion even in death.

Where's the line between prolonging life and dehumanising another's end? When do we accept it'll all one day be over? How can we reframe the fear and regretful psychology we've designed around death and dying? We deny death's existence while simultaneously working overtime to master and control it. This has to change if we hope to evolve. Imagine if we invested the same kind of attention and emotional energy into mastering life as we do in fearing and feebly attempting to command the inevitable.

So, condemnation of death is not sudden but developed over time. It combines folklore, parenting, media and medical intervention, religion, and our inherent leaning towards attachment. Our conditioning results in an illogical fear of something we logically know to be impermanent. My, while pertinent, how dark a subject this is! Though, together, we can change this status quo, curating and practising numerous methods that will result in a paradigm shift. All of which is to come.

CHAPTER FOUR

Prepared to Die

I'm not afraid of death; I just don't
want to be there when it happens.
— Woody Allen

Death sucks, and its associated grieving is a messy process. While for some, it's highly destructive, others experience phenomenal transformation in its wake. What are you doing along these lines? Have you ever considered training for your death and that of those you love?

We are emotional beings. Relinquishing all sense and sovereignty to them will amplify what is likely to be a painful experience. It's death, after all. But we can be more than human — superhuman when we put our minds to it. Or, more precisely, when we relegate our minds in favour of activating consciousness. With practices, including yoga, breathwork, and meditation, we can learn to master our emotions — including death-related anxiety and grief. Not to the point of dulling them but training them to the point where we identify our emotions as internal responses to inevitable events. The game is to get ahead of that response, prepare ourselves for death's inevitability, and be less surprised when it comes around.

In the movie *Saving Private Ryan*[1], in the memorial cemetery, old Mr Ryan stands in front of his fallen comrades' graves and pleads with his wife: "Tell me I had a good life". Increasingly anxious, he adds: "Tell me I'm a good man". Her affirming response puts him at ease, as it likely would for anyone's search for meaning

1 *The feature film Saving Private Ryan (written by Robert Rodat).*

and worth when contemplating life and death simultaneously. So here are some questions: would you deny death when your turn came if you felt you'd lived well? Would your anger be less fierce if you had long since come to terms with the fickleness of mortality? Would depression's grip be as firm if your daily practice enabled the conscious control of your ego? When we learn to accept happenings merely as events within a rich and beautiful life story, a transformational perspective is obtainable. This is a utility for how to die happy. There's just the small matter of doing the work to pave the way.

Perhaps death can only be frightening when one's actually dying? But then, we're all dying, aren't we? I know I am. The only variant is velocity. Hence, with acceptance, we can live in such a way that at day's end, we can be thankful for the gift of another 24 hours in this big, beautiful shared theatre of experience. As you'll learn later, gratitude plays a fundamental role in the anatomy of happiness. So perhaps begin to think about the simple things that give you joy — things the healthy and young often take for granted. The framework for such a mindset for conscious living is what this book endeavours to introduce.

What if death is not the end? There's fierce debate about what happens when we die among the eight billion souls inhabiting planet Earth. Depending on these perspectives, some folks are far more prepared than others. So, next, we'll briefly discuss some ideas surrounding life after death.

CHAPTER FIVE

Death and Religion

If there are no dogs in Heaven,
then when I die I want to go where
they went.
— Will Rogers

There is no denying fear has been weaponised by certain religions since their inception, and I'll arm-wrestle any priest who says differently. Depending on your beliefs, you're either going to Heaven, Hell, Purgatory, a higher density dimension, or coming back here for more lessons about how to love in a world of separation. Perhaps you're coming back out of choice, to help awaken others. Or, you're done for good; lights out; the end. Where are you in this mix, and how does your consideration of this affect the quality of your life? When did you last lend any meaningful thought to the topic? Perhaps the debate surrounding the soul's existence is one of our species' most significant discussions. Or, at least, what happens after death.

Just as the sun will set on this day, around 178,000 people will die somewhere on this spherical wonder upon which we reside. Setting aside the apparent fact that we're all in one state of decay or another, how does our global community feel about our Earth Rovers eventually crawling to a stop?

Whether your Hindu soul works to cleanse its karma through the Samsaric cycle of rebirth or your one-shot Christian spirit winds up in Heaven, Hell, or Purgatory, death is not the end for many. Interestingly, different variations on the reincarnation story might be the most significant held concept among our world religions. Thus, Islam, Christianity, Judaism, Buddhism, Hinduism, and Scientology all pursue spiritual salvation, sharing the goal of saving one's soul. As is written in the Hindu Bhagavad Gita: "It is born not, nor does it ever die, nor shall it, after having been brought into being, come not to be hereafter. The unborn, the permanent, the eternal, the ancient, it is slain not when the body is slain". So, by this rationale, we are not our bodies but infinite energy residing in flesh and bone for as long as it may last. Long enough to experience and learn from an exciting life story.

It's not for me to judge or argue one way or the other for the existence of an afterlife. Such a debate is not entirely necessary when contemplating the meaning of happiness in life or death. Indeed, it dramatically helps, but lessons of the metaphysical only open hearts and minds when ready to receive. Note that I say "metaphysical", not "religious". While the two might feel separate, they are very much intertwined.

Actually, what of our atheist brothers and sisters? They would say that believing in an afterlife is a convenient way to allay one's fears about dying. This is a great idea. They would say: "Prove there is life after death!" For the atheist, death is nothing short of total nothingness. Perhaps ironically, I see nothing to fear about nothingness. In a place of no things, there can be no thing to fear, right? Fated for such, we have no senses in the void. Thus, the end is just the end.

Those disinterested in an afterlife might find the entire discussion much more straightforward. Without such preoccupation, you're more likely concerned with the present. Perhaps, therefore, you're already developing a fine plan to ensure a good death. Here's a thought, though: just as we experience darkness through our knowledge of light, how do we know what life feels like without first knowing death? Which comes first? The chicken or the egg?

Throwing his hat into the ring, of this debate Alan Watts said:

"When you die, you're not going to have to put up with everlasting non-existence, because that's not an experience. A lot of people are afraid that when they die, they're going to be locked up in a dark room forever. Try and imagine what it would be like to go to sleep and never wake up. And if you think long enough about that, it will pose the next question: what was it like to wake up after never having gone to sleep? That was when you were born, you see. You can't have an experience of nothing, so after you're dead the only thing that can happen is the same experience or the same sort of experience as when you were born".

So, we have to wonder, how could a place of permanent nothingness exist, since we can only envisage this concept based on our acceptance of the alternative of somethingness? Furthermore, life experience tells us that even in nothing, there's something to find.

Where Shall We Go?

In 2011, a global research company conducted an online survey to ascertain how the world felt about the existence of God (or other "Supreme Beings") and the afterlife. The study of around 18,000 people from 23 countries showed that 51 per cent of the world believes there's life after life. In contrast, 23 per cent think they will "cease to exist", and 26 per cent have no idea what will happen when they die.

Regardless of our current beliefs, it would appear there are three common themes:

1. We are afraid of dying.
2. We do not want to die.

3. We'd rather not think about it.

Shout out to all *suicidal readers at this point. Wanting to die but being too afraid to kill yourself is, I know, mentally taxing. Please stick with me, at least to the end of this book.

*If you're having suicidal thoughts, please, please reach out to someone — anyone. I know it's hard to see now, but you bring a gift to this world; you just have to find out what it is. You are loved, and you are seen. I love you. Life can change for the better in a heartbeat, but only you can make it so. I promise there's a future where you can be head over heels in love with being alive.

So if most of us fear what death will bring, how might I help alleviate that dread? I cannot. I can tell you about the many mystical incidents I've had during meditation and breathwork, my intermittent interactions with "ghosts", the near-death experience, and many other profound (what some might refer to as "religious") adventures I've had with plant medicine. Still, I don't think that's the way to go, as it ultimately requires your unfettered faith in me and my story, and we're only just getting to know each other.

By now, you may have gathered that this isn't a book about death but about life and living. After all, the unpleasantness of dying likely comprises the ponderance of how we could've lived. This book is littered with utilities to help you prepare for death by making wholesale changes to how you live, so read on.

In the event that you are terminally ill with very little time left to tackle this book's many utilities, I offer some straightforward advice: love and be grateful to yourself. Hold your hands over your heart, and forgive yourself. *Let go*. Contrary to popular misconception, it is never too late to change. Right up to the very end, to the last days or minutes of your life, you can embrace, respect, and fully understand that you always have a choice. And what better things to choose than forgiveness and love?

With this intention, bask in self-gratitude for making such a choice. Be thankful for your awareness and presence. Then maybe skip to this book's concluding chapter to maximise the precious time you have left. Or, God willing, there's an audiobook of my ramblings. For efficiency's sake, perhaps listen at 1.5x speed. And when you've finished, consider giving it to someone else. Pay it forward.

Reckoning Death

Eventually, and perhaps inevitably, I leapt from the religion into which I was born and forced to follow into the disillusioned arms of atheism. Then, despite various metaphysical experiences throughout my childhood and early adult life, I wound up on the fence with the other agnostics. I had no faith in God, gods, or anything beyond material phenomena, and with this lack of belief, I could only hold up my hands and declare: "I just don't know!"

Sobriety changed everything. Regular meditation and fitness cleaned my body and mind. These wholesale modifications in lifestyle brought transformation in my understanding of the esoteric. I could see and feel more by clearing my mental and physical fog. Then I discovered Ayahuasca, which frankly blew the lid off everything I thought I knew. We'll discuss that in a later chapter (36) about teacher plants.

So I went from believing I would never believe to a profound position of questioning the existence and reality of all things. I suspended judgement of that which I did not know. I now have no doubt whatsoever that death is not the end. "It's just getting out of one car, and into another", as John Lennon once said. "I'm not afraid of death because I don't believe in it", he declared. You and me both, John.

Prepared for Death

In Eastern philosophy, death is more of a welcome friend and its relationship to living is altogether more significant. Between the Hindus, the Buddhists, the Taoists, Shintoists, and the Confucianists, there is a rainbow-coloured world of untold wisdom available for anyone who wishes to consider better ways to live and die. However, it is a painful reality that much of this incredible wisdom is fast becoming archaic as the illusory world of technology, consumerism, and distraction romps on. Despite their profound treasures, modern society has set aside much of its interest in ancient philosophies in favour of an alternate, arguably vacuous pursuit of happiness.

Thanks to the rise in podcast popularity, Eastern philosophies are experiencing a renaissance, via recordings of timeless wisdom from the likes of Ram Dass, Alan Watts, and many more. Such content reminds us that religions and philosophies of the East have a lot more in common with contemporary psychology than those from the West. Save, perhaps, Stoicism, which is a beautifully logical school of philosophy, dedicated to achieving happiness and well-being. Western religions tend to focus more on dogma, doctrine, and instructions regarding what one should believe and how to behave if one has any hope of reception in Heaven. They're often somewhat scary.

Far from focused on fire and brimstone or a vengeful God with a penchant for smiting, these teachings from the East are as old as time. They provide guidelines for mastering the art of being human. They are as relevant now as they were when created and encourage the expansion of one's consciousness and self-awareness. The result of which cultivates harmony with everyone and everything else.

Much Eastern wisdom speaks to the journey of personal development, avoiding the suggestion of worshipping anything other than life itself. We do well to invest time and energy in re-evaluating the vast collections of ancient wisdom, asking how and when we might apply it to our lives today. Because apply it, we can. So much of this knowledge is timeless, because it focuses on personal development and the human condition. We all have a vested interest in this topic, do we not?

I continue to find a wealth of practical wisdom within these teachings. Unsurprisingly, the knowledge I speak of often uses similar ideas about simplicity, emotional management, interaction, pragmatism, and practising how to empty one's mind. Doing so creates space for fruitfulness, positivity, and creativity. And above all, love.

The Death of Reason

Thanks to fundamentalist and draconian practices, we've arrived at a point where many of us find the ideals of organised religion to be contradictory, intolerant, oppressive, and in some cases, absolutely nonsensical. Their existence therefore drives us away from inward inquiry.

Today, distanced from oneness, humanity misinterprets religion and spirituality as one and the same, while they are often not. We wage wars in the name of faith while forgetting that the "Word of God", undistorted by ego, can be simply defined as the vibration of love — a shareable truth by all. Dissonance cannot exist in this frequency. Man-made dogma distorts it, and Chinese whispers are set in its place. One ought not to consider this as an attack on faith; more an invitation to contemplate how religion can ironically muddy our openness to unity and the concept of the afterlife. Death existed before religion, after all.

Omnism is the idea that no one religion is the truth, but there is truth in all religions. You must discern for yourself. Omnism respects and recognises all religions and their gods. It encourages one's acceptance of another's truth without requesting belief. I do not follow a religion, but you and I need not agree on a faith structure to walk a path together. To find common ground, we've to step back and ask ourselves what fundamental things we might say and do to generate healthy minds, bodies, and communities. Harm no one. Treat others with equal respect. That's it. How might we adopt philosophies that put the needs of the many first, never seeking to serve the few? What course can we take to bring us closer together, setting aside petty differences? And can we see that such thinking cultivates a happier, healthier way of life?

So, you see, there are rich pickings in ancient philosophical and religious texts, but we must discern that which seeks to control versus ideas cultivating healthy and mindful living. To reduce such wisdom to being "outdated", "made up", and "hocus-pocus" stories about "sky fairies" is to grossly underestimate the collective wisdom of countless great thinkers. If we can get past the senseless arguments about whose god is better, or whose prophet is more pious, we can begin to make real progress as individuals and a community. Now, more than ever, as mental illness and suicide skyrocket, our focus must be on individual and collective healing.

Newsflash: a man called Jeshua (Christ) did and said some extraordinary things. Stripping back the supernatural legend, he was a sage, a wise man who articulated beautiful ideas about life, suffering, happiness, oneness, and love. Multi-faith spiritual leaders and prophets have expressed similar opinions throughout time. The Buddha, Lao Tzu, Muhammed, Marcus Aurelius, Confucius, Maharaj-ji, Isiah, and the list goes on. All these people have shared insightful parables about suffering and the human experience. Religion and dogma aside, they shared wisdom about existence and our transmutable ability to evolve using our heads and hearts. They encouraged us to love ourselves and one another — a highly subscribable ideal. Yet such simple notions remain immensely difficult since, married to the material, secured to separation, humanity rejects divinity. We must change our direction, one person at a time. The route to expansion is through self-inquiry.

Perhaps the most practical wisdom surrounding death originates from the Buddhists. Please note, however, that I am not a Buddhist. Though I doubt the Buddha would have a problem with that. Buddhism tackles death in a pragmatic, frank, and straightforward way, as it does life; hence there's much functional wisdom to be gleaned from its philosophies. The Buddhists invite us to embrace impermanence while reminding us that we cannot predict the time and date of our end and should thus appreciate life's gifts accordingly. Buddhists cultivate an appreciation for the preciousness of life through their heightened awareness of death. It was, in fact, Sogyal Rinpoche's *Tibetan Book of Living and Dying* that first inspired me to create the *How To Die Happy* podcast and the subsequent ramblings in this book. And since Buddhists believe that when a person dies, they'll be reborn as something else, they're one of many religions upholding the concept of rebirth. Thus it's relevant to dive deeper into this topic, briefly exploring the philosophy and science surrounding reincarnation.

Take a Breather

Sit with your spine straight.
You might like to close your eyes.
Relax your jaw, neck and shoulders.
Soften your belly.

Inhale through the nose for one, two, three, four, five.
Exhale through the nose for five, four, three, two, one.

Pause.

Repeat another nine times, with your attention
focused on your breath.

CHAPTER SIX

The Reincarnation Story

If you're really a mean person,
you're going to come back as a fly
and eat poop.

— Kurt Cobain

What if death was scientifically proven not to be the end? Can you imagine what such a revelation would do to the collective psyche? Perhaps millions would end their lives overnight, with plans to "respawn" like a character in a computer game.

Along the journey of expanding heart and mind, one must suspend judgement wherever possible, opening to possibilities one might traditionally refuse. It's more complicated than it sounds, but they don't call this self-improvement business "the work" for nothing. As adults, most of us reach a comfortable limit of knowledge. With plenty of distractions, little motivation or a teacher, it's easy to lose interest in learning. We decide, therefore, that we know what we know, and our life will thus operate specifically on this premise. However, to ignore the invitation to learn is to grossly limit one's potential. Since my first Ayahuasca journey exposed the superficiality of my previous existence, I have a newfound drive to learn with humility. My new topics of interest are philosophy, theosophy, spirituality, and how to better care for our bodies and minds. The more I learn, the less I know. Perhaps it's more that I know what I don't know. Without actually knowing it, if you know what I mean?

There's a surf shop and cafe in my current Balinese backwater.

Drifter, a mecca to the spirit of surfing, also has an impressive book collection ranging from colouring to religious to outright esoteric. During a podcast discussion, *Drifter's* co-founder, a living master of the art of happy, Jake Mackenzie, told me of the book, *Many Lives, Many Masters* by Brian L. Weiss, MD. This mind-blowing account details how Weiss, a prominent psychiatrist, had his worldview warped during a seemingly innocuous hypnosis session with a female patient. What followed took him on a most unexpected journey through the patient's many past lives and deaths.

What's most interesting about this story is that the patient occasionally channelled the voice of "The Masters" from a place referred to as the "space between lives". These higher-dimensional entities explained to Weiss that we are all here (on Earth) to experience the vast array of human traits through many lifetimes. As The Masters explained, life on Earth is a sophisticated construct, an experiment to bring us closer to God (source). This is a religion-free reincarnation story. The Masters described how we work together in "soul family" teams, returning and playing alternative roles, assisting one another in settling karma. For example, a soul family member may play your mother's role in one life, then in another, play your wife, child, saviour, victim, or even murderer — whatever the lesson requires. As outlandish as this seemed to the first sceptical Weiss, his disbelief was quashed as his patient channelled information containing remarkable revelations about Weiss' family and deceased son.

While astonishing, this story is not unique. Hypnotherapists around the world regularly report helping patients revisit their past lives. Plato spoke of an immortal soul with many incarnations. And as we've learned, many religions, including those originating in India, believe the non-physical essence of a living being is reborn in a new physical form or body after our biological death. But what do you think? Can you accept that you don't know what you don't know, and therefore there is more to know? If not, why not?

Proof of Life After Death?

Cosmologist and astrophysicist Carl Sagan, a famously "hard" scientist, said: "Reincarnation deserves serious study". In fact, there have been many investigations into reincarnation in recent decades. Ian Stevenson, MD, was a Canadian-born American psychiatrist. He founded the Division of Perceptual Studies at the University of Virginia School of Medicine. Professor and eventual chairman of the Department of Psychiatry and Neurology, Stevenson worked at the university for 50 years. Fascinated by the phenomenon of reincarnation, he carried out extensive research studying children who apparently had memories from past lives. It would appear that Stevenson has scientifically proven that reincarnation exists.

During his research in Europe, India, Alaska, America, Lebanon, Brazil, and more, he discovered countless children as young as two and three years old who recounted memories from past lives. He wrote hundreds of papers and fourteen books on the subject, including *Twenty Cases Suggestive of Reincarnation, Children Who Remember Past Lives, Cases of the Reincarnation Type,* and *Where Reincarnation and Biology Intersect.*

What makes Stevenson's work so fascinating is that he followed up on the children's past life accounts with people closely associated with the deceased, who thus verified specific information from the children's reports. In some cases, these interviews uncovered murder locations, going so far as to identify murderers. Peers reviewing his work were unable to explain his painstaking and factual studies. They confirmed the overwhelming data to be something that simply could not be ignored. And while inexplicably overlooked by mainstream science, his many books and papers gathered much praise and interest within the scientific community.

Perhaps even more fantastical was the weight of evidence in his 1997 tome, *Reincarnation and Biology: a Contribution to the Etiology of Birthmarks and Birth Defects.* This work detailed the presence of birthmarks or defects in children with past-life memories. The marks (and more) matched wounds (usually fatal) on the deceaseds' bodies whose end-of-life stories the children recalled as being their own.

Still think it's nonsense? As we've seen, science suggests otherwise, so it's up to you. Perhaps it's time to switch gears and take a metaphysical adventure into the reincarnation wilderness. Buckle up.

So if reincarnation is commonplace for the dead, what's its point? And who the fuck are we? If we're not humans that live and die once, then perhaps the more pertinent question is, *what* are we? The theme of remembering (and forgetting) runs like a salmon stream through the reincarnation story. The idea is that while children can often see through the Veil of Unknowing (an energetic veil between the physical and metaphysical), that visibility lessens. Why? Because brick by brick, family, religion, and society burden us with their belief systems. And as we fully embrace the illusion of individuality, we forget our true nature. Imagine if you spent every day with others projecting their fears, expectations, neuroses, and identities on to you. Wouldn't this make knowing your true Self more challenging? All that ego blasted at you like snot from a sick kid's nose would undoubtedly be a thing to contend. Actually, I just described reality, didn't I?

Perhaps, as a youngster, you saw or heard things you could not explain. Or did you have dreams about flying that felt much more real than the usual nighttime visions? The veil was thin. But as the wall of conditioning grew thicker and higher, until you no longer remembered, you became a fully fledged citizen of the game of life. And by forgetting yourself, you can have another run around Samsara without metaphysical preconceptions. Forgetting is what keeps us in play. The aim of the game is to remember.

A Story About Reincarnation

A fair question of reincarnation is what point it serves if, upon our next life, we (usually) remember nothing of what's passed before. Does a repeatable, failed experiment empty life's meaning? Does it render a life valueless that you may simply hit the "repeat" switch? Well, no. Far from being a waste, all is gained. To comprehend how and why, we must go back to the beginning — *before* us, before our Universe. Before the Multiverse. It's a complex concept to comprehend and requires open-minded deliberation of four fundamental ideas:

1. We are much more than highly evolved animals that live and die once, with no meaningful purpose other than survival (and shopping).
2. Our perception of existence is limited solely to our senses.
3. We are one of countless sentient life forms in the multiverse.
4. Sentient life does not always require a body.

And so, assuming you've momentarily suspended all judgement, I can tell a story that goes something like this:

Once upon a no time and no space exists a super-conscious energetic being of immeasurable power with the ability to create anything from thought. By its nature, this omnipotent entity contemplates myriad ways to be. Then at some point in no time, the entity asks itself: "What am I?"

Wowsers. Three small words spelling boundless possibilities.

This line of self-inquiry launched a wondrous journey that would focus the entity on the most fascinating and timeless mission there ever was. And so, using fractal creation and infinite patience, it began creating. Then those creations thus created yet more creations — all with the ability to create. Very different flavours, mind. Many possessed the same sentient power of self-inquiry. And amidst this vast and complex system of systems made of the frequency of love is an order of the mathematical kind.

Here, in the dualistic Third Density, Planet Earth, The Universe, as individualised fractal expressions of The One consciousness, we are governed by Universal laws of polarity, free will, impermanence, cause and effect, and more. Since, at our core, we are love, we practise aligning with that frequency — *learning how to love* — in unfavourable conditions since the construct of this game favours separation by design.

Still with me? Hold tight.

Maybe the *Brief to Self* went something like this:

"Learn everything there is to know about me, by breaking myself into a million little pieces, giving each piece the power to create ('in my image'), and scattering them to the far corners. I may experience myself through infinite facets possessing many truths. Hence, I can know myself better".

So, inside this scientific [hippo]campus with infinite laboratories, there is two-way communication from the prime node (the entity) through the entire neural network (its creations and the creations' creations). Keen as they are on the phenomenon of identity, certain groups of lower-density nodes call themselves "human" and get busy creating various sub-groups with which to identify. With some understanding of the system's design, while they're at it, they also dub the prime node "The One", "God", "The Divine", "Brahman", "Allah", "Tao", "Source", and "Creator". And with more fractal groups come more names and doctrines.

Aware or unaware, the smaller nodes transmit data back to the prime node through each energetic density in the chain. Meanwhile, simultaneously, the prime node and sub-prime nodes send data back the other way. Some nodes understand the data, others only partially or not at all. Not at first, anyway. But they learn and create. So there's a back-and-forth where all nodes self-analyse, grow, remember, and share. Thus, the network grows ad infinitum. *Fractals.*

All nodes are sentient energy. They are perfectly imperfect by design, so the prime node can experience itself through myriad facets. It must have the ability to "succeed" and "fail". But there is no failure, only learning. By this rationale, whether positive or negative, learning is true success. The system's design allows one to learn a greater understanding of itself until each individualised sentient expression comprehends to the point of levelling up. New opportunities to learn are unlocked at each juncture.

Levelling up does not refer specifically to ascension from Third Density or what is commonly known by some nodes as "going to Heaven". That would be to skip many more subtle, invisible layers of ascension within this dimension. Hence these nodes learn how to "bend the Matrix"[1]. The closer one becomes to The One, the more One-like one becomes. The more one surrenders to The One, the more one flows with *The Way.*

The bountiful byproducts of these microlessons are forgiveness, peace, prosperity, tranquillity, and unconditional love. Add a healthy spoonful of acceptance to this magical melting pot, and unity shall prevail.

And so they might all live happily ever after.

The end.

Kudos, Creator! If I'm not very much mistaken, you've co-constructed the most imperfectly perfect system to better know thyself. It is, I suspect, the very definition of ingenious. It is divine.

1 *Observe and understand how to weild the illusory power of life on this plane.*

Well, that's a story of the Universe and reincarnation's functional role. If you managed to stay with me through that wild ride, you might wonder why people forget that they are a spark of divinity. That's a blimmin' good question. Why? Because, according to this idea, each thought, each choice, and experience is a new behavioural variant of an expression of The One. We forget so that we can upload these authentic experiences of the Self *to the Self* without the hindrance or memorial influence. So, lesson after lesson beams up the pipe, thus expanding every entity's understanding of itself. If one remembered all there was to know about their relationship with The One, then one would have nothing left to learn. Hence one would not participate in the game. At least, not in this density. Nevertheless, one question always remains relevant.

What Am I?

This fantastical story's theme is entrenched in the miracles of growth, learning, and change. The system in this tale welcomes bold self-inquiry and the logical and unconditional forgiveness of mistakes. After all, a mistake is only a mistake if one learns nothing from it.

So is this story religious or metaphysical? We might think it an impossible leap of faith to open our minds to the latter since many choose only to trust that which we can see. However, with the void rapidly closing between science and spirituality, the study of metaphysics and consciousness is exploding, alongside our newfound understanding of the energy connecting us all *(the Unified Field)*. Who knows what discoveries lie ahead? Who knows what we don't know? Funnily enough, the ancient masters, yogis, and mystics knew. *Prana, Qi (Chi), Life Force, Ki,* and *Anima* (all meaning energy) have existed in their world since the dawn of man. The cultivation of these practices has been scientifically proven to transform mental and physical health.

In the meantime, perhaps consider how your worldview would shift if you suddenly found, beyond a shadow of a doubt, that life after death isn't just possible but that each and every one of us dies and is reborn hundreds and thousands, if not millions of times. How would you view your role on this planet in this time and space? Would it influence your choices? Would you throw caution to the wind and embrace a full life, playing the game so you might experience the following unknown levels? Or would you waste it just because you could? Might you smile as you bask in the light of learning who you truly are? Or all of the above?

If regardless, you see the reincarnation story to be fanciful nonsense, then life on Earth is a one-shot opportunity. So with this truth in mind, how will you spend the remainder of your time? Can you learn to love yourself and others, forgive and do no harm? If you can treat people as you would hope to be treated, who cares whether life after death or reincarnation is real? What matters is that we co-exist with new levels of love, respect, and appreciation for one another. Such mastery of the art of living is undoubtedly enough.

CHAPTER SEVEN

The Art of Dying Well

**When death finds you, may it find
you alive.**
                    — African Proverb

Carl Gustav Jung was a world-renowned psychiatrist and philosopher whose work cannot fail to inform and inspire. He conceived *Individuation, Synchronicity,* and the famous *Jungian Archetypes* — traits of conscious human behaviour characterised as manifested personalities. You'll find reflections on the latter later in the book.

In his essay entitled *What Preparations for Dying Should Include*, Jung wrote:

"The title of this essay most likely strikes the modern reader as bizarre, if not obscene. With our American focus on youth and our medical system regarding death as some sort of 'enemy' to be defeated, we do not regard death as either an 'art' or something one might try to do 'well'. Given the profound materialism of our culture, with its stress on the tangible, the body, and the physical plane, few people indeed give much thought to death, other than to shudder at the prospect".

Jung's blend of spiritual-psychological thinking greatly appeals to me. His perspectives are open-hearted, leaning heavily into more esoteric concepts of Self. He's open to metaphysical elements of human life, and for good reason.

In the April of 1944, Jung had a heart attack and remained at death's door for almost three weeks. During this time, he had a profound and prolonged near-death experience. Below are excerpts of his account of returning to life and the living:

"It is impossible to convey the beauty and intensity of emotion during those visions. They were the most tremendous things I have ever experienced. And what a contrast the day was: I was tormented and on edge; everything irritated me; everything was too material, too crude and clumsy, terribly limited both spatially and spiritually. It was all an imprisonment, for reasons impossible to divine, and yet it had a kind of hypnotic power, a cogency, as if it were reality itself, for all that I had clearly perceived its emptiness. Although my belief in the world returned to me, I have never since entirely freed myself of the impression that this life is a segment of existence which is enacted in a three-dimensional box-like universe especially set up for it".

Such an elegant and accurate description of existence in the planes outside of time and space — *reality*. He later adds:

"It was only after the illness that I understood how important it is to affirm one's own destiny. In this way, we forge an ego that does not break down when incomprehensible things happen; an ego that endures, that endures the truth, and that is capable of coping with the world and with fate. Then, to experience defeat is also to experience victory. Nothing is disturbed neither inwardly nor outwardly, for one's own continuity has withstood the current of life and of time. But that can come to pass only when one does not meddle inquisitively with the workings of fate".

Perhaps unsurprisingly, Jung's ethereal experience was pivotal, inspiring him to re-evaluate life and living. By his admission, "a fruitful period of work began" following the event. The result was his creation of many principal writings. He concluded: "The insight I had had, or the vision of the end of all things, gave me the courage to undertake new formulations". I can relate. Is death the only gateway to transformation? Not physical death, no. Every beginning needs an ending, but the opportunity can be cultivated voluntarily through many living practices, including meditation, breathwork, yoga, and psychedelics. Hence reinventing a life within a life deserves much celebration. It's a precious gift.

While many are familiar with the expression "surrender to the flow", often perceived as a seemingly superficial, spiritualised cliché, these words often carry little weight. However, Jung's transformational account of the near-death experience is a beautiful example of a rare gift given, or perhaps one we give to ourselves, enabling us to re-evaluate our perspectives on living and dying. That is to say that Jung resurfaced from his experience, choosing no longer to fight fate but to accept and surrender to it, thus fully surrendering to the flow of life. One could argue this turned out well for the man and humanity as a collective.

In learning to submit, we can revolutionise our enjoyment of life, more of which we'll discuss later on. Suffice it to say that in ceasing to focus on destinations, one is indeed living, learning, and embracing the beautiful and idiosyncratic nuances of life's rambling journey. And when you open this door, alchemy occurs. You're discovering the secrets that manipulate gameplay. Where once you were a non-player character, now you have a shot at becoming a conscious architect — a game maker. Curiously and somewhat mysteriously, the game senses your change in strategy and responds favourably to your newfound level of acceptance. Why? Acceptance removes friction.

We don't all have the luxury of knowing when we'll die. While some terminally ill folks might wish they did not know, the majority are eventually grateful to have had a heads-up. So what about those who'll be hit by a bus or fall down the stairs this week? Or a mindless murder en route home from dinner? What are such unfortunates supposed to do? Well, the answer really is relatively simple. And if you listed your regrets at the beginning of this book, you've already begun your journey. As I've said and will say again: the secret to dying well is in living. Moreover, it is in being. But now you're at a crossroads. Andy once told Red in *The Shawshank Redemption*[1] that you "get busy living or get busy dying". Thus, our old friend choice enters stage left.

1 *The Shawshank Redemption (novel by Stephen King, screenplay by Frank Darabont).*

CHAPTER EIGHT

Everyone You Know is Going to Die (Part One)

As life is, death is. The awareness
of this fact allows you to live life
fully and intensely.

— Sadhguru

A lot of folks say we can do nothing to prepare ourselves for losing a loved one. Such thinking has us lost in a void that envelops our ignorance and lack of preparation for the inevitable. There are many things we can do to reduce such suffering. I say this with love.

There's a significant chance that you've already lost someone — perhaps one or many. Maybe your parents, friends, or even your children. Possibly your partner, grandparents, or a beloved pet. Maybe someone died recently, or death looms for you or someone close, and you seek answers, meaning, and alleviation. All such loss can cause us to experience devastating emotional injury, none of which is less significant than the other in the eyes of the grieving.

One incredible gift from the dying, should you choose this perspective, is that the event often triggers a renewed interest in living. We question our reality more deeply, perhaps choosing significant introspection for the first time. Or at least, that's what happened to me.

The last time I saw my mum alive was Christmas Day, 2013. I was still a high-functioning alcoholic then — a habit inherited from her. She'd drank my whole life, you see. We all had a lovely day, a rarity for our family during Christmas. Since there was more alcohol in the homestead in the festive season, the Christmas tree dramas were aplenty. On this occasion, it was a short visit, with plans for dinner in my own home. As frail as she was already, Mum seemed fine enough for a woman with advanced *Chronic Obstructive Pulmonary disease (COPD)* in her early 70s, who'd recovered from a double mastectomy the year before. I hugged her when I said goodbye; I might've even managed a kiss on her cheek — a rare moment of intimacy between us.

Monday, January 6th, was my first day back at work. During the holidays, I'd made plans to start a new creative agency — *Fist of Fury* — a solo venture that would eventually provide many lessons alongside my third breakdown. I was about to go to a meeting when my older brother called with the news. Peter was bereft, mumbling and sobbing as he forced the words: "Martin, our mum's dead". Immediately shocked, yet pausing only momentarily, I said I would go to a meeting and then travel to my parent's house later. He was understandably surprised. I put the phone down, packed my bag, and left the house like nothing had happened. Loading the car, I bumped into my friend and neighbour, and the moment she asked how I was, I broke down, spilling the news with a pond full of tears. She suggested I might instead drive directly to my family. I'm thankful she was there for me that morning (blessings to you, Caron). Without her, I would've made a six-hour round trip to avoid the inevitable, neglecting my suffering family for a pointless business meeting.

Still wearing his pyjamas, my broken dad answered the door, collapsing into my arms as he sobbed. He couldn't speak. I asked when the ambulance had removed her body, and at that point, realised that only the family doctor had been to pronounce the death. She was still in her armchair in the back room. "What am

I going to do, Martin?" he asked. I packed him off upstairs for a shower, took a deep breath, and entered the room. It's strange to see a dead body — especially when you know the person well and with whose every expression you are intimately familiar. It's like they're there, but they are not there. I didn't feel like she'd ended so much as she wasn't in that body anymore. Pat's story was over. Her Earth Rover was a greenish-yellow, and her closed eyes were sunken into deep, dark holes. I wasn't sure whether the doctor had done that, but I remember feeling grateful for not having to look into such emptiness that would likely overwhelm.

With no detectable life force, her frail body rested peacefully in the black leather *Lazy Boy* chair. I suppose her nothingness was the oddest aspect of the scene. I tentatively approached and, through tears and trembling lips, mumbled: "Oh, Mum". I kissed her cold forehead, and as I observed her through streaming eyes, I noticed she'd died with a packet of cigarettes in her hand. A chuckle escaped. I don't know what made me do it — shame, perhaps — but I gently took her hand and pried the carton from her grip.

The doctor had left details for the town undertaker (a kind and gentle man), so I called and made arrangements. By the time my older brother arrived, dad was showered and dressed, a shadow of his former self. There were tears and hugs aplenty during that moment of quiet. Then we put the kettle on and rolled a joint the size of a whiteboard marker pen. We spent around three hours in the room with her, telling stories of her idiosyncrasies and adventures, chugging coffee, smoking weed, and remembering whatever good times came to mind. She was pretty quiet, obviously, but we laughed a lot. It was nice. I coordinated the removal of her body with a much-needed family visit to the pub, since none of us were overly keen on being around for it.

We were all pretty broken the following days — though I worked hard to hide it. We planned the funeral together, and I stayed organised and busy. On the day we cremated her — after a great deal of drinking at the wake — I finally crumbled. Now it was my turn to fall into my dad's arms. I honestly don't think I've ever cried like that in my whole life.

After keeping it together relatively well in the following weeks, the cracks in my psyche became all too visible. Though, similarly with my childhood and adult life, I put on a brave face — bizarrely pretending everything was fine. One by one, however, the wheels of the Martin Express came off. And boy oh boy, that train derailed. *[Ding-ding] All aboard!*

I'd not long been separated from my second wife, a victim of my cheating with an employee with whom I eventually shared a home. Said new partner and I had flirted outrageously from her first interview. We both lied to friends, family, and colleagues as we carried on our messy affair with no real thought for anyone other than ourselves. My actions destroyed my relationships with my wife and my former business partner. Both became unwitting victims of my ongoing self-destructive behaviour, which increased with intensity. Understandably, my partner Don asked me to sell my share in our successful firm; I had broken our seal of trust. It was a needless end to an excellent partnership. Years later, I sought Don's forgiveness with a new perspective on my actions; he promptly asked whether I was dying! Rumours of me apologising to folks had spread like wildfire; thus, there was some speculation about whether I was not long for this world. Funny. Thanks to Don for accepting my apology with empathy and humility. How might the world be if we all learned to let go of grudges?

Not for the first or last time; I used a lot of cocaine back then and drank and smoked heavily. I confided in very few — including my closest friends — some of whom tried their best to overcome my defences. No one could, not really. Thus, emotionally incapable of seeking intimacy from my former employee-cum-partner, and being the self-destructive narcissist I was, I sought attention elsewhere. Relationships borne from dishonesty will be plagued by insecurity and mistrust until their inevitable demise. So it wasn't long before my suspicious partner discovered my indiscretion, naturally breaking her heart.

When caught red-handed, a narcissist's best course of action is to gaslight and sling buckets more drama with the hope of assuming the victim's role. So I drank a bottle of neat gin, put my head through a window, and sliced my arm repeatedly with a kitchen knife to release the shameful pain. Perhaps, as unconsciously anticipated, the event garnered her sympathy. The distraction worked a treat. Of the many lows I have had, this was one of the more significant. It was also pivotal to the journey of accepting responsibility for my actions. And so, having realised that the common denominator amidst all my bullshit was, in fact, me, I made the life-changing decision to begin therapy sessions with a wonderful man named Michael.

Regrets for the Dead

We all have valid reasons for being broken when someone dies. We're human, after all. Some will miss the deceased and suffer a deep sense of emptiness and loss. That wasn't my major malfunction; mine was regret. My guilt had nothing to do with my last encounter with my mum since I was grateful for it. Rooted like cancer, my shame was tied to my role in the abusive and dysfunctional relationship we shared for 39 years prior. I carried so much regret for the lack of a resolution, and that dark energy consumed me to my lowest. The maggots of shame and guilt for not working harder to fix us bore into me. I had not said "I love you" anywhere enough. I never once said, "Thank you for bringing me into this world and doing your best", or "Please talk to me about what drives you to self-harm so". Nor did I accept responsibility for my own human shortcomings during our countless negative interactions.

And then we'd run out of time.

I'd spent most of my adult life holding on to hatred, anger, frustration, fear, blame, or blatant disinterest in her well-being. Now, she was dead, and my love for her no longer had any place to go. I was on a tightrope, with each step switching between plans of survival and suicide — a heady and tiresome mix that might well yet be my undoing.

When something happens — regardless of being a direct result of something we did, that event carries a lesson. The lesson is for you and you alone. Each event, each exchange we have — no matter its bittersweet flavour — is a gift. The gift of trauma. The work is in learning how to see that. I was far from understanding this concept in the stories I've shared above. However, while I had no idea at the time, I had taken the first essential steps on a new path. And what a glorious adventure it would turn out to be.

CHAPTER NINE

Everyone You Know is Going to Die (Part Two)

Choose to die well while you
can; wait too long, and it might
become impossible to do so.
— Musonius Rufus

So how can we better prepare for a loved one's death? As the Stoics know all too well, we can do many things to empower ourselves and those we love in preparation for our parting ways. But first, are such thoughts morbid? The definition is "an abnormal and unhealthy interest in disturbing and unpleasant subjects, especially death and disease". Frankly, it's unhealthier to pretend it's not going to happen. How is interest in your or another's death anyone else's business? All too often, we bend to the pressure of others, reticent to express our true feelings, therefore stifling our authenticity. Let's not do that. Alas, the "morbid" objection is part of the problem regarding our view of death. Hence we might take a leaf from the Tibetans' book mapping the entire process for death, for which one should prepare long in advance.

Allowing my mum to die without making my peace was immensely unhealthy. Returning to that situation takes a different understanding, self-awareness, and practice. Think about it: they're gone. That's it. You'll never be able to say another word to them. They will never hear from or respond to you again (not in the traditional sense). You've no more chances. This will break some of you, causing irreparable emotional damage to you and those close to you. Why put yourselves through an extended phase of trauma and grief that can be avoided? Even if the words you wish to say are to get something off your chest, then do it — clear the air. Then see what's left when the dust settles. At least you will have spoken your truth and given them a chance to respond in kind. Carrying the weight of a grudge right up to a death isn't healthy for anyone. Avoid it if you can.

Perhaps all of this seems obvious. Or maybe you see the death of someone close as an event we must accept and "get over", ultimately just "getting on with it"? It's not always as easy as that, though; such dismissal will often result in shock, anger, and depression. In fact, you might make yourself very sick indeed.

The Burden of Loss: Unexpected Death of a Loved One and Psychiatric Disorders Across the Life Course in a National Study was published in 2014 by Katherine M. Keyes, PhD, Charissa Pratt, BA, Sandro Galea, MD, DrPH, Katie A. McLaughlin, PhD, Karestan C. Koenen, PhD, and M. Katherine Shear, MD. The paper mentions the relationship between a loved one's unexpected death and subsequent symptomatic elevations in multiple forms of psychopathology. It considers whether unexpected loss creates the novel onset of psychiatric disorders such as mood, anxiety, and substance disorders. The result? According to the survey, unexpected death was the most common traumatic experience and most likely to be rated as the worst, regardless of other traumatic experiences. The study also demonstrated the potential for major depressive episodes, including panic and post-traumatic stress disorder. "Unexpected death..." Isn't that a funny expression? How can the inevitable be unexpected?

As we've discussed, a lot of folks and scientists believe that we revisit Earth repeatedly, living multiple lives. In this case, an early death might well be an experiment from which the souls involved have the opportunity to learn. So in this scenario, the person's passing is not early. *It's right on time.*

There's no such thing as an unexpected death, even in literal terms, since all things die. In writing, "… In this world, nothing can be said to be certain, except death and taxes", Benjamin Franklin nailed the coffin shut on this point. Like all things in this world, death is a constant — the ultimate example of the transformative nature of our very being. If we fully embraced the myriad realities of death, there would be very little to no surprise when the time came around, as it so often does.

According to the aforementioned study, bereavement and the onset of psychiatric disorders go hand in hand. The paper's authors suggest this as "an important emerging area for clinical research and practice". I tend to agree.

The science also points to another psychobiological aspect of grieving that most of us will never consider. A clinical review by Annina Seiler, Roland von Känel, and George M. Slavich observed the effects of spousal loss. The study states that bereavement following such a loss triggers an increased risk of multimorbidity and mortality in the immediate weeks and months. Specifically, it can lead to an elevation in inflammation-related health problems, including but not limited to cardiovascular disease and cancer. Wowsers. Imagine if you lost someone to cancer and grieved so much that you gave yourself cancer. That's what's happening. It's not the dead or them dying that makes us sick. Our grieving becomes the catalyst for our ongoing physical and mental illness.

Seiler and colleagues' review considers a framework called the *Social Signal Transduction Theory of Depression.* This mouthful of a multilevel approach describes physiologic, neural, molecular, and genomic mechanisms (body stuff) that link a human's adverse socio-environmental experiences with biological processes that create and drive depression. The theory centres around the hypothesis that interpersonal stressors involving social threats increase internal inflammatory processes, thus creating several depressive symptoms that can, in turn, affect the body's health.

In conclusion, the review states:

"The death of a spouse is considered one of the most stressful life events a person can experience. In addition to increasing risk for depression, spousal death can lead to increased risk for various somatic and physical diseases and early mortality".

So our response to another's death can profoundly affect our minds and bodies in ways we cannot comprehend. As it transpired, this happened to me. Though then, I didn't fully understand the extent of my mental illness.

CHAPTER TEN

Good Grief

**You cannot prevent the birds
of sorrow from flying over your
head, but you can prevent them
from building nests in your hair.
— Old Chinese Proverb**

There's *normal* and *complicated* grief, the latter of which is a recently recognised condition occurring in about seven per cent of the bereaved. Below is an excerpt from a paper by Myrna M. Weissman, John C. Markowitz, and Gerald L. Klerman, which sums it up nicely:

"Grief is a painful emotional experience, and some individuals find their emotional response too overwhelming to deal with. The death of a significant other tops the life event stress scales. Perceiving the feelings of mourning as dangerous, too painful to contemplate, they try to 'keep busy' with other activities, numbing themselves in the hope that the feelings will subside. They may avoid their feelings by occupying themselves with funeral arrangements and taking care of other mourners rather than mourning themselves. The sadness of the loss may feel dangerous. If the relationship has been a conflicted one, for instance, the death of a formerly abusive parent, the patient may feel guilty about feeling angry at the deceased ('What a terrible person I am to be angry at the dead, someone who can no longer defend herself!'). These patients suffer from not grieving. Avoiding the emotions leads the person to try to go through life containing them, distancing herself from emotional life, and consuming great emotional energy. This postponing and avoidance of grief is characteristic of complicated bereavement, a long-recognised form of major depression".

The paper mentions the phenomenon of those who have become "professional mourners". These people devote an unhealthy amount of time and energy to remembering the dead (shrines and all). I've had many interactions with such folks by publishing previous articles about suffering and grief. "I'll never get over the loss", they'll say. "It destroyed me, and I will never heal", they finitely declare. No shit. All the science points to such a mindset as giving us more illnesses with which to contend.

So is it morbid? No, giving due thought and attention to your relationship with those around you and focusing early on how their death will affect you is not morbid. It's common sense. The big question is, how on earth does one do it for all the people in one's life? Who have we to consider here? Mum, dad, brother, sister, significant other, best friends, pets, gran, your children. What about Mary in Accounts? Wayan, your favourite barman? The list goes on. Is there anyone you're holding back from sharing your truth? To whom are you eternally grateful? Who needs to hear something from you? Who loves you? *Who do you love?*

Think back to that list you wrote in the early pages of this book. Does it involve them? I've left a blank page for the people you care about in the spirit of consistency. Take a moment. Dig deep. Be honest.

People I care about

Now, some of the folks on your list will be easy. Perhaps your relationship with your dad is first-class and always has been. You tell him you love him every time you speak. You've no secrets from him; he knows you cheated on your wife, of your alcohol issues, and that you saw a therapist for depression. You even told him that you like to use cocaine on weekends. Perhaps he even did a line with you one time at Christmas? Let it snow. What a fantastic relationship! But did you ever sit him down and tell him that for most of your childhood and early adult life, you held him co-responsible for your mum's alcoholism? Did you express that for such a long time, his fear of exiting their toxic marriage likely caused more harm than good? Have you told him that, despite the circumstances, you realise he was doing his best? Do you forgive him for his role in the mental illness you developed as a child? And have you created the space for him to express his truth to you, ensuring he feels fully heard?

And what about the ex you haven't seen for 15 years? She's rarely on your mind because "that was a long time ago", and there's no point crying over spilt milk. But deep down, you know how much your selfishness hurt her. Sure, you were broken and unconscious back then, so to a large extent you couldn't help yourself. What about now, though? Do you think she might deserve an apology without any attempt at mitigation? Can you make amends for your part in the emotional trauma she still carries 15 years after your split? You might still do some good.

Is a list of people you'd be sad to lose enough? How about another list of those who will die while deserving acknowledgement, admission, or an apology from you? You know the drill by now. See the next page.

People who deserve an apology before one of us dies

All this points to certain inevitabilities. They're going to die, and you'll be sad. If their death is unplanned, you'll likely be significantly more devastated, perhaps even crippled by guilt and regret. According to science, you will likely develop physical and mental health problems.

Here we are again, at the crossroads otherwise known as choice. Yes, some inevitabilities come with interpersonal loss. Will this happen to you? Yes, it certainly will. Perhaps many times. Will it suck? Yes, big-time. Depending on who you lose (a child, for instance), you might even wish you'd never been born (the irony). Are there any practical utilities we can embrace to lessen such incredible emotional pain and mental and physical illness? Yes. There are a whole host of options available to us. That's the point of this book.

Obvious ways to avoid a mess when people die:

1. Tell people you love them every time you say goodbye.
2. Tell the absolute truth to everyone close to you.
3. Be yourself with them. Hold nothing back.
4. Forgive them — no matter how harsh their crime.
5. Spend more time with them! Even if it's only via video call.
6. Rise above falling out with them.
7. Own your shit. If you're wrong, admit it.
8. Invite them to do the same.
9. Let it go and move on. None of it will matter when they're dead.
10. Be love. Cultivate devotion within all of your cherished relationships.

How does this list feel at this juncture in your life? Doable or altruistic bullshit? If the former, then *BOOM*! If the latter, keep reading. There's hope for us all.

Only Human

The pragmatic approach to suffering in this book may disconcert you, but as discussed, i didn't always feel this way. Feelings are merely a functional aspect of the mind. While emotional responses are normal and sometimes healthy, all too often, they enslave us. So what is to be done? To walk the line between our humanity and proactive emotional observation, we must learn mastery from the masters.

The old Zen saying, "The obstacle is the path", nicely sums this up. The way of the Buddhists, Taoists, and Stoics isn't devoid of emotion; it's rooted in self-love. However, these philosophies offer mindfulness utilities that help us master and even befriend our emotions, thus becoming captains of our fate. Far from *beating down* or *shrugging off*, mastering requires complete and one-pointed immersion. It's a craft. So just as we apply ourselves to the expert execution of a trade, we must do so with our minds. Humans have human experiences and express very real human feelings. Grief is an adversarial emotion — of that, we can be sure. Emotions usually arise alongside seemingly impossible or unwelcome situations. Though, isn't every great story littered with challenges? Life wouldn't be life without an appropriate number of obstacles, so perhaps we'd do well to expect and welcome them with open arms. Stoic bestselling author Ryan Holiday wrote a brilliant book called *The Obstacle is the Way*. Aligning completely with Eastern philosophies in this regard, the Stoic method is to turn that obstacle into an opportunity to search for the lessons. As the Stoic Roman emperor, Marcus Aurelius, once wrote, "What stands in the way becomes the way", thus, obstacles bear alchemic gifts should we choose to see them. Along these lines, the 13th-century Sufi mystic and poet Rumi's "The cure for the pain is in the pain" offers layers of wisdom for review.

The obstacle is the path.

To put a storm in our rear-view mirror, we must drive through it, regardless of the terrain. We must seek opportunities to learn despite the lesson's probable and unpalatable pain. So trauma sufferers wishing to simply forget will, at some point, be haunted when the emotions they once pushed aside inevitably resurface with a notable degree of potency. It's not the way.

We can't all naturally see the world through this logical lens; such pragmatism takes contemplation and practice and embodies Zen. Grieving takes as long as grieving takes. Nothing can stop that unless you've had a near-death, psychedelic, or other such altered consciousness experience that presents you with an alternative understanding of death's ephemeral nature. All that said, it will not do to simply drown ourselves in sorrow. As sure as eggs are eggs, everyone you know is going to die. They will no longer be available to you in this life. Your traditional two-way interactions will cease. So what to do?

We must learn better ways to work through our suffering. We have to embrace it more healthily. I'm not saying don't grieve. Absolutely do grieve. Don't rush the process; try to experience it with zero expectations. Grieve for however long it takes, but be mindful. Grief is not something you should attempt to set aside. Your protective ego might work overtime to convince you otherwise; however, grief is not a facet of death that should be buried. In fact, if you proactively externalise it, the blocked emotions can flow. There's a quote whose unknown author I cannot accurately credit: "Grief never ends, but it changes. It's a passage, not a place to stay. Grief is not a sign of weakness, or a lack of faith. It is the price of love". What a wonderfully compassionate reminder of the power and impermanence of grief.

Side thought: it's strange to continually bear sorrow on the anniversary of a death. This is an unhealthy version of time travel. Celebrate their life, sure. But carving out time once a year to feel sorry for ourselves the whole day at least once a year is a curious thing indeed. Who does this mental torture actually serve?

So have in the back of your mind that, at some point, your grieving will curtail. Don't guilt yourself when this happens; it's not a case of no longer loving or forgetting the dead; it's merely energy, changing, as all things do. I remember suddenly realising it was February, and the anniversary of my mum's death had passed entirely without my attention. That was a good day.

The dead are not sad about their predicament; only those left behind suffer. We're attached to our memories of the deceased because they play such significant roles in our stories. We cling to anyone or thing that offers a sense of who or what we are. As such, they're perceivably fundamental aspects of our identities. So what's the alternative? What does it mean to be nobody? Can we imagine such a thing? The Buddha said: "Attachment is the root of all suffering". Through personal loss, we suffer. Just as we cling to people, we cling to possessions and status because we feel our story lacks foundation or an engaging plot without them. But none of those things is *us*. Part of our egoic story, but not the real and true us. What if we could learn to be connected rather than attached? The game is to allow your suffering but observe it for what it is — your emotional response to an event. The Buddhist's *Four Noble Truths* are helpful utilities that speak to this phenomenon; we'll discuss them in detail in Chapter 24.

Drawing a line under our grieving process doesn't mean we forget or stop caring. The frequency of love is a timeless vibration. It comes at a cost because all relationships end, but grief dissolves, too, if you allow it. It's been nine years since my mum died and three since my best buddy Macy. Despite early fierce sorrow, I mourn neither now. Grief is love, and my affection for them never ends. As for the internal suffering? I detached myself from that long ago.

So what's so good about grief? Well, for one thing, it's evidence of the potency of our love. Knowing as we do that those we cherish will die points a finite finger at the time we have left together. We can preempt grief by being more mindful of how often we interact with people. Because, in the end, our degree of presence with one another defines the successes and failures of our relationships. Since grief is love transmuted, and a bearer of gifts supreme, then grief, in my book, is a good thing indeed.

Disciples of Life

We are born gentle and weak.

At death, we are hard and stiff.

Green plants are tender and filled with sap.

When they die, they are withered and dry.

Therefore the stiff and unbending are the disciples of death.

The gentle and yielding are the disciples of life.

Part Two

Doing

CHAPTER ELEVEN

The Art of Living

To be able, under all circumstances, to practice five things
constitutes perfect virtue; these
five things are gravity, generosity
of soul, sincerity, earnestness, and
kindness.

— Confucius

Not all of us share the same fear of death. And while religion is a core root of our differences, there are many more in applied philosophy. What other philosophies might open our minds to new perspectives on life and death? Many schools have encouraged introspection so that we might better navigate the world outside. One such philosophical model to cultivate conscious contemplation of the art of living is Confucianism. Though, we must be prepared to go back in time to uncover such lost yet profound wisdom. People use the phrase "new-age thinking" along these lines, which is somewhat of a misnomer since such philosophies amount to knowledge that's existed for thousands of years. Though, since much was relegated to history's annals by the savage spread of the global Christian machine, perhaps it's no surprise that we're only just reconnecting with this wisdom. Consider, if you will, the Mayans and Incas. Profound secrets of living and dying were obliterated alongside their untimely ends.

Confucius, who died aged 71, was born in 551 BCE. He was a hugely influential Chinese educator and philosopher, often associated with the Chinese sage stereotype. Confucius wanted people to regard their interaction with others more than money or material possessions. The man's teachings became the stuff of legend, leading to the philosophy of Confucianism.

The central Confucian concept is that every one of us wishes to become superior to our past and Self. As such, we aspire to transcend (level up). These guiding principles encourage the ongoing propulsion towards the evolved (Higher) Self. Confucianism, therefore, invites people to master the art of living. For us to "abide in the highest excellence", we first must learn and present at least the following attributes:

1. Purpose.
2. Truthfulness.
3. Prudence.
4. Poise.
5. Firmness.
6. Charity.
7. Self-sufficiency.
8. Earnestness.
9. Thoroughness.
10. Sincerity.
11. Purity of thought and action.
12. Avoidance of sycophancy (being fake).
13. Love of truth.
14. Openness.
15. Mental hospitality.
16. Rectitude (decency).
17. Composure.
18. Moderation.
19. Fearlessness.
20. Ease and dignity.

21. Lowliness.
22. Growth.
23. Capacity.
24. Benevolence.
25. Broadmindedness.

The Confucian Golden Rule is "What you do not want done to yourself, do not do unto others", and it's more common than you think. The principal notion of treating others how we would hope to be treated features prominently in Buddhism, Taoism, Hinduism, Islam, Judaism, Zoroastrianism, and Christianity. The Stoics too. It's the world's most influential ethical tenet.

Confucianism focuses on philosophies surrounding our interaction with family, community, and the adoption of social order. Unlike its rather more free-flowing philosophical sister Taoism, government and employment also featured in the Confucianist framework.

The Confucian Five Relationships

Confucian philosophy tackles relationships with family, friends, and leaders. Three out of the five relationships relate to family, and the complete list is as follows:

1. Father and son (loving and reverential).
2. Elder brother and younger brother (gentle and respectful).
3. Husband and wife (good and listening).
4. Older friend and younger friend (considerate and deferential).
5. Ruler and subject (benevolent and loyal).

You might wonder where are the sisters and mothers, the LGBTQ+, the gender-neutral, and generally unsure? *Protest not, friend!* Gender inclusion wasn't really a thing in 500 BCE China, so while perhaps in need of an update, the thinking is still sound, assuming we sidestep identity politics.

So the Confucianists invite one another to identify, accept, and conform to their collective roles within the family and community. In this practice, everything falls into place for them to live happy and fruitful lives. Harmony in life is, therefore, the goal.

Respecting familial relationships isn't exactly exclusive to the Chinese Confucianists, as many Eastern cultures prioritise family. How many might read the list above and struggle to reckon with it? Have we all experienced a happy and healthy relationship with our father (and mother)? Did your older brother (or sister) protect and treat you kindly? Or did their early childhood trauma materialise through their subsequent abuse of you? Does your husband or wife hold space for you, keen to ensure you feel heard? Do they respect your truth despite contrasting beliefs? How about your friends, are they attentive and respectful of your opinion, and is their fellowship offered free from judgement?

As for the last on the list (number five), your relationship with your "rulers" is likely altogether more complex. After all, respect is earned. Or is it indisputably deserved? Regardless, I propose the hypothesis that we are no one's "subject".

So, Confucianism is one example of an Eastern philosophy embodying the art of living, not just theoretically, but with practical guidelines and utilities. Alas, the relational rules cannot apply to all families. Why? Because the Western family structure is primarily broken. As we continuously plough head-on into a turgid sea of distractive consumerism (now also gripping the East), society is developing a great sickness.

To openly discuss life, happiness, and death, we must also traverse the rugged terrain that covers family's effect on our psyches and how we live our lives. The Western family model is built on a different foundation. But then, what should they look like now? All things considered, I remain optimistic that there are genuinely happy families in the world. However, it cannot be denied that mental illness spreads like wildfire throughout our society. Granting that a low divorce rate does not necessarily indicate a healthy family unit, the point remains that Western families are often subjected to different cultural and religious stimuli. In most developed countries, we have many more distractions available after all.

In 2020, there were 109,000 divorces in the UK, nine out of every 1,000 marriages (compared to just three in China). Over in Australia, there was an increase of 200 per cent in divorce petitions, while the Turks witnessed a whopping 400 per cent rise. At the same time, in the US, almost 45 per cent of first marriages end in divorce. Sadly, such statistics are by no means unique to the West. While Eastern divorce rates are lower (the lowest being in Hindu populations), divorce and single living are rising globally. And, of course, one cannot overlook the obligations and social stigma attached to divorce and separation by most of the world's religions.

Does none of this come as a surprise? As humanity changes, perhaps it's natural for the family unit to transmogrify. Is marriage a contractual construct of control? Perhaps broken family structures are one of life's norms and evidence of natural transition.

The same could be said for child abuse (mental and physical), narcissistic personality disorder, domestic violence, gaslighting, addiction, and adultery. The toxic baton of unhealed trauma is passed from generation to generation like a shitty stick. Yet we see such societal disease as nothing out of the ordinary. We may have gotten the whole thing wrong, and we don't necessarily need marriage or a fully functional family structure. Maybe we're destined to live in separation, in service to self? Or is society sick simply because we do not naturally fit into the societal model meticulously crafted by the system's architects?

So with these rife ills comes wave after wave of traumatised generations, ironically keen to express how they're "living their best life" via the illusory miracle of social media. This projection of false happiness involves crafting an endless stream of stories. Location, sculpted bodies, latte art, breakfast, lunch, and dinner, their crafted eyebrows, the cars they drive, planes they fly, houses they occupy, make-up regime, squat routine, and every other material thing. Every moment and experience is presented in an online exhibition to ensure the world sees just how happy they are. How heavy my heart as I contemplate that our younger generations are growing up believing this is a reality to which they must aspire. I say this with love, you understand, but how low we have fallen, to the point where our perception of happiness is now so perversely distorted beyond recognition.

CHAPTER TWELVE

Out With the Old

Grey hair is a crown of life.
— Lailah Gifty Akita

Confucianists also believe that age gives all things worth regardless of their nature, so the young should respect the old. Can we unquestioningly respect our old folks? How many of us bore witness to world-class parenting, anyway? Thanks to my childhood's chaos, I stopped obeying my parents' instructions early on.

Any mandatory direction to follow anyone without question is questionable.

There are millions of wise and wholesome old folks capable of sharing truths and experiences of untold societal, familial, and individual value. By 2050, we'll have two billion older adults living on the planet, accounting for twenty per cent of the population.

On the island of Bali, all the family's generations live in a collection of buildings surrounding a pagoda and temple, protected by a walled compound. It is unheard of for grandparents to live elsewhere or be placed in the care of others. In the Balinese Hindu tradition, the grandparents stay with the family, and depending on their age and physical capabilities, household chores and work are delegated accordingly. As with many Eastern countries and traditions, grandparents become active carers of their grandchildren, sharing wisdom and life experience that nurtures growth. In turn, the whole family cares for the grandparents until they die in a way that might often be considered an excellent death. What a way to go out.

Elsewhere in the world, we have an entirely contrasting approach to treating the aged. According to a government study in the UK, the life expectancy of care home residents between 65 and 79 is lower than that of non-care home residents. Arranging for older relatives to move into senior care facilities or assisted living centres is commonplace.

As of August 2022, over 408,000 people over 65 in the UK lived in residential care and nursing homes. That's 16 per cent of older people over the age of 85. Contrastingly, only 0.46 per cent (roughly 1.5 million) of elderly people live in nursing homes in America, with 0.21 per cent (1 million) of elderly adults in assisted living facilities. Why such high figures in the UK? Several factors are apparently at play, including couples in their late 40s or early 50s having young children and elderly parents, with spiralling housing costs and children usually taking priority. Fair points that they are, such issues concern the East less. In China, just one per cent of the elderly population lives in care, but as Asian countries rapidly follow the ways of the West, the old patterns dissolve, and elderly folks are being shipped off to care in increasing numbers. In Korea, one-third live alone, and South Korea has the worst senior poverty rate among developed nations. Japan is similar, so gone are the days when a family should live close enough to its senior family members for one to carry a bowl of soup. Perhaps family values are crumbling alongside the wisdom of old.

I do not judge anyone who struggles to look after their ageing folks. But what does it say about our society that we would acquiesce in the removal of our ancient advisors from view and proximity, and into the care of others than find a way to look after them ourselves? Do we not move heaven and hell to host our children? I imagine many more families would welcome their elders into the home if money were not an issue.

Or am I being naive? Did your mother's aggressive and abusive behaviour guarantee her a place in that care facility? That would make sense. Perhaps you'd rather gnaw your toes off than spend your days looking after Grandad — cantankerous as he doubtless can be. Or possibly watching Grandma knock on heaven's door is a most unwelcome reminder of what's just around the corner for the rest of us?

Old folks can be cranky and the creators of deep-rooted and widescale familial misery. They can be utterly toxic. But is it loving to reject them in their latter stages of life? Is it kind to deprive them of the serenity exuded by a home in the bosom of a family? And in future, when we're the ones two steps from kicking the bucket, how will we be treated? Might our actions become a heinous regret later down the road?

The old have much to offer the young; if only we realise their value. The alternative? Out of sight and out of mind, a void forms between us. They've always been around to call or visit whenever we needed them, and while fantasy, part of us expects that will never change. We're lackadaisical and complacent like that. Hence the surprise when people die. We're not ready for it. Of course, we're too busy to notice that we've drifted apart, but it's happening all the same, and it's just life, isn't it? Do we discard the elderly because they remind us of what's in store for us all? Wrinkly skin, brittle bones, white hair, failing eyes and ears. Perhaps their words and actions have slowed; maybe their memories have failed. Such physical cues bring home the brutal truth that our bodies and minds will be the same one day. It's a scary thought. After all, it's one thing to hypothesise about humanity's impermanence, but it's another to witness the signs of decay.

There's a potential future where we collectively embrace impermanence and live accordingly. We reconnect with our old folks with presence and awareness. Inquisitively, we dive beyond the superficial — immersing in meaningful conversations about living, loving, and learning. About what it feels like to be in the latter stages of life. Perhaps we're teaching them about our new ideas, sharing techniques and methodologies for self-realisation, mindfulness, and connecting with one's authentic Self. Maybe these things never occurred to them or were thought too late to learn. I imagine such interactions would provide comfort and contentedness — perhaps even bring us closer together while sharing wisdom and rekindling purpose. This game would have upsides aplenty since all parties would surely die happier with such mutual love and appreciation. In this future, we support each other's growth to the very end. A wholesome crown of knowledge passes from one generation to the next.

CHAPTER THIRTEEN

The Tao

Happiness is the absence
of the striving for happiness.
— Zhuang Zhou

Life need not be a constant uphill battle. Taoism (pronounced "Daoism") is a Chinese philosophy that offers guidance for living a long and healthy life in harmony with the Tao. Lao Tzu, the founding Taoist philosopher and author of the *Tao Te Ching*, said: "Life is a series of natural and spontaneous changes. Don't resist them – that only creates sorrow. Let reality be reality. Let things flow naturally forward in whatever way they like". You will see similar thinking later in this book since acceptance (surrender) is a crucial pillar to happiness.

Philosophers and theologists the world over have sought to define the Tao, while amusingly, Taoists would argue it cannot be determined using the primitive construct of words. Hence wordless teaching is a part of learning Taoism. "The Tao that can be told is not the eternal Tao. The name that can be named is not the eternal name", says Lao Tzu. All the same, his 5,000-word book tells the Tao's story and is well worth reading if you're keen to learn more about this mystery and its philosophies.

Just like many of you, I've communed with this energy. The Tao is the source, the pattern, and the substance of everything that exists and does not exist in the Universe. The Tao is everything, nothing, whatever was, whatever will be, whatever won't be, and whatever — if there was ever anything — in between. The energetic system connects and contains all things within the constructs of existence and non-existence.

Simply put, the Tao is the way. And perhaps, the reason it cannot be defined with words is because the Tao is a frequency, the frequency of love. Therefore, it cannot be seen or heard by traditional means. Or rather, if we know what we are looking for. We must learn to feel it. Though it can be seen and heard. Each of us, the ground on which we walk, the sea in which we swim, and the birds and insects whose microstories we witness daily are all intrinsic expressions of the Tao.

Sharing the Confucianists' Golden Rule, a Taoist lives day-to-day, practising the core principle of kindness. Guilty, as we often are of self-neglect, compassion for oneself is paramount. Taoism invites us to consider our essence (frequency) and connect with the same life force energy (chi or qi) as those around us. Hence we should always keep our intrinsic connection in mind. Another beautiful Taoist idea (among many) is that any act of unkindness creates an imbalance in our own life. Thus, vice versa.

Taoism invites us to surrender to the flow. This is not to suggest that we all wander around smiling like lunatics. Such behaviour might well have us out of balance with our authentic selves. Consider it more an invitation to observe the times we find ourselves at odds with life's flow — fighting a losing battle or attempting to swim up the stream, so to speak. Perhaps at this point, an alternative choice would be to pause and evaluate our status quo, then reapply kindness to our thoughts and actions. This book contains a multitude of utilities for such practice.

Remember, this includes kindness to Self, which means we must be ever-mindful of how we judge or criticise ourselves. We spend a significant amount of time in our own heads. Try to ensure that it's a healthy place to be. There is no place for judgement in an open heart. Perhaps it's easier to see how life

("The Universe") reflects our actions back at us? What we transmit, in turn, we receive. The man who blinded me offered wise words along these lines and I remain grateful for his lesson. More of which I'll share later.

Taoists neither fear death nor welcome it. They simply enjoy living in harmony with The Way. One of the oldest books of Taoism, written by Zhuang Zhou, the *Chuang Tzu*, says:

"The true men of old did not know what it was to love life or to hate death. They did not rejoice in birth nor strive to put off dissolution. Unconcerned they came, and unconcerned they went. That was all. They did not forget whence it was they had sprung, neither did they seek to inquire their return thither. Cheerfully they accepted life, waiting patiently for their restoration (the end). This is what is called not to lead the heart astray from Tao and not to supplement the natural by human means. Such a one may be called a true man. Such men are free in mind and calm in demeanour".

I have a 100 per cent vibe with Taoism and its celebration of simplicity and peace. The Taoists believe that the secret to happiness lies within the *T'ai Hsü* or the *"Great Nothing"*. In his utterly charming book *The Tao of Pooh*, Benjamin Hoff makes many remarkable observations on this topic, brought to life through conversations between Christopher Robin, Pooh Bear, and friends. Quoting from the Chuang Tzu, Hoff shares the following wisdom:

"Consciousness asks someone named Speechless Non-Doer what it can do, think, and follow to earn the wisdom of the Tao. But Speechless Non-Doer doesn't answer. Consciousness asks someone named Impulsive Speech-Maker the same questions, and Impulsive Speech-Maker starts to talk but forgets what he is saying. Finally, Consciousness asks the Yellow Emperor, who says, 'the secret to the Tao is doing, thinking, and following nothing'".

One final story springs to mind about two monks sitting

together in the forest. The older monk is calm and one with the nature around him, which he peacefully observes. Troubled, the younger monk declares: "Nothing makes sense". Without shifting his gaze, the older monk smiles and says, "It does, doesn't it". I smile every time I read this.

These tales are not an invitation to immediately shift your self-development strategy towards the sofa. In Taoism, nothing is something. And so, by practising the attainment of an empty mind *(the Great Nothing)*, you may well make space for something great. As Hoff wittily observes: "I think; therefore I am... Confused". I imagine Descartes chuckling over that little riff on his nugget of wisdom.

This chapter has introduced how we might reframe our view of life and living, how we treat ourselves and others, and our focus on *being* rather than *doing*. Taoism offers much to the anatomy of happiness and a focused way of living. These philosophies help us prepare for a good death. There are unfathomable depths of wisdom within these teachings. Although only a flying visit, we'll discuss more of Taoism's divine intelligence later.

The philosophies briefly mentioned are lifelong practices. So you need not necessarily dedicate all your focus to one. Perhaps consider simply following your heart, keep your mind open to all truths, retaining whatever resonates with you. Anything not serving you might not be your truth, but is no less true. The Tao is as relevant now, as it ever was. It's timeless because it is human as much as it is divine.

There are many more ancient utilities to uncover. A little later, we'll explore *Dukkha, Anicca,* and *Anatta* — the Buddhist concepts that, when fully embodied, can forever transform your fear of living and dying into a calm, connected, pragmatic, and sustained status of peace.

CHAPTER FOURTEEN

A Sidenote About Suicide

If you know someone who's depressed, please resolve never to ask them why. Depression isn't a straightforward response to a bad situation; depression just is, like the weather.

Try to understand the blackness, lethargy, hopelessness, and loneliness they're going through. Be there for them when they come through the other side. It's hard to be a friend to someone who's depressed, but it is one of the kindest, noblest, and best things you will ever do.

— Stephen Fry

A good friend and coach came to visit me soon after I moved to Bali. She arrived precisely when I needed her brutal yet objective advice. Coincidence? No chance. I have no doubt that the Universe puts people and events in our paths at the right time and place. Sarah had her own needs for space and sunshine to reflect, so her last-minute arrival suited us both. So there she was, on the *Island of the Gods*, for a spot of mutual healing.

During our initial catch-up, I nonchalantly told Sarah that I'd come very close to suicide a few years prior. As the waves crashed and the cicadas chirped, I spewed my dramatic tale of woe like a bowl of bad mussels — all in the unsuspecting face of a woman fresh in-country after 24 hours of transcontinental travel. My bad.

The following day, Sarah told me of her sadness following my admission, and how sorry she was that things had gotten so bad for me. It made me think about how dark and guarded those days were — and how little of that darkness I shared with anyone around me. We don't, do we? Allowing the feeling of depression was counter-intuitive to the usual warrior-comedian persona I worked so hard to present to the world. I wanted everyone to see water running off this duck's back. I tried to impress people with my resilience and ability to laugh at harsh lessons, while spitting in the eye of depression. Despite quietly and regularly considering my own suicide, putting on a brave face had become one of my very best skills. Opening up was a weakness. Plus, on the rare occasions that I did open that door, more often than not, people would say, "It's just a phase!" or "Pick yourself up and dust yourself off", or (my own personal favourite) "You always land on your feet, Martin!" Bless their hearts. I always landed on my feet because I was always in *fight-or-flight* mode and running away from shit. One foot in front of the other at high speed was the only way I knew how to operate. Half the time, I ran so fast that you couldn't even see my feet — like that old *Roadrunner and the Coyote* cartoon.

My predominant suicidal phase was around the time I'd successfully completed the ruination of my business partnership with Don and my second marriage — the latter lasting less than six months. My mum had died; my girlfriend (the one with whom I cheated) had left after my alcohol and cocaine abuse went too far. And all the while, I was under criminal investigation for tax evasion, money laundering, and fraud. I was never charged for these crimes, but it weighed heavily on my mind and body. It's safe to say that I'd brought a great deal of drama to my table, and my mental platter was full.

I'd already self-harmed during this time. Head-butting that kitchen window put a nasty, deep gash on my forehead. It had been a long time since I hurt myself like that. Violent self-harm was more prevalent in my youth.

One night, I could no longer pick myself up or dust myself off. I drove home from my local bar a little high and a lot drunk, and in a fit of deep despair, I drank a whole lot more. And then it occurred to me that I'd ruined my miserable life beyond all belief; I'd hurt everyone with whom I ever came into contact. I had taken this life too far down the wrong path, making too many mistakes to fix. And then I had the bright idea to load my shotgun. I was alone in the dark — where I deserved to be. The light was far, far away — too far to get back to in this lifetime.

I'll share more details of this story in the next chapter; this introduction aims to highlight some recurrent thoughts and feelings that overwhelm and drive many of us to suicide.

I was lucky. I didn't pull the trigger for reasons that will become apparent. So after my dice with death, aged 39, I began my long journey of self-awareness and personal development, which began with me acknowledging that I needed professional help.

Despite being unaware of my suicidal thoughts, the therapist I was lucky to meet suggested I "seek care". He invited me to share my shit with a chosen few I must realise loved and cared about me. My friend Jane was a crucial player in that process. At that time, she was like a sister to me, and I her brother. While she did know of my suicidal thoughts, I did tell her a lot, and she listened — intently, lovingly, and without judgement — distraught yet determined to help. She was familiar with the famous "brave face" and knew I could take flack. She also knew that for things to get so bad, the situation was indeed serious. No more warrior-comedian. Time to work on being authentic and honest and to admit I needed help. Time to chip away at years of conditioning. Time to unlearn. I'll never forget those events, as it was a period of great realisation and awakening.

How to Commit Suicide

At the time of publishing this book, in a typical month, 677,000 people around the world research "suicide" online. That number has increased by 13 per cent since 2019. Around 89,000 use specific terms, including "how to commit suicide", and "how to commit suicide painlessly". This purpose-driven (monthly) number has increased by a shocking 78 per cent since 2019. The US, India, Philippines, the UK, and France rank high in the league table. I wonder whether you know any of these people personally.

This problem is not going away. It's getting worse because more of us feel out of place while trapped inside this illusory system. We're conditioned to be perfect — successful, and live our "best lives" — whatever that means. All the while, life on Earth loses its appeal to many. We're encouraged to be in debt, to work 60-hour weeks, to binge-drink on Fridays, and max our credit cards on Saturdays. And as the layers of fakery pile on to our frail, confused, and screen-addicted psyches, we chase the utterly pointless wonders of materialism. We focus less on being mindfully kind to ourselves while turning an apathetic, blind eye to what's happening to us and those around us. Perhaps we numb the pain with banal distractions because we simply do not know what else to do. Society is sick, yet our programming still stigmatises and marginalises mental health issues. This is not okay. We are not okay.

According to the World Health Organisation, around 800,000 people take their own lives annually. That's one suicide every 40 seconds. There's also hard evidence to suggest that for every person that succeeded, another twenty tried and failed. Do the maths on that. Perhaps you were affected or even involved? Maybe a family member or a close friend or colleague? Or a school friend? Or just a total stranger you passed in the street — your eyes meeting for a nanosecond, and then they were gone.

Then they were gone.

Factoid: it really is okay to not be okay and, no matter how broken we feel, to share that with others. It's okay that we're none of us bullet-proof, and it's okay to freely admit that with a woeful lack of support, this business of life often breaks us all in so many unspeakable ways. What's not okay is that so few of us talk about this openly enough and that putting on a brave face has become a universally accepted and positive trait.

All too often, we simply don't see people's behaviour as a sign of mental illness. The "damage" is a stigma or marginalised flaw and more likely dismissed as an attitudinal dysfunction. This has to stop. We must start seeing mental illness for what it is: an all too common aspect of today's society. It's too prolific to be anything else. Furthermore, as this pandemic touches people in almost every corner of the world, we must ask ourselves, what about our societal models drives an increasing number of people to want to end their lives?

Joel Osteen once wrote: "Know that the depth of your pain is an indication of the height of your future". It's a perfectly agreeable idea, but it doesn't mean we all have the same capacity to manage that pain, free from suffering. Nor do most of us have a beagle in the next room (this will make more sense in the next chapter).

So the issue of suicide must be cracked wide open by as many willing to have this conversation. With the right help reframing it, perceivably negative aspects of our rich life stories can become an aspect of our uniqueness — and a positive part of our development. Though not if it's suddenly and meaninglessly brought to an end.

One of the ways to counter this is for us to become collectively more aware. To be less focused on individuality and more on community. We must listen more to what our intuition says about what's happening with those around us — looking past brave faces. The world's a much better place with our favourite people in it. Just as we hope they've got our backs, remember to remember to have theirs. Consider this a double-barrelled reminder.

Since shotgun night, I've worked hard to practise new methodologies to think, feel, and live better. To *be* better. It hasn't been a walk in the park, nor is it over. I'm a work in progress. We all are. And we should be freely encouraged to forgive ourselves and openly share the things that have damaged us without shame of fear of vilification. Only then can we help ourselves and be supported by others. Only then can we heal. We can't hide our flaws. After all, they're part of our history. Part of what makes us so beautifully unique. We must learn to embrace and accept them.

CHAPTER FIFTEEN

Last Night, a Beagle
Saved My Life

Grief is just love
with no place to go.
— Jamie Anderson

I found Macy at what I learned to be a puppy farm in an anonymous sea of grey houses amidst the urban sprawl of north-west England's Greater Manchester. It was early in 2013 when I visited the unkempt house. I remember entering the lounge with trepidation, realising the so-called "breeder" had been far from honest.

Eight or nine puppies were in the corner of the room, all huddled around the side of a cruddy cream sofa long past its sit-by date. Seemingly spoilt for choice as the super cute welcoming wave of tri-colour and lemon beagle pups all scarpered towards me, one of them stood out — the runt. As the others bullishly rushed to the front of the pack to be the first to greet me, the little one shyly held back, staring inquiringly. It was almost as if she already knew me.

As she tentatively shuffled my way, I did the same — cautiously parting the sea of eager fluff-muffins and providing nonchalant head pats to the others until Macy and I stood toe to toe. The moment I picked her up and brought her face close to mine — feeling the tiny, cold, wet black button nose touch my own, I knew that this potbellied pup and I would be friends for life. And so, regardless of the lacking paperwork, I handed over a wad of cash and exited gladly — the squeaking fur-ball safe and sound in my arms.

For six and a half years, she was by my side.

My play-pal, sofa-sharing hug-buddy, and pub-visiting partner in crime stuck with me through some of the darkest years of my colourful life. What a pair we were.

Free of even a whiff of anger or irritation, Macy O'Toole was a friend to all. Because she came to work with me every day, she was a fond favourite on the dawn trek from Peckham to my south London offices. Brightening the early mornings of the downtrodden daily commuters, Macy trotted carefree across London Bridge train station, keen to arrive at work to check in with her "pack" (my fantastic *Fist of Fury* team). We gave her a job title at the creative agency — she was the *Head of Tails and Barketing*. The daft mutt even starred in YouTube videos, which we dubbed *Macy's Paws for Thought*. Often, my ex-girlfriend and I would proudly declare: "Everybody loves Macy!" We even had a song for it.

When Baguette-Nose and I arrived in Bali in 2019, my little friend (who would swim fanatically in the River Thames) had the gleeful epiphany that the Bali Sea was now in her back garden. She quickly became famous and beloved by the many faces along the beach. Locals, tourists, fishermen, and hospitality workers waved and greeted her on our daily walks. She would cause people to laugh out loud as she wandered up and down the beach with sticks so ludicrously oversized that pedestrians would dive from the path to avoid a shin-battering. Part-beagle, part-dolphin, my marginally mad mutt, would unsubtly and relentlessly encourage people to throw sticks in the ocean for her, just so she could rescue them repeatedly. Her passion for the sea often made me wonder whether she'd been a sentient sea creature in a past life.

In the last chapter, I began describing how close I came to killing myself. As many of you know, when one is gripped by the insurmountable wall of depression, it's common to lose all sense of rational thought. And as the mania and crushing weight becomes unbearable, it's easy to conclude that you're doing everyone a favour by ending your life. Alas, with a bottle of gin and various narcotics inside me, I'd also conceived this a sensible option.

So there I was, on the sofa, in the dark, with two cartridges in my double-barrelled gun; safety off, and the scary end of the bang-stick pointed in the wrong direction. I surmised I would feel nothing. And if it did hurt, I deserved it. Besides, it would be worth it to erase the incessant vortex of guilt, worry, and shame swirling in my head.

I swayed due to being so pissed and heavy with sadness. As I tried to settle with the gun pointed squarely at my forehead, darkness and silence crept around me like an insidious influence. And suddenly hinges creaked, letting light in as the door slowly and slightly opened. My furry friend ambled in. Macy had watched me skulk off into the lounge with a bottle and a gun; had heard me sobbing, mumbling, and spitting obscenities, apparently at no one. Clearly disapproving of my plan, she walked in, plonked herself next to the gun, and looked up at me. I don't know whether it was a "Don't do it", look or "What's for dinner?" Perhaps it was both. Either way, when I looked down at that little sandwich nose, I immediately moved the gun from my face, broke the barrel, unloaded, and placed it down. "Safety first..." I whispered to her, nervously chuckling through snot and tears.

So like that, my course was changed by the unconditional love of a beagle. If she hadn't been there, perhaps I wouldn't be here. And you wouldn't be reading this. Macy saved my life; it's as simple as that. Losing her four years later highlighted my penchant for suffering once again. However, it was also (ironically) a powerful lesson in grasping the Universal concept of impermanence.

In June 2019, just two months since we'd traversed the planet to start a new life in Bali, my little sandwich-nosed compadre went missing from our garden on the beach. I launched and maintained an island-wide search for her, gaining national coverage and even making several appearances on Bali TV's evening news. Despite a hefty reward and so much unfathomable loving kindness from people all over the island (and friends and strangers worldwide), Macy didn't come home.

As the days went by with no news, an old pal Dan (a Buddhist) contacted me from England, suggesting I might wish to prepare for a grave lesson in impermanence *(Anicca)*. I remember internally questioning whether I had already accepted the worst, or perhaps the thought was entirely inconceivable. Nevertheless, I reluctantly took heed of his words and, for the first time, began entertaining the idea of what life would be like without ever seeing Macy again having never said "goodbye".

Weeks went by without a word or sign. Then in August, my friend Terae introduced me to Angela, a respected and compassionate animal communicator in South Africa. *Animal communicator?!* I had no idea such a profession existed, but a little research told me they're a widespread phenomenon, as surprising as that may be. Out of options and open to anything, I contacted Angela. I gave her the bare minimum of information; some photos, the dog's name, and where she was last seen. I asked if she might help me find Macy's location. Two days later, I received the following message:

"Dear Martin, I have picked up that Macy has crossed over the rainbow bridge. I am sorry to tell you that your 'Anum Cara' (soul friend) is not here anymore. Not in the physical sense. I am deeply sorry for your loss of this friend and soul mate, though she does wish to talk to you".

I was sceptical yet curious to hear more and requested as much. A few days after, I received another message:

"From Macy: I am grateful to speak. To let Martin know what my story is. That I miss him and am grateful for the friendship and love he gave me. We have travelled a long journey together. We have an opportunity to shine our souls in unison... Once again. To extend ourselves into a new future.

On the day I left him, I woke up tired. A deep tiredness in my heart. The tiredness became a stress and the heat of the day seemed to make it worse, so I walked to find deep shade. I needed the cold earth against my body.

She says that you are not to feel guilt. You are not to feel despair. You are an incredible human who cared for her and put her needs as equal to your own. Your service and love are so gratefully received.

She says that you needed the release of loyalties to an old life. That you needed a clean break. A reset of sorts. She merely facilitated the shift and took the ends to be tied off on the 'other side'. She has created an opportunity for nothing to pull you backwards out of alignment with this new life you are creating".

Angela added:

"Also, know that while you might experience her body as gone, her spirit is an intrinsic part of your life purpose. To honour yourself completely with compassion and forgiveness opens new avenues for your souls to walk on the earth together again. She says that you can let go of sadness. She can only come back when you look for love inside".

I received this bittersweet note at the end of a long road trip across Bali. My dead dog's WhatsApp message filled me with joy and broke me in two simultaneously. I didn't want to believe it, yet the details and depth were so uncanny — especially coming from a complete stranger who knew nothing of mine and Macy's lives together. *A WhatsApp message from my dead dog?!*

That night, my sleep was busy with dreams. I was with Macy again. She was curled up in the diamond-shaped space between my crossed legs as she always had in the past as I meditated. We were happy. We were love.

Angela's message also mentioned the location where Macy died. She'd identified an area close to my house, where I'd find a bamboo bridge in the deep shade of the trees. The following day, my friend Richie, his kids, and dog (Macy's friend, Rascal) helped me search for her. As we trudged through the constant mesh of knee-deep green, I wondered how far her tired heart might've taken her before she succumbed to the overwhelming pressure, eventually seeking solace in the deep shade. The sun blazed that day; my tee shirt stuck to me with a mix of dirt and sweat, and despite its strength, the sea breeze could not alleviate. Whenever I found a cool spot under a densely covered tree and parted the branches and tangled creeping vines, I fully expected to see my little buddy — dust-covered and curled up, her eyes closed and her sandwich-snout resting on her front paws — finally at peace. But despite uncovering the ruins of a bamboo bridge hidden in those trees, I did not find her. She'd been missing for months after all. And so, after many weeks, I reluctantly gave up the search.

Macy never came home, but I picture her at peace every once in a while, resting in the deep shade, becoming part of the earth once more. And while I miss her, my heart sings as I contemplate the character she was, her unconditional love during my darkest days, and the gift of life that she gave to me.

Call me crazy, but all things considered, I choose to believe the fantastical message I received from my four-legged friend. I have no doubt that our bond transcends physical form and that the love we shared has an unseen mystery one might never fully understand in this lifetime. A type of energy, if you like. We all share it. I like to think we'll meet one day again, or perhaps another moment — in no space and no time. I choose to believe that my little mate knows my feelings and also knows I am happy for her to be free from her canine form and grateful for saving my life.

Jamie Anderson once wrote: "Grief, I've learned, is really just love. It's all the love you want to give but cannot. All that unspent love gathers in the corners of your eyes, the lump in your throat, and the hollow part of your chest. Grief is just love with no place to go". I think there's a great deal of truth in this. Moreover, if one believes that love is transcendent, and that the ripple effect of that frequency can be felt through any and all boundaries, then, like me, you will know that our love does have somewhere to go. And so whenever our hearts sing (as mine regularly does these days), there can be no doubt that vibration will be sensed far and wide on some level.

Believing in Angela's message isn't really the point, though. My lesson was likely, as my Buddhist friend forewarned: to accept the loss simply as another event in my life. To receive further proof of a Universal law: that nothing in life is permanent. A test inviting me to choose to suffer — or suffer not. Thus this lesson in impermanence was delivered, eventually welcomed, and learned at a curiously timed juncture of my life's journey. An opportunity to see the good in the situation instead of being consumed by the bad.

Had this happened to me a year earlier, it would've been a different story. My previously woeful and self-sabotaging mind would've leaned into suffering as I unconsciously focused on the negative, wilfully adopting the role of victim. But this time, there was no crippling fear nor irksome and extended suffering. I met this lesson head-on, and sitting with it, taking what I felt I needed,

I let go and observed a more profound sense of understanding of the reality of things. A pacifying realisation that form is an illusion and nothing Earthly lasts forever. *Anicca.*

CHAPTER SIXTEEN

The Pursuit of Unhappiness

Maybe you are searching
among the branches, for what
only appears in the roots.

— Rumi

So, as we further explore the anatomy of happiness, it's prudent to observe humanity's pursuit of life, living, and doing, while neglecting to enjoy the magic of simply being, as the Taoists and Buddhists would welcome us to consider.

Remember *The Bucket List*[1]? It's a charming movie about two fellas who share a room in a cancer hospital. Morgan Freeman's character is a mechanic with an encyclopedic knowledge of the world, despite never travelling or experiencing anything remarkable. His roommate, expertly portrayed by Jack Nicholson, is a cantankerous billionaire, wealthy beyond dreams yet lacking happiness or love. After a bumpy start to their relationship, the unlikely pair embark on a beautiful journey of adventure and self-discovery as they travel the world, checking off numerous experiences before their imminent demise. Perhaps unsurprisingly, in the end, the message is about finding joy in all aspects of life — not just through fantastical, material events and experiences.

The thematic aspects of fear and distraction are two common denominators amidst the conundrum. The extraordinary dichotomy is that many of us are scared of death, yet we're equally afraid to live. Fear keeps us in a low vibrational state, existing from one day

1 *The Bucket List (screenplay by Justin Zackham).*

to the next, often convinced we should not dream of stepping outside our comfort zones and inviting actionable change. Then there's society's curated view of living. If you think about it, we're assigned a name, nationality, neighbourhood, race, and religion from birth. We'll spend years defending these facets, despite them being entirely fictional identities. Knowingly or unconsciously, our life choices ensure that we remain anchored and hardwired into a framework demanding unhealthy volumes of attention and life force energy. Born into such systems of control as we are, it is no wonder many people spend their entire lives never getting around to living. The bar is low because downtime has become a hard-earned reward rather than a God-given right. The so-called "hustle" has been glorified to the point that entrepreneurs are worshipped. And thus, the centre of our aspirations encircles graft, status, acquisition, entertainment, and similarly superficial distractions. It's a lot of doing and what many folks misinterpret as living. Thus, more wholesome aspirations like financial freedom, sovereignty, good health, stillness, emotional regulation, conscious communication, learning to love, be loved, and spend more time with those we love are often overlooked. Imagine how existence could be redefined if we removed participation from the current model.

Is one happier wanting for nothing, or wanting nothing?

We all strive to possess, and we want what others have. Isn't that a crucial component of what life's about? To accrue possessions and thus arise in status. Then ultimately, in our sixties or seventies, we can enjoy them and some well-earned rest, too, if we're lucky. This model into which we've all been born and conditioned to accept is absolutely fucking insane.

As soon as we're old enough to understand a mortgage, our

parents push us on to the property ladder. So we borrow a few hundred thousand from a financial institution with 25-year-plus payment terms like it's no big deal. The lender professes to be by your side, so why not? We need a nice new car to park outside the new place, so another amicable monetary establishment lends us 10, 20, 50, or even a 100,000 to scratch that itch. *Ta-da!* You're driving the car you've always wanted. Everyone dreams of an Audi, right? Even if it's not vorsprung durch technikally yours.

What about a new bathroom, lounge set, and dining suite? We need stuff to fill the new home we don't own. Fret not; you can have that all on interest-free credit. Buy now, pay later, no problem. Next up? The wardrobe! Do those shoes make the correct statement about the person occupying this new house, with the fancy new car and furniture? Best upgrade the duds. No worries, though; your credit card will sort that lot. After all, there are some things money can't buy. For everything else, there's Mastercard. So now you're 300,000 in debt in a house you can't afford, driving a car you could never buy, dressed like someone who can afford it all. *Illusions layered upon illusions.* And every day, you have the newfound, crippling pressure to produce enough bravado, energy, and income to pay for all this shit you bought using someone else's money. This trap does not promote inner peace. The fragility of the system and its profound effects on people and families cannot be overlooked. In 2010, following the financial crisis of 2007-2008, there were 2.9 million mortgage foreclosures in the US alone. And again, in late 2021, foreclosures surged as COVID mortgage bailouts ended abruptly. A literal house of cards. In the next chapter, we'll discuss debt's effects on our mental health.

Meanwhile, let's say you're cash-rich. You bought the house, the car, the clothes, and the watch outright. Your wealth has you surrounded by friends — you're a baller. Is that what defines happiness? The world is full of millionaires and billionaires distinctly dissatisfied despite their brimming treasure troves of trinkets. Though, you might still say, "Yes, actually, I'm ecstatic", and if that genuinely is the case, then I'm happy you're happy. Regardless, money is not the key to happiness. Cash gives us choices and financial freedom, which are facets of material happiness. But we cannot simply choose happiness with money. More investment is required in this process.

This *Tao Te Ching*[1] passage sheds light on this phenomenon:

> "Pursuit of name and fame rele-
> gates true person to second place.
> To crave property harms the
> person.
> Pursuit of gain injures life.
> Undue love of sensual beauty and
> pleasure waste the spirit.
> Wealth invites misfortune, inciting
> robbers to ransack the warehouse,
> to rifle the grave.
> Whosoever does not pursue game
> and knows content, is free of desire,
> incurs neither harm nor disgrace.
> To know when to halt, to be dis-
> entangled from gain, to be unper-
> turbed by the senses, is to avoid
> peril, is to befriend fortune.
> Self-cultivation keeps the spirits
> safe from harm".

To understand the abundance in nothing is to know true success. We may live happy and healthy lives minus much money and stuff. Enjoying the absence of energetic ties to debt, unaffected by fears surrounding status, one can live a distinctly

1 *River Master excerpt: Lao Tzu's Tao Te Ching, translated with an introduction and commentary by John Minford.*

more peaceful and minimalistic life. I've been fortunate to travel. I've visited townships in South Africa, impoverished island communities in Indonesia, tribal villages in Brazil, and remote rural farming territories in Turkey, where people all live in the most basic ways possible. The inhabitants of all these places greeted me with ear-to-ear smiles, offering some of what little they had without a second thought. They enjoyed a life of simplicity, where abundance comes in the guise of peace.

Is money an illusion and debt a weapon? They are, after all, never-ending energetic distractions. Debt is the most enslaving invention ever created by humanity for humanity. We can all adopt a more healthy en masse relationship to materialism, thus forcing the system to change. The way to do this is to turn your back on it, audit, re-evaluate, and then return as a conscious consumer who consumes less.

There is a profundity to happiness that one will never perceive while one seeks bliss in the vacuum of stuff. We are not our possessions. While we may feel that we are indeed defined by such, this could not be further from the truth. People judge one another by haves and have-nots, but as you will realise, what others think of you is none of your business. Possessions belong to another egoic class which we must identify, isolate, and dissolve so that we might cease searching endlessly amongst the branches and continue on the more meaningful journey inwards.

We can't do away with money; we need it. Earning money doing something we love is a gift. As long as we're not killing ourselves in the process. Money is stored energy — a physical (often non-physical) representation of our activity and energetic application. Currently, it's a necessary systematic function. However, we must avoid an unhealthy pursuit of money. Ultimately, this path will only satisfy the superficial while burning time, attention, and energy we can never get back. Money has everything to do with distraction, while happiness has nothing to do with possession.

Over a decade ago, I paid off or negotiated deals on all my debts. I chopped up my credit cards, deciding only to buy what I could afford. I would later discover the incredible catharsis of owning virtually no possessions, embracing the life of a minimalist. This excellent existence we'll explore later. But first, we must connect the dots between material possession, attachment, and suffering. And how, through self-mastery, we can observe these illusory states, finding happiness regardless.

An Introduction to Suffering

Arguably, one of the world's foremost authorities on suffering was Siddhartha Gautama (the Buddha). Hence, understanding and overcoming suffering is central to the Buddhists' path. There is a saying from the Buddhist Pali canon, which translates as "Attachment is the root of suffering". Another translation of this expression is: "Acquisition is the root of stress". "Stress", in this case, is suffering.

So, this is the study of attachment's attachment to unhappiness. We've a massive box of thinking to unpack, perhaps asking a lot — conditioned as we are. We need to adopt two significant ideas to get to the guts of this crucial concept. Firstly, we must grasp the relationship between attachment and suffering. The next challenge is to learn how not to suffer. A straightforward walk in the park, right? No, it's really not.

You might not know this, but "The Buddha" means "Enlightened One". My limited understanding of Buddhism has convinced me that pigeonholing this belief system as "religion" does a heinous disservice to this incredible, Universal wisdom. And since, similarly to Jeshua, the Buddha never wished for worship, we do well to observe core philosophies while not becoming entangled in dogmatic weedery. Within these teachings lies a handbook and blueprints for inter-dimensional travellers having a human experience at Earth School. Assuming you're not ready for that chat yet, let's just say Buddhism offers exceptional guidelines for any human being interested in the arts of living and dying well. While ancient, these teachings do and shall always stand the test of time and are thus well worth further exploration. At the heart of Buddha's teachings lie the Four Noble Truths as follows:

1. The truth of suffering.
2. The cause of suffering.
3. The end of suffering.
4. The shining light of truth on the path that leads to suffering.

So, suffering is a thing; caused by things; it can be ended like all things, and there are things you can proactively do to end it. Observe, evaluate, and consciously act.

Jeshua once said: "The Son of Man must suffer many things". Contrary to some die-hard Christian ideals, this wasn't a call to eternally self-flagellate or remain contritious or fearful from birth to death. It was an invitation to see that suffering is a gateway to rebirth, reinvention, and spiritual evolution. Suffering places us at the juncture of a forked path. One route leads to ongoing suffering, the other to regeneration, having sought the lessons provided by suffering's root cause.

We are at the mercy of our emotions. As illusory as they are, their power makes them absolute, often to the point where we are powerless over their might or trajectory of travel. Many of us thus refuse to accept we can end suffering. Hence, we pursue unhappiness. Sometimes the pain is so unbearable that we see no way out of it, and in so many tragic cases, the logical choice is suicide. Trauma, anxiety, and depression are wicked foes like that. But a lot of our mental illness is absolutely avoidable. We must prioritise our evaluation of what causes 3.8 per cent of the world's population, approximately 280 million people, to suffer depression. The answer, by the way, is not to prescribe antidepressants. Incidentally, as if those figures weren't depressing enough, just six months after publishing them, the WHO also announced that the COVID-19 pandemic had triggered a 25 per cent increase in anxiety and depression worldwide. And we've already discussed our increased interest in suicide. We are suffering. We might not be directly responsible for the source of our depression. However, our ongoing participation in a system exponentially breeding mental sickness is a shared responsibility. Salvation is within our reach but will not be forthcoming from the system.

CHAPTER SEVENTEEN

The Illusion of Debt

We may idealise freedom, but
when it comes to our habits, we
are completely enslaved.
— Sogyal Rinpoche

I once knew a man concerned with what others thought of him. Though his emotional immaturity made him paradoxically unpopular. He had a successful business, a big country house, two new luxury cars, and even a sit-on mower for his expansive lawn. His employees were loyal, friendly and diligent. He had a loving wife and two beautiful children. All the same, he was suffering, so as a subsequence of his ongoing unpleasantness, those around him suffered too.

Eventually, good people left the firm. His wife and children moved on, too. Interestingly, he dove headlong into the online dating scene and began entertaining a string of women in his big house and taking them for expositional drives in his cars. Despite his false confidence, his internal pain was evident to me. In a rare instance of vulnerability, he confessed that the big house had a hefty mortgage, and both cars were financed via hire purchase. The payments for it all cost thousands of dollars a month. This debt excluded other loans, credit cards, and general living costs. Can you imagine having to service debts of many thousands of dollars a month before considering food, utilities, clothes, savings, holidays, or anything else? Perhaps so. Many live similar lifestyles even though we can afford none of it. Moreover, we are often unaware of the real cost that such pressure creates in the name of identity and status.

Debt is a mighty energetic chain and anchor we take for granted, primarily because programming informs us it's a normal and entirely acceptable part of life — much the same as so many other unsound societal facets. We refer to debt as a "burden" or "weight" because, unable to discount its existence, most of us carry it every day, everywhere we go. For some, that feeling is embodied; it's a heavy sensation in the chest or a constant and most unpleasant fluttering of toxic butterflies in the gut. The weight is so unbearable for an unacceptable number that they take their lives rather than face bankruptcy and reputational ruin when they cannot repay. Have you ever wondered how the transference of zeros and ones on a screen can result in such undesirable, sometimes crippling or fatal physical effects?

Debt is always on your mind, even if you're unaware. A percentage of your mental "hard drive" is constantly dedicating time and energy to calculating your debt while considering its ramifications. According to a 2022 debt relief study of 2,000 people in the US, the average American loses around 200 hours of sleep yearly due to their debts. Furthermore, they experience three "debt nightmares" a week. Designed to highlight the effects of debt on mental health, the study showed that 38 per cent of the test group reported an increase in anxiety, 33 per cent in stress, and 32 per cent admitted to "moodiness" because of their debt problems. And despite 77 per cent of them feeling guilty about leisure spending while remaining in debt, three in five conceded that they felt pressured to continue spending to conceal their worsening financial situation. Also, in the US, the *Lending Club Paycheck-To-Paycheck Report*, August 2022, states that nearly half of all Americans making a six-figure salary are living pay cheque to pay cheque. The money arrives, the monthly repayments leave, and little is left.

Meanwhile, in the UK, a bank's 2020 study of the same number found that the group generally thought about their finances four times a day for 28 minutes, which is 170 hours annually. So a year in the life of the average Brit is dedicated to worrying about debt. The same goes the world over. Perhaps the most depressing revelation in recent times is the vast wave of collaboration between governments, banks, and fintech companies. They aim to introduce technological platforms to the developing world that will ultimately result in the widespread global distribution of financial products (mainly loans) to the unbanked via smartphones. What do you see here? Are you beginning to understand how debt profoundly impacts our energy, mental health, and, therefore, our happiness?

Setting aside the frightening amount of lost time, unbeknownst to most, we're dedicating a crucial portion of our life force to the most mindless endeavour of consumption in the history of our species. You see, wherever we put our attention, we put our energy. Our addiction to the material feeds debt. We believe these chattels are all we are — vital building blocks of our identity, yet we are so much more. But to understand this fully, it is necessary to analyse and transform certain aspects of life that keep us intrinsically connected to materialism.

How much of your stuff do you actually need? Furthermore, how much could you afford to buy (and own) outright? Why buy it at all if you cannot afford to do so? Is there an alternative? Wanting and needing are not the same. This is another form of attachment. Letting go of such distractions requires a pivotal shift in mindset because when significant change is necessary, we often feel we have no choice but to remain in the status quo. Fear of the unknown is a powerful foe. However, you do have a choice. You always have a choice.

The first stage is realising how much physical and mental energy you are burning to service your debt. How much undue pressure are you piling on yourself? How does this affect your relationship with others? The second is to see the illusions associated with debt and ownership. The third is the realisation that a vast amount of the stuff we own goes mainly unused, serving no real purpose, nor providing true joy. We don't need it.

Debt is yet another often needless obstacle that slows us down, distracting us from more enjoyable aspects of being and enhancing the illusion of identity. Just because these things are an intrinsic part of our system does not mean we must accept them as a reality — not as long as we retain the power of critical thought. As we've seen, debt can significantly affect one's mental health and, in extreme cases, lead to death. So while this invitation is far from profound, consider where you are in the debt and consumption story. There's no need to walk away entirely; merely acknowledge that our relationship with material possessions determines much more than we likely consider. Solving or removing one's debts is one of the simplest ways to improve one's mood. Likewise, reframing a more mindful approach to debt, money, and consumption can only be a good thing. This is basic stuff that we've to address before we can get anywhere near the real guts of the anatomy of happiness. So thick are the layers of illusion.

CHAPTER EIGHTEEN

Was The Matrix a Documentary?

A wise man, recognising that the world is but an illusion, does not act as if it is real, so he escapes the suffering.

— Buddha

The Rat Race, The Hamster Wheel, The Daily Grind. Living in the Matrix has many metaphors, all amounting to the same thing. Of course, you know all about it. There's a good chance that your life has revolved around the same apparatus for some time. It may still do.

The Matrix[1] movie presents a world of drudgery. The protagonist works all day in a job he loathes, for a thankless employer, in a city filled with millions of other people living parallel lives of similar dissatisfaction. The people in this world are controlled quietly and subtly by an invisible and insidious group of highly organised, self-serving elite puppeteers. The system's rules are enforced by "Agents", who keep order.

The people plugged into the Matrix are unknowingly born into a highly sophisticated system that keeps them docile and placated inside the illusion of reality. At the same time, and unbeknownst to them, their life force energy is harvested to feed the invisible machines. *Work, consume, sleep, pay taxes. Repeat.* Very few living in this dystopian world contemplate an alternative to their grinding existence, yet some (the protagonist included) instinctively begin

1 *The Matrix (screenplay by The Wakowskis).*

to consider alternate possibilities, ultimately asking the big question: how can this be all there is?

Taking the Red Pill

If you've watched this movie, you'll know that those who asked the question were invited to take a blue pill (remaining in the fake reality) or a red pill (awakening from the dream). So it came to pass that the red-pilled people were unplugged from the Matrix and faced head-on with their true nature stripped of the glossy illusion. They were free to live an alternate life in a non-superficial reality.

From Fiction to Reality

Setting aside the fundamental tenet that our very human existence is nothing but a dream, the movie's analogy proposes a shared perspective that our current societal system is also a construct. An energetic prison of sorts, offering the illusion of freedom. While we experience degrees of liberty, it cannot be said that we are entirely free. It's a worthwhile debate. We are, after all, plugged into and manipulated by debt-based financial systems built on illusory foundations, where our movements and choices are, in some cases, severely limited. Encouraged to borrow and spend slowly and incrementally, the system siphons our energy. And whatever we wish to do, there's a fee, permit or license or fine, assuming we're allowed to do it at all. This is heavy stuff, but can you see tendrils of truth in that thinking? Do you feel trapped in the rat race? Do you question whether there is more to life and living? It would be perfectly normal if you did. You're looking for answers and utilities that might help you discover ways to live a more fruitful life, are you not?

All over the world, regular people choose to unplug from our archaic, draconian system. They ignore the news and grow their own food. Unshackled by materialism, they choose a minimalist and mindful life, consuming less and doing something they love. Looking inwards, they design a life of financial and societal freedom. Making alternative plans to create a new and decentralised reality where the needs of the many can be better addressed, and equality provides the opportunity to bloom.

Stepping Out of the Illusion

There are many ways to unplug and reset, and each person's journey will determine how and when is best and to what possible degree. First, you must ask whether you enjoy life as it stands. Are you free, or are you somehow a slave to a model of control? If you realise that you are not fulfilling your potential, you might be ready to consider a new plan that will do away with any possible regrets over failing to live freely and on your terms.

Why write about such things?

Practically addressing our connection to such a system can drastically improve your work-life balance. You can work when you want to, doing something you love; that people appreciate, for which you're paid. No more Monday-Friday, 9-5 grind, or obediently following rules pretending to be laws. Instead, live a simple, wholesome life. You might not be financially wealthy, but for the first time in decades, you will be free.

Achieving this kind of liberty requires self-realisation, sacrifice, and reframing the concepts of materialism altogether. Above all, it takes self-belief. I had to *believe* I could unplug from the system and trust there was a better, more balanced, healthier way to live. The trick was letting go of what I thought to be the only route to happiness. The pursuit of which, as we've learned, has nothing to do with our fascination with endless flavours of consumption.

A Check-List for Financial Freedom

If any of the above feels remotely appealing, some of this might be helpful:

1. Picturing Freedom

Ask yourself what freedom looks like and what might give you the time and space to do the things you'd love. Perhaps it's a three-day week, turning your passion into a career, or an achievable plan that means you can pick and choose when you work.

2. A Personal P&L

Carry out a no-nonsense profit and loss analysis of your finances. Consider what you're earning, what you're spending, what you're borrowing, and what you're saving.

3. Learning is Earning

Also, ask yourself what you're learning. If the answer is "Nothing", then perhaps contemplate why. We are all teachers and learners; to grow, we must always be learning. It's in our nature.

The two straightforward ways to begin your financial freedom journey are reducing spending and stopping borrowing altogether. The quicker we realise we don't need much of anything, the faster we'll see excess money in our bank accounts at the end of the month. If this triggers a "But I need to pay for *XYZ*", perhaps figure out a plan to remove *XYZ* from your life entirely. We'll talk more about *Minimalism* in Chapter 23.

So now you're saving money. What will you do with it? Invest in assets or retraining? If the latter, then for what will you retrain? Both are precious opportunities for a bright future of financial freedom.

4. Find Your Ikigai

Find your Ikigai — a Japanese model designed to help you consider a new vocation: something you love, something the world needs, for which you can receive an income. You can read more about this beautiful Japanese philosophy in Chapter 30.

You might find it helpful to write your plans in the form of SMART objectives that look like this:

1. Specific (clear and straightforward).
2. Measurable (meaningful, actionable, and motivational)
3. Achievable (sensible and attainable).
4. Relevant (specific to goals, realistic, and results-based).
5. Timely (time/cost limited and time-sensitive).

This may be overkill, but it's an excellent practical utility and will help you get in the flow. Things will change, and as you cut more ties to debt and possessions, your newfound attitude will remove significant burdens alongside the realisation you no longer need (nor want) as much.

Right about now, self-doubt might creep in. Maybe some people close are judging you for making these seemingly radical changes. Ignore the doubt and anyone not supporting you. While at it, audit your relationships with anyone (family included) criticising how you live.

What do you want for yourself and your family? Is it more peace and more love? If that's the case and you want it enough, you'll make the necessary changes. It all starts with that red pill. Don't let that thing you want — or dream you have — be anything material. Let it be a state of mind or doing something you love — that makes your heart sing. Let it be happiness, healthiness, and balance. Abundance will naturally find its way if this becomes your focus.

There's a line of wisdom often attributed to the Buddha yet refuted by experts. The ambiguity of its origin means I cannot accurately credit the author, but it is Buddha-like wisdom nonetheless: "Pain in life is inevitable, but suffering is not. Pain is what the world does to you; suffering is what you do to yourself. Pain is inevitable, suffering is optional". Lest we forget, attachment is the root of all suffering. We choose attachment.

In this realm of duality, we must also have pain to have pleasure. According to the *Seven Hermetic Principles*, this is known as the *Law of Polarity*, outlined by Hermes Trismegistus. Incidentally, Hermes was his Greek name, while the Romans called him Mercury. The Egyptians also worshipped this deity, otherwise known as Thoth. Check him out; his story and teachings are worth further investigation.

The Buddhists' pragmatic view of suffering is not heartless nor robotic; merely the logical observation that suffering is an inevitable part of life that requires our conscious attention. Just as suffering is impermanent, pleasure is subject to the same Universal law. Ergo, in a way, happiness can never be permanently experienced. Though when one fully embodies this truth, one can remain happy regardless. Thus, while we cannot stop events that will cause pain, we (and we alone) have the keys and capabilities to modulate and end our suffering. What an exquisite paradox.

To be clear, we need not relinquish all interests in growing and succeeding as working professionals or entrepreneurs. It is not better to give up all aspirations of having a lovely home, niceties, and the ability to travel and be free. One day I'd like to build a cosy cabin in the woods near a like-minded community where I can write more and my family and I can enjoy a life of peace and simple pleasures. So even I have such desires. I'm actually giving serious consideration to buying a washing machine.

Perhaps we can aspire to a future where financial success

assumes a collaborative and mindful balance between reasonable amounts of wealth for all and a healthy lifestyle promoting personal and community wellness. And in parallel, we develop philanthropy funds and projects to serve the greater good through enabling (not rescuing) like-minded communities. Success looks different to us. We're growing something sustainable together, and we live minimalistic lives. When we have enough, we slow down, live in service to others, and enjoy life more peacefully — with myriad more choices.

We've discussed the unhealthy focus on wealth, money, and debt to highlight the apparent pitfalls of a dogged pursuit of something that doesn't necessarily create happiness but significantly drains precious time and energy. Naturally, such a life might result in regrets regarding health, goals, spending too much time at work and not enough with family, friends, or even oneself. Our societal relationship with money is undoubtedly co-responsible for rising mental illness. Illusion or not, consumerism has claws in our hearts and minds. Assuming we want this to change, then change it, we must.

Part Three

Being

CHAPTER NINETEEN

Who Am I?

As all living beings desire to be happy always, without misery, as in the case of everyone, there is observed supreme love for one's Self, and as happiness alone is the cause for love, in order to gain that happiness which is one's nature and which is experienced in the state of deep sleep when there is no mind, one should know one's Self. For that, the path of knowledge, the inquiry of the form "Who am I?" is the principal means.

— Ramana Maharshi

In the forecourt of the Greek Temple of Apollo at Delphi is an inscription that reads, "Know thyself". Philosophers, scholars, and truth-seekers the world over have sought to rise to this challenge, keen to understand human nature at the deepest levels. Self-realisation, also known as self-knowledge and self-discovery, is a natural stage of our journey. Though the motives of how, when, and what drives this introspection are different for all of us. For some, it's a coming of age, which others refer to as a "midlife crisis". Perhaps such critics are thus so because they fear introspection.

Some lucky souls are supported to develop such awareness in youth, while others must reach the brink of annihilation before taking a long, hard look at themselves.

I didn't realise it back then, but vast aspects of my dissatisfaction with my world were intuitive expressions of feeling like a stranger in my mind and body. An unfamiliar and barely audible voice was whispering — inviting me to begin the undesirable work of knowing myself. But did I listen? I did not. Apparently, even I felt I had no place inquiring about life, love, and the Universe. I should instead stick to being drunk and distracted, blissfully unaware of all such profundities. I was not a philosopher; I was in advertising. And so I continued grinding the mill.

Never allow anyone — family, partner, friend, colleague, or institution to vilify you for asking big questions about life, love, and the Universe. It is your God-given right. If we all spent more time on self-inquiry, the world would be a happier place. Besides, we already put plenty of barriers ahead of our progress without needing additional assistance from others.

Jeshua said, "deny thyself", the suggestion being that we address the illusion of ego and ultimately deny its control. He knew some stuff, did Jesus. This wisdom was an invitation to engage in self-realisation so that we might learn to know ourselves. How confident are you that you know your true Self at this moment?

The process of unfuckery is by no means welcomed by the average adult — assuming one's even aware of its necessity. It's unlikely that many of us simply sit up in bed and decide, "Today's the day I'm going to fix myself!" As dysfunctional as things may be, we get comfortable with the chaos. We learn psychologically intriguing coping mechanisms that do a satisfactory job of helping us get by. But they don't work, do they? Not in the long term. Stressed folks show signs and eventually break. Pressure cookers blow. And through the process, those around us are scolded or, more seriously, burned. It's the price of associating with psyches in need of repair.

The first significant stage of the Anatomy of Happy is self-realisation. So how does one begin the process of self-inquiry? We usually do this following intervention from loved ones or from a healthy internal sense that we could improve. Or because we hit rock bottom and the reality of our bullshit splashed unceremoniously all over our shoes. The creator being inside gnaws at our mask's interior — keen to be seen and heard. Whatever the stimulus, self-realisation is the process of pausing and finally asking the big question, "Who am I?" And with that, a can of worms promptly spills across all you see. Have you ever tried putting worms back into a container? After the initial hot wave of despair, mindfulness and patience are required in abundance. And since many a worm is surprisingly athletic, you must look out for the ones that get away.

For me, self-realisation eventually began with therapy, because I realised I was doing rather a poor job of therapising myself. This was the second time I tried it. All in all, my therapy sessions lasted around a year and a half. Being a pragmatist, I told my therapist, Michael, that things could only improve for me if he "explained the science". And so he did. Our time together was the beginning of my *doing the work*.

The contract:

I promise to make a weekly 30-mile round trip to openly and honestly discuss my actions, feelings, and increasingly random thoughts. I have to pay whether I attend or not, and punctuality is crucial.

He listens; tells me about PTSD, trauma, childhood abuse, self-harm, synaptic pathways, *fight, flight, or freeze, Transactional Analysis Theory*, and more. This psychological smorgasbord offered glorious life lessons that I ought to have been taught as a child.

They were certainly not encounters where I might spill my guts to a nodding quack who writes and rarely speaks. Sometimes we laughed; sometimes, I cried. Sometimes I squirmed in the silence.

So through our weekly get-togethers, I learned much about myself and the human condition. Never before had I been so forthright and vulnerable with someone so compassionate while never judging the swirling soup of my broken mind. Although, regardless of our progress, I remained entirely dishonest. Early on, Michael was concerned I had a severe substance and alcohol problem, about which I continually lied to his face. I missed several sessions due to being drunk, high, or both, offering lame excuses via SMS. I withheld my suicidal schemes for fear of facing my truths. Although great therapists will never judge their patients, I was so ashamed of myself that, even with Michael, I could not be candid. Throughout the years, speaking to others about counselling, I've learned that lying to one's therapist is a ludicrously common occurrence. According to one study, 93 per cent of us do it. Clearly, this isn't a great idea. If you decide that you need a therapist, find a great one and tell them absolutely everything. Lying to them sets you up for failure or grossly hindered success, at the very least.

Self-realisation does not necessarily require the support of mental health professionals. However, be mindful that when one attempts to therapise oneself while not necessarily knowing one's neuroses, one might wish to consider the quality of such advice. *Beware the echo chamber.* Furthermore, beware of self-prescribed attempts to heal — be that yoga, meditation, microdosing, breathwork, or blasting yourself off to another dimension in search of subconscious reparation. Some of us are simply incapable of healing alone, and that's okay. Accept it; set aside any pride along these lines, reach out and seek support. It feels good when someone else lightens your burden. A problem shared is indeed often a problem halved.

There are many spiritual and scholarly opinions on the stages of self-realisation. Mine are relatively simple:

1. Self-Inquiry

Voluntarily or forced to face the realisation that you can live a more wholesome and connected life, you ask yourself: "Who am I?" This is usually borne from a deep discomfort in one's skin or environment. Something's just not right in your life. There's plenty of friction but no flow. Perhaps it feels like all you've ever done is run from one toxic person or drama to the next. You suffer more than others and suppose you were dealt a bad hand. Maybe you constantly declare: "Nothing's going my way!" Relationships and events come crashing down; you feel like the Universe is always conspiring against you.

These are all significant instances where, instead of abrogating responsibility and slinging blame at others *(that damned Universe!)*, you must stop and truly observe yourself. What do you see? Who are you? Don't enter this phase expecting to "fix" anything. Instant gratification has no place here; it's not how this works. However you do it, suspending judgement or mitigation, you must assess the reality of your truth. Who have you been up to this day?

If you're really stumped, try this exercise as a warm-up:

If I could do anything, I would _____.

The only personal barrier stopping me from doing _____ is _____.

If I didn't _____, then _____ would happen.

If I did _____, then _____ would happen!

The thing I dislike the most about myself is _____, because _____.

The thing I love the most about myself is _____, because _____.

Repeat this every morning, as soon as you wake up, instead of switching on your phone. Every day you'll feel different; thus, you'll paint a picture of self-inquiry over time. Be mindful that there's a fine line between negative self-talk and being aware of an aspect of Self requiring attention.

2. Honesty

Candour with oneself is actually rather tricky. Which is odd if you think about it. We can lie to everyone else, but why would we lie to ourselves? Well, ego doesn't like self-realisation because it drops defences, inviting unwelcome change. Ego doesn't like change any more than it likes criticism. As misguided as ego often is, everything it does is to protect you. Therefore, what one must consider here is how does one know whether one is lying to oneself? Intuitively, you will always know, though depending on your ego's power, such intuition might only be a dim and indistinguishable light. While this skill requires practice, one rather obvious litmus test is considering how others generally respond to your behaviour. What does the data say? Suppose through this statistical line of inquiry, you note that the common denominator in a boatload of negative experiences is, in fact, you. In that case, it's safe to assume that you've been lying to yourself unbeknownst to yourself. Isn't that a trip?

So we lie to ourselves to stay safe in our comfort zones. However, this work requires that we stand vulnerable and naked. Without absolute, unbridled self-honesty, your self-realisation journey will be nought but smoke, mirrors, and bullshit. Lying to yourself will only serve to hinder your progress. Be truthful with yourself and others, or don't bother at all.

3. Self-Acceptance

Get out of your own way. Acknowledge that you've been

co-responsible for the events in your life. How? Mentally revisit previously painful exchanges, and observe them from a higher seat of consciousness. By that, I mean that inside a maze, you can only see what's right in front of you. From above, you see much more. Try to look further than the version of events you recall; view it from the perspectives of the others involved. For best results, use specific meditation techniques. There's also therapy, of course, and psychedelics too. Though do not try the latter alone.

The work in self-acceptance aims to understand your ego's response to situations and how such exchanges have impacted others. Was it really "all their fault"? Do you not bear any co-responsibility? Do you acknowledge you have room for self-improvement and thus seek sustainable practices and processes? Or are you reading this book because you hope to find a list of happiness hacks — sick as you may be with what Carl Honoré [1]deftly refers to as "the virus of hurry"? If so, set aside any such fantasies and get ready to face the music.

Bearing witness to oneself brings peace to taking responsibility for your actions and who you are. Through self-acceptance, you can let go. You can contemplate who you want to be and how you might become this new version of yourself. With your slate of previous experience clean, you can move in this new direction, mindful of your human traits and willing to own your shit.

4. Action

Stepping to a fork in the road is one thing; having the courage to choose a new path is quite another. When it comes to success, we dream and speak of dreams, yet act on them less so. And as Tolstoy once said: "Everyone thinks of changing the world, but no one thinks of changing himself". The former might be easier than the terrifying prospect of self-realisation. However,

1 *Carl is the unofficial founder of the Slow Movement. Check out his excellent book, In Praise of Slow.*

somewhat ironically, if we all actioned change in ourselves, such transformation would absolutely be felt by others.

To change, you must act. Test and learn. **Be bold.** This will be a series of messy experiments, filled with learning in the guise of mistakes. Don't be put off by that voice in your head — ego, asking, "What if?" Instead, hear Lao Tzu's reassuring words, "The journey of a thousand miles begins with a single step".

A word of warning about this inward journey. In the early stages of self-realisation, getting carried away with your fledgling understanding is expected. Try to avoid wearing your awareness like Joseph's technicolour coat. Let humility be your guide since while you're on a journey to know yourself, paradoxically, the game is about stripping away identity's layers until you are nothing.

You'll find much wisdom in this passage from the *Tao Te Ching*[1]:

> "To understand others is wisdom,
> To know Self is illumination.
> To vanquish others requires force,
> To vanquish Self requires strength.
> To know contentment is true
> wealth.
> To persevere requires will.
> Not to lose one's place is to endure,
> To die but not to perish,
> Is long life".

And so, the way towards illumination is to persevere as one vanquishes Self with patience and love, assuming nothingness at every turn. Be kind to yourself. The road to learning to love begins with pointing loving kindness inward. If you judge and beat yourself up for your perceived failures, you've missed the

1 *Knowing Self excerpt: Lao Tzu's Tao Te Ching, translated with an introduction and commentary by John Minford.*

point of the exercise.

Welcome to self-realisation, self-awareness, and unlearning. All of which requires the prerequisite phase of activity commonly known in the community as "Shadow Work".

CHAPTER TWENTY

Shadow Work

Shadow work is the path
of the heart warrior.

— Carl Jung

It was in early 2019 that, broken and Bali-bound, I left the UK. I had sold or given away everything I owned, and with just two bags and a beagle, after an arduous road trip across Java, I arrived at a seaside town on Bali's east coast with little inkling of what lay ahead. I'd gravitated to the *Island of the Gods* with no real plan whatsoever. No strategy, mentor, family, friends, or clue about how I would spend my days. Nevertheless, I was instinctively cognisant of where the real work should begin. And so I initiated what I later learned was to be my Shadow Work.

While not exclusive to the island, an expression known as "spiritual bypassing" regularly makes its rounds in Bali. Introduced by the Buddhist psychotherapist John Welwood, the term is defined as using "spiritual ideas and practices to sidestep personal, emotional 'unfinished business'; to shore up a shaky sense of Self, or to belittle basic needs, feelings, and developmental tasks". When spiritually bypassing, we use such practices to cover up our emotional and psychological shortcomings; a spiritualised smokescreen for us and others. We dive into new techniques, skipping the critical healing phase known as Shadow Work.

So what is it? Well, it derives from another Jungian concept, *Shadow Self*, essentially getting to grips with the parts of our personality that we reject out of fear or shame. Whether we acknowledge it or not, we all have a shadow, and the self-reflective work necessary is a deep dive into one's Shadow Self. The purpose is to fully see and know it, to sit with the searing pain of "who" that Self is and has been, and to ultimately embrace it as a welcome and most beloved part of us.

Honestly, it's no fun.

In hindsight, I dove into my Shadow Work in two tranches. The first was during the previously discussed therapy sessions, commencing shortly after my mum's death in 2014. The second was after my inaugural introduction to plant medicines, including Ayahuasca and Huachuma (San Pedro), in February 2019. Next was some early work with meditation and yoga. All that to say that in linear terms, having leapt into other practices first, I may have been guilty of a little spiritual bypassing too. However, if it started out that way, my spiritual-cum-metaphysical training quickly led me to a place where embracing solitude, I began the painful process of self-reflection. Observing past behaviour honestly, I eventually accepted co-responsibility for all of it. Now, there was no one left to lie to other than myself. Perhaps it was the meditation or the plant medicine. Maybe it was the self-prescribed removal from my former toxic environments. Using this new mindset, I deliberately situated myself in a place where silence came far easier. And so I began surfing tsunami after tsunami of melting hot lava-like truth in the form of memories I'd previously worked hard to repress. Perhaps I was lucky. Along an extended, dark road, I altered my course, embracing the work with an overwhelming desire to change because there was frankly no other option. Besides, having learned a great deal about the dark, I felt compelled to acknowledge its teachings about the promise of the altogether more appealing light.

My Shadow Work process involved spending weeks and months revisiting and reflecting while simultaneously reading tomes of psychological and spiritual teachings. This enriched and transformed how I viewed my darkness. With time on my hands, I audited many of my life's darker moments. This was no longer through the traditional lens of masochism or self-pity; it was with an emerging belief that I could dislodge the pain of these memories — moving that stuck emotion. The practice I used (and a practical utility) was to place all my attention and energy on these memories one by one, safe in the knowledge that they no longer had the power to hurt me. In fact, they would shift in shape, size, and potency as I observed them with love and without judgement.

While an ancient practice amongst meditators, this idea also belongs to quantum mechanics. The so-called "Observer Effect" is the disturbance created in a system through observation. In physics, instruments measuring something often alter the results. Not to get too scientific, but one example is how the observer effect occurs during the Double-Slit Experiment, demonstrating that light and matter can display classic and defined waves and particles. What does that even mean? Don't worry about it. The point is that during such experiments, physicists have discovered that their observation of quantum phenomena can change the measured results. In layman's terms, we direct energy wherever we place our single-pointed attention. Thus, observing a situation or phenomenon (in this case, a memory's latent energy) changes it because everything in this world is impermanent.

I paralleled my newfound mental nourishment with regular physical and spiritual practice, including yoga, breathwork, sound healing, and eating clean. And then there was sleep — 8-10 hours every night. Lest I forget, the most powerful ally I introduced to my daily routine was one of the most profound teachers of them all — *silence*. We'll talk about this more later on. Or maybe not. Should I just leave a metaphorical blank page?

In a matter of months, I immersed myself in what I eventually came to call "the work"; my self-made programme designed to go inward and heal. And so it was in Bali, of all places, that I did the most challenging work I've ever done. Was it hard? Yes, it was. Was it worth it? Would I recommend it? Unequivocally. It changed my life. Having finally put my demons to bed, I paved the way to unlearn my conditioned behavioural traits, eventually learning for the first time how to forgive, love, and accept myself for who I am. I said goodbye to the darkness and welcomed the light. More accurately, I embraced a future where the two can live happily and healthily ever after.

Now then, there are some words to highlight as we tread carefully around the minefield of Shadow Work. The first is "repressed", and the second is "bullshit".

Repressed

There are three sides to every story: my version, your version, and the truth. One could elaborate by saying there is no truth other than *All That Is*, but let's just settle on the third truth being defined in this case as the Universe's non-dualistic perspective of the event. *All truths.* So my memory of the events where I, shall we say, neglected to practice *Right Speech, Thought*, or *Action* might well have been corrected by my ego (AKA "Monkey") to protect myself. Or, as my narcissistic brain switched into *Machiavellian Strategy Mode*, perhaps we (Monkey and me) chose to tell ourselves a different version of the story that painted us in a somewhat better light. Which, if you think about it, is another form of self-protection and control.

So our recollection of how we've conducted ourselves in the past can be repressed. We subconsciously push memories far away from our awareness. On the other hand, we can *suppress* our memory of an event. In such cases, we deliberately try to forget what we said or did. We proactively shove painful or shameful memories into a mental box, subsequently tossing them on to a cerebral conveyor belt transporting the painful ponderings for long-term storage. **Newsflash:** such energy remains in the body and mind, festering, giving off an unpleasant smell, and eventually making its presence known to all and sundry. Oftentimes and regrettably, this materialises as a breakdown, the "popping" of one's lid, or as disease (it's dis-ease, after all). Naturally, we believe we'll never see it again, but that's rarely the case. Sharing the resilience of the *Fast & Furious*[1] movie franchise, it shall thus return.

Bullshit

And what about bullshit? Well, a crucial part of Shadow Work is to own your bullshit. To fully embody the process is to wholeheartedly accept that you've been a bit of a dick. There's no skirting around it. No "Well, I might've done this", or "there's a chance I did that", or "it's conceivable that I said this, but..." Nope, none of that. Steps Eight and Nine of AA's (Alcoholics Anonymous) 12 Steps are referred to as "making amends". Written in the past tense, they read like this:

> **Step Eight:** [we] made a list of
> all persons we had harmed and
> became willing to make amends to
> them all.
> **Step Nine:** [we] made direct
> amends to such people wherever
> possible, except when to do so
> would injure them or others.

Take heed of the last line of Step Nine. If there's an outside chance that reaching out might cause them more harm than

1 *The Fast & Furious movie franchise, created by Gary Scott Thompson.*

good, then don't do it. Let those sleeping dogs lie. Assuming you continue, then exercise humility and honesty. It is imperative to own one's bullshit. An apology with mitigation is an excuse. For those of you brave enough to reach out to the people you've hurt, I salute you. Having done this many times, it was often more painful than rewarding. My amends were met with a bittersweet combination of "Fuck yourself", "I'm not interested", "I'll never forgive you", "Have you had dental work?!", and "You've honestly no reason to apologise, Martin, but thanks". Perhaps the worst response is total silence, but we must accept it all the same. Acknowledging our bullshit and the co-created drama we birthed and crafted is tough, tough work. Expressing heartfelt remorse is challenging too. Expecting nothing in return while instead fully embodying the true definition of forgiveness is a skill reserved for Jedis. All this and more lie ahead in the Shadow Work fun palace.

Actually, now's as good a place as any to share an excerpt from Russell Brand's most excellent *Recovery: Freedom From Our Addictions*. Much of his somewhat salty and down-to-earth version of the 12 Steps could well be applied to anyone interested in the work, addictive tendencies or not. They read like this:

1. Are you a bit fucked?
2. Could you not be fucked?
3. Are you, on your own, going to unfuck yourself?
4. Write down all the things that are fucking you up or have ever fucked you up, and don't lie or leave anything out.
5. Honestly tell someone trustworthy about how fucked you are.
6. Well, that's revealed a lot of fucked-up patterns. Do you want to stop it? Seriously?
7. Are you willing to live in a new way that's not all about you and your previous, fucked-up stuff? You have to.

8. Prepare to apologise to everyone for everything affected by your being so fucked-up.
9. Now apologise. Unless that would make things worse.
10. Watch out for fucked-up thinking and behaviour, and be honest when it happens.
11. Stay connected to your new perspective.
12. Look at life less selfishly, be nice to everyone, help people if you can.

As sweary as some may find this list, Russell's fun and forthright tone deserves appreciation. Can you see how they could apply to all humans rather than just self-professed addicts? How would it be if we all did this work?

A Shadow Work Starter for Ten

1. Sit with your darkness; feel the pain until it transmutes.
2. Master your emotional responses, so you are no longer easily triggered.
3. Free from shame or judgement, acknowledge your negative behavioural emotions.
4. Free from guilt or judgement, recognise your negative behavioural traits.
5. Master assertiveness minus rudeness.
6. Learn to appreciate others' truths.
7. Observe and accept yourself; laugh at yourself.
8. Observe and avoid passive aggression.
9. Arm-wrestle adversity; seek out and analyse the lessons.
10. See yourself in others (and others in you), thus minimising your predilection for judgement.

So that's a wee introduction to Shadow Work. While the process most certainly sucks, done properly, the end results are nothing short of glorious. Furthermore, if you attempt to skip this stage of your healing, you will likely never know true happiness. Remember: during this process, do not judge yourself. To do so is to create yet more inner conflict. Knowing and owning the dark things you've done — even only to yourself — is massive healing work. Taking it that one step further, reaching out to those who were hurt by your words or deeds is epic.

Despite having gone to great lengths to make amends to those I wounded, the brutal truth is that I hurt so many. Thanks to my own honed skills of repression, I cannot even remember them all. With that in mind, please indulge me as I sincerely apologise to anyone I injured during my first 40-odd-year bumbling rampage. I couldn't meet your needs because I was emotionally miles behind — a wounded child without the life skills. I didn't listen to you because the roaring noise of my ego shut out anyone else's feelings other than mine. I didn't want to look at you because observing the unspeakable damage I caused filled me with shame. I couldn't let you get close because my heart was shored, secured, and perversely protected. I am unreservedly sorry for anyone whose heart I broke or whose feelings were injured through my words or deeds. The version of me they met was emotionally unskilled; a scared, angry, and wounded little boy. Even if he wanted to, he could not love. He couldn't even love himself, so you see, no one else had much of a chance. But we forgave ourselves and chose to change.

Okey-dokey, with all that said and done, let's dip a timely toe into the turgid pond of apprehension, otherwise known as *fear*.

The Ho'oponopono Hawaiian Prayer

Sit with your back straight.
Be comfortable.
Relax your face, jaw and shoulders.
Soften your belly.

Take a long, deep in-breath through your nose.
Make an audible sigh as you breathe out through your mouth.

Repeat two more times.

This prayer (this vibration) is from you, *for* you.
You can say these words with your eyes closed.
Or face a mirror.
Say them out loud:

I love you.
I'm sorry.
Please forgive me.
Thank you.

Repeat as many times as it takes for you to *feel*.

CHAPTER TWENTY-ONE

A Sidenote About Fear

> Tell your heart that the fear of
> suffering is worse than the suf-
> fering itself. And that no heart
> has ever suffered when it goes in
> search of its dreams.
>
> — Paulo Coelho

While observing various human traits, we've yet to stand toe to toe with the phenomenon of fear; but stand close and firm, we must! We have to wrestle with humankind's most prevalent and brutal foe to outline a meaningful path towards happiness.

Socrates said: "I shall never fear or avoid things of which I do not know". This is a welcome reminder that in life, we should garner fearlessness while avoiding fearful choices. Furthermore, beware of the futility of fearing the unknown. We're a mixed bag like that, though, aren't we? Some of us fear nothing, while others' choices are driven wholly by fear.

How about you? Do you throw caution to the wind in all unfamiliar experiences? Does fear pull you from pillar to post like a Labrador puppy hell-bent on marking its territory? Do you welcome the unknown with open arms and a maniacal smile, or are you reverent and cautious? Ah, fear, we welcome your unwelcome presence with simultaneous respect and indifference.

According to psychotherapist and author Amy Morin[1], the top ten fears holding people back are:

1 *The Top 10 Fears That Hold People Back in Life, Inc.com, written by Amy Morin.*

1. Change.
2. Loneliness.
3. Failure.
4. Rejection.
5. Uncertainty.
6. Something bad happening.
7. Getting hurt.
8. Being judged.
9. Inadequacy.
10. Loss of freedom.

All truths about fear are naturally valid. Fear's a reality, but that's not to say it should be our ruler — especially when fearing that which has not yet occurred. Fear can and should be used healthily, but to evolve, we must learn to overcome it, as more often than not, fear is nought but an illusion that holds us back. Hence, the challenge is to concurrently observe from the perspectives of ego and consciousness. One looks out for legitimate dangers, while the other exposes fear's many falsities.

My past is peppered with many a scary moment. I remember snowboarding off-piste and being stuck half a metre from the edge of a 100-foot drop to a rock mattress below. I narrowly cheated death, pulling myself to safety by grasping sapling trees. Could I have avoided the situation altogether? Of course. I could've stayed on piste. Better still, I might've decided not to get on a snowboard at all, thus removing myself from any related risks or injuries. Though playing victim to my fear to such extremes would deprive me of countless incredible experiences, witnessing stunning snowcapped mountain landscapes in a way one can only do by riding down them at speed on a hardwood and fibreglass plank. I recall a teenage street fight; three of us had small, wooden bats to use against a much stronger young adult. My friends struck the older kid's head fearlessly with their bats. I refrained through concerns about seriously injuring him, even if he was a misguided and brutal bully. I was afraid. Could this have been avoided? Yup. Moreover, it should have. Putting myself in such a situation was foolish; here, my fear was righteous and deserved to be heard.

Fear rarely stopped me from trying new things, but it hampered my progress in other fundamental ways. And as you'll learn later, perhaps the thing I feared the most was opening my heart to love. Through this inherent failure, I rooted myself in a place where I could not develop emotionally, psychologically, or spiritually. So fear drove me, as it does all of us, for far too many years. I allowed it to rule me as fear can.

Suppose we believe the anecdotal deathbed regrets outlined in Chapter Two. They infer that fear is at the heart of many people's inability to truly break through and experience new horizons. Fear is ingrained in our collective and individual psyches, a crippling emotion that prevents us walking paths of transformational discovery. As our hearts remain closed and guarded, fear stops us from expressing our true feelings, undoubtedly stunting growth and personal development. Especially if it stops us from better connecting with one another for fear of being hurt in some way by the unknown. And so, it would appear we stick with what we know, what continues to make us feel safe. They call it *The Comfort Zone*, one of three psychological states where we feel safe or at ease, devoid of stress.

Getting Comfortable

Life in the Comfort Zone provides illusory control of one's environment. Brené Brown describes this behavioural phenomenon as a place, "where our uncertainty, scarcity, and vulnerability are minimised — where we believe we'll have access to enough love, food, talent, time, admiration". Put that way, it doesn't sound all that bad, does it? Rather comfortable, in fact. After all, in an era so warped and drowned by stress, who needs more? Life in the Comfort Zone is a relative breeze, wherein a steady level of performance is achieved. But what of the other two states? According to the traditional model, the Comfort Zone has two relational partners that help define the psychology surrounding our barriers to growth.

Popularised in the 1990s, the Comfort Zone model rose to fame thanks to Judith Bardwick, PhD's international bestseller, *Danger in the Comfort Zone*. According to Bardwick, the Comfort Zone is "a behavioural state where a person operates in an anxiety-neutral condition, using a limited set of behaviours to deliver a steady level of performance, usually without a sense of risk". The alternatives in this model are the "Optimal Performance" and "Danger" zones. Wowsers, no wonder people are afraid to take chances when a potentially extraordinary future path is marked by a neon danger sign! Another version, developed by psychologist Lev Vygotsky in the early 1930s, was the zone of proximal development (also known as the "Learning Zone" model). This tool helps plot the distance between a learner's capability unsupported and what's possible when supported by someone with more expertise or knowledge. The thinking around this subject has somewhat evolved, so we now have a new model moving through four zones — *Comfort, Fear, Learning,* and *Growth*. And so, to evolve, we are thus encouraged to push ourselves into the zone of growth. But is that easier said than done? And why should we wish to grow anyway? To answer these questions, we must face them with authentic analyses of the alternative. What does dwelling in each of these zones offer?

As outlined, the Comfort Zone offers safety and control, but the personal cost is a ceiling restricting potential and maturation. Inside the Fear Zone, we're concerned with what others think of us. We lack self-confidence and are likely capable of creating a long list of mitigating excuses for not moving from this space. However, new riches await us if we're courageous enough to take a leap of faith to the Learning Zone. Here, we're invited to overcome personal challenges, be open to discovering new skills, and thus progress to where the magic happens: the Growth Zone. To be clear: new skills aren't exclusive to one's work or vocation; learning how to love one's Self healthily is, perhaps, one of the most essential skills of all, and one's career has no bearing on this incredible superpower.

So what's in the Growth Zone box of delights? Perhaps the more appropriate question should be, what isn't? How does finding your true purpose sound? Or realising your goals and aspirations? Is the idea of living one's dreams in any way appealing? With trying comes failure as much as success. So it's not all rosy. But if we only do what we always did, then we'll always get what we always got. And as Einstein once said: "Insanity is doing the same thing over and over and expecting different results". If your fear is presently working on a rebuttal, I'll throw in a hat-trick prose for you: mistakes are only mistakes if we learn nothing from them. By that rationale, there's no such thing as "failure", there is only learning. *Boom.* And if we're occupying the space of learning — failing or not — then we're already out of our Comfort Zone.

What's the utility? Action is the utility. Either a solo flight or with an instructor by your side. When we overcome the fear of admitting we want or need help, such vulnerability can reap massive rewards. We're more likely to leave our Comfort Zones with the assistance of others' knowledge or expertise. In this regard, Vygotsky had a point. Perhaps my words are moot since your reading this book already demonstrates a sincere interest in learning.

The irony of the entire debate around whether or not to stay in one's Comfort Zone is that inaction is the root cause of many people's regrets. So you see, we simply *must* roll up our sleeves and challenge fear to a blimmin' good arm wrestle. The only way to grow and witness the beauty and awe of new experiences is to learn how to observe and beat fear. We've discussed that it's a good idea to fear steep cliffs and baseball bat fights, but what of the fear of expressing oneself? Or fearing opening our hearts to love? Perhaps you know someone terrified of failure, crippled by concerns about what others think of them? While not exclusively, these latter fears' origins will likely be found in one's early childhood. You fear expressing yourself because someone close to you constantly dismissed you — perhaps they still do now. Or worse still, they ignored you altogether. You fear opening your heart because someone was careless or cruel to a younger version of you. You fear defeat because the idea that failure is not an option was unreasonably ingrained in you.

Trauma and abuse come in many forms. Neglect, bullying, a lack of intimacy, or a parent (or close adult) passing on their own learned emotional perversities imprints on a child's mind. We take the toxic baton handed to or thrown at us and carry on, sometimes through entire lifetimes, without being truly cognisant of these neuroses or their harmful effect on our lives. Naturally, upon realising this, one might resent people close to us for their role in cultivating our fear. Avoid such feelings. These people, whoever they are, could only do what they could with the life skills they had. In all likelihood, they were treated in exactly the same way. Nothing good can come from focusing on historical suffering. Instead, be grateful that you've had this life-changing revelation. Make amends, change, and move forward fearlessly. This is the very definition of the phrase "breaking the cycle". You may not be responsible for how your neuroses were learned, but be under no illusion you are 100 per cent accountable for what happens next.

Is overcoming fear as simple as invalidating the unknown and thus beginning the journey of what it is to know? We can believe a thing; we can intellectually know a thing.

From there, the obvious step is experience. And in such, we can finally see the object for ourselves before judging whether to entertain the idea of further exploration. Of course, this is not necessarily the place to say, "Right, I've tried that, and it's not for me". In fact, this is precisely the time to try again! If, at first, you don't succeed, etc. It's not about how we get knocked down but how we get up again. But you've got to wrangle your fear to enter the ring in the first place. All that said, surrendering to the flow means we can also get up, leave the ring, and go do something else instead. Only you can know if it's appropriate or timely to do that. But be honest about how much effort you put into making those changes that will most certainly lead you to new avenues of personal growth.

CHAPTER TWENTY-TWO

Cha-Cha-Cha-Changin'

**If you realise that all things
change, there is nothing
you will try to hold on to.**
— Lao Tzu

What makes us want to change? Perhaps we feel stuck, lost, keen to level up, or, having hit rock bottom, it's our only chance for a new beginning. Whatever the inspiration, the more critical question is why we don't change despite appreciating its benefits, necessity, and inevitability.

Intransigence is undoubtedly a factor, though the predominant barrier is fear — a word unsurprisingly featured in this book almost 100 times. In the *Tao Te Ching*, Lao Tzu tells us, "There is no illusion greater than fear", though, to most of us, fear feels far from illusory. And since it affects the mind and body, it's a tangible adversary. Fear fights for the leadership role of human emotions and regularly comes out on top. So crucial to the transformation story, fear got its own chapter. Hence, here we'll speak more generally about our emotions' impact on our inability to change.

There's a common truth overlooked by many in this age of the "hack", where even personal development is expected to deliver life-changing and sustainable results quicker than an Amazon drone. Herein lies the conundrum. Innate or learned, emotions are ingrained. Events and the subsequent feelings we attach to them are deeply rooted in our psyches, and the business of change requires that we undertake the equally demanding work of unlearning. Since it takes years to learn who we think we are, the notion it can be unlearned with little effort is utterly preposterous. Of course, deep down, we know that. Hence our reluctance in the first place. So through intransigence and fear, we reject change, fighting the natural order of things — swimming against the tide; yet change is coming whether we like it or not. The only question is: are we prepared, or will it take us by surprise?

How can we evolve from the material dream spell? We can spend our whole lives operating in *fight-or-flight* modes. We can cling to one external distraction to the next. We might never see nor understand any alternatives to our attachment. We often search for happiness in all the wrong places, thus failing to connect with our true Self. Ego and illusion stand in our way, both needing to break down. We're talking about the second stage of The Anatomy of Happy, where we learn to unlearn.

As a wise man once said: "We are human beings, not human doings". Consider for a moment what life would be like with fewer physical and mental complications. To achieve such a state, you must unlearn the illusion of you — the story created by the trauma, your family, the church, the state — whatever your coatings of conditioning. Stripping layer by layer, you get closer to the core until you find stillness. Inside that place of peace lies a dormant cryogenic chamber of consciousness.

AA Milne's Pooh Bear once said: "People say nothing is impossible, but I do nothing every day". He adds, "Doing nothing often leads to the very best of something". A Zen fluff-ball if ever there was one. Along these lines, Ram Dass said, "The game is not about becoming somebody; it's about becoming nobody". To become something new, we must let go of what no longer serves us. In this incredible action of self-love, we make space for something else. Better still, we make space, then leave it — as space.

An essential utility in unlearning is acknowledging our egoic states' impermanence. We have to believe we can change. Eradicating all illusory facets of the Self weeds out the ego. So we must sit in silence and observe it for what it is — a changeable illusion. Ego works overtime to protect us from facing the unknown. By removing distractions, addictions, possessions, drama, or mental chatter, the "I" is muted, leaving only "me". This is a terrifying thought for ego, but ego is not the sum of us. We are pure consciousness — infinite energy. We must work through the challenges of silencing ego to enjoy an evolutionary existence of peace, love, and connection.

At some point in your journey, you will realise that to be anything and everything, you must endeavour to become nothing. Learn of your essence by unlearning your many layers of conditioning. It's like peeling an onion. And yes, your eyes will water, but you'll be altogether more cheerful. Benjamin Hoff articulates this idea perfectly in his excellent book, *The Tao of Pooh*, when he says: "When you discard arrogance, complexity, and a few other things that get in the way, sooner or later you will discover that simple, childlike, and mysterious secret known to those of the Uncarved Block: life is fun". The Taoist "Uncarved Block" refers to a primordial mind state of pure potential before the emergence (and interference) of experience. Its Chinese character means "Wood that is not cut". The Uncarved Block is an essential or unfettered and natural condition. Transmuting to such a state is worthwhile work with surprising benefits for all.

There's a metaphor about "bringing the weather", illustrating people's awareness of our energy as we walk into a room. Folks gravitate or feel repelled depending on what signals we're consciously or unconsciously broadcasting into the field. Thus, connected as we are, when one of us makes positive personal changes, it's experienced and felt by others. It's like the ripple effect from a stone in a pond. We radiate when we adopt new practices that improve our mental or physical health. People see it and, more often than not, want to feel the same. "I'll have whatever's in her tea!" they might joke. Others see how happier you are and naturally become more inspired to learn about it. Hence the expression "Be the change you want to see in the world" is a literal instruction to quit focusing on the external, do the work of self-introspection, and watch what happens inside and out.

So change, and unlearning, go hand in hand, benefitting the few and the many. Beware the difference between practising acceptance and the more common traits associated with an avoidant personality. In the latter, we make frequent and significant life changes, nimbly disappearing like ninjas or covering our escape with a flash-bang grenade. Here, we're not running boldly towards new goals; we're fleeing the scene. Like fearful, wounded children, we employ change to obscure emotional ineptitude. Thus, this style of change is another shrewd deception from the ego.

Lest we forget, your intuition is a phenomenon to observe along this tricky transformational track. Your heart knows when you do not belong in certain relationships, partnerships, or places. Learn to discern the difference between intuition and ego. Stillness is your superpower here. And in cases where change is good for your health, consciously uncouple if you can.

Change is difficult to accept — impossible for some. Fear of loss and unknown alternatives often drive decision-making and values. *Self-realise, unlearn, forgive, love yourself,* and *connect.* This is the anatomy of happiness. Without change, we can go no further; and stagnate, we assuredly shall. Unlearning and healing are not linear. One minute we make progress; the next, we falter. We must appreciate the impermanence in every state. No magic bullet. Surrender. Keep showing up. By welcoming change healthily, we invite the beautiful realisation that perfectly answers attachment's problem.

There are many practices to unlearn and stimulate the mental state of nothingness. Psychedelics, psychology, meditation, breathwork, yoga, and more. We'll talk about some of them later in this book. Meanwhile, since we've identified that all things come to an end, so must this chapter. Let's move on.

Taoist Peace Prayer

If there is to be peace in the world,
There must be peace in the nations.
If there is to be peace in the nations,
There must be peace in the cities.
If there is to be peace in the cities,
There must be peace between neighbours.
If there is to be peace between neighbours,
There must be peace in the home.
If there is to be peace in the home,
There must be peace in the heart.

CHAPTER TWENTY-THREE

Two Bags and a Beagle

Are you not entertained? Are you
not entertained? Is this not why
you are here?
— Maximus Decimus Meridius[1]

I raced Lamborghinis in Rome, vacationed in Elton John's
safari lodge of choice, and had many similarly quite bizarre
experiences and trappings that only come with a life of privilege
and excess. I've had German and British sports cars in the
driveway and elegant Swiss watches on my wrist. An entire room
dedicated to storing schmancy Italian and Savile Row suits.
There were homes filled with luxurious Scandinavian furniture
and stacks more stuff to boot. Perhaps, as an addict, it stood to
reason that my penchant for materialism knew no bounds, or
was it perfectly normal? Either way, I was an expert in the art of
distraction.

In this lifetime, I've blown an obscene amount of money
on possessions. But the decision to leave London for a new
and mindful existence, reluctantly giving away or selling almost
everything I owned invited a strangely delightful and most
freeing sensation. It came as a complete surprise. The last night
I spent in my Peckham flat, Macy and I shared a sleeping bag
in the centre of the empty lounge. In the corner were two large
barrel bags packed and ready to go. So, perhaps befitting, it was

1 From the feature film, Gladiator, screenplay by David Franzoni, John Logan, and
William Nicholson.

April Fool's Day when I set off for a new life on the Indonesian island of Bali with just two bags and a beagle. And for the first time in decades, I had never felt so free. This was my introduction to life as a minimalist, which I continue to enjoy to this day.

As we continue to explore the myriad drivers behind our more superficial feelings of unhappiness, we continue to consider the plights and challenges we face in our so-called "advanced" 21st-century society. Because whether we know it or not, we are victims and active participants of a daily assault manifesting as marketing, consumerism, and materialism. One might wonder how one can concurrently be a victim and active participant. That's a recurring theme in the book since, through profound apathy, we have allowed our social conditioning to amplify our Samsaric existence, thus eroding our sovereignty. The word "sovereignty" does not merely refer to physical independence; it includes our mental and energetic freedoms and our supreme authority over ourselves as sovereign beings. Brick by brick, we're giving that away.

Artist Hugh MacLeod once created a doodle that said: "If you talked to people the way advertising talked to people, they'd punch you in the face". Dan, an old friend of mine, had this printed and mounted on the wall of his marketing agency. Despite being well and truly entrenched in the advertising industry, I realised that I agreed wholeheartedly with Hugh's message. As an ad man, I suppose I ought to have felt some irritation or inherent need to leap to the defence of the industry, but I couldn't. Though I had not the courage to express these feelings at the time, the business of unwanted advertising made me sick.

Advertising has exponentially evolved since I started in the business in the mid-90s. In the 1970s, it wasn't unusual for us to be exposed to between 500 and 1,600 ads a day. Fast-forward to 2023, and the average person in a developed city is exposed to a staggering daily number of 10,000+ ads. Incredibly complex marketing strategies employ creating and optimising sales funnels, user-experience analytics, and tracking pixels. Using enterprise-grade sales and marketing automation technologies, brands can now get inside your head in incredible ways.

Do consumers even stand a chance with such sophisticated practices in play? The data marketing industry's now championing personalisation strategies as the future. There are highly targeted ads, emails, and omnichannel messages for those abandoning baskets or unsuspecting Googlers searching just once for an item. There's a funnel for it. For the folks passing a geo-location tracker with the wrong phone privacy settings, there's a funnel for that too. The recipient of an email who clicks on one link versus another? Yep, more funnels. It's not even a case of attrition; global consumers are now so used to being advertised at that we respond favourably to personalised messaging — with gratitude and appreciation. *We want it.* The air is thick with consumption apathy.

The messages come hard and fast, driven to buy, inferring short supply, never-to-be-repeated deals, or aspirational positioning convincing us that purchasing a thing will make us happier and more complete. Ah, the irony. Lest we forget Black Friday: where, every year, the internet spikes with multibillion dollar daily sales; followed shortly thereafter by a flood of videos capturing folks in stores, physically fighting over the last remaining discount TV or toaster.

We live in unprecedented times where almost anything we can imagine owning can be on our doorstep in hours. But with this newfound ability to own so much stuff, are we asking ourselves whether we need it? Moreover, is everything we want really what we want? Do we even know what we want? And do we unknowingly contribute to a wasteful and careless society through our mindless consumerism?

When we've come to a place where 108 million people watch a YouTube unboxing video of a "Rare Neon Water Barbie", is it not time to ask whether we might be just a little bit fucked? Just kidding. We're all free to watch whatever we want, of course. However, perhaps if I replace judgement with observation, I can better articulate the point. Could it be that in our role as 21st-century consumers, we might be focusing on things less likely to create a meaningful and sustainable state of happiness?

The Minimalists

Joshua Fields Millburn and Ryan Nicodemus are the self-dubbed "Minimalists". Authors, documentarians, podcasters, and spokespeople for the minimalist movement, the pair pose the primary question: *how might your life be better with less?* Defining minimalism as "the intentional use of the resources you have", the movement invites society to stop and consider some healthy and timely questions. For instance, what are the real costs of consumerism to our physical and mental health, relationships, and spiritual and personal development? Does *stuff* help us grow, or more likely impede such aspirations?

Minimalism invites us to re-evaluate our consumption, thus acquiring and using items aligned only with our basic needs. That is to say, just because we can afford a huge $5m house, do we need one? Regardless of whether our income could finance a Porsche 911, do we need that? How about ten pairs of shoes when we only have two feet? Is it healthy to be attached to these things? Beyond the superficial, what is the benefit?

Minimalism teaches us to detach ourselves from lifestyle and possessions. Far from being about decluttering your household, minimalism is a movement. One might venture to suggest it's an accidental spiritual movement, teaching the art of simplification — a step towards nothingness and the Uncarved Block. It demonstrates ways and methodologies that would help us let go. Hence, there is something altogether Zen about minimalism because, at its heart, it promotes inner and exterior peace.

So what about the science? Well, in the 1970s, a chap called Brickman conducted a study investigating whether having more money resulted in happiness. The findings showed that millionaire lottery winners in the group were no more happy than others living altogether more frugal lifestyles. Having lived on both sides of the track — possessing lots of money (and stuff) and having very little money (and less stuff) — there's no denying that money offers choices. However, as the research indicates, it's not an automatic happy pass.

Dunn et al.'s 2008 *Spending Money on Others Promotes Happiness* paper showed a direct correlation between happiness and gifting to others. Here's a short excerpt:

"Specifically, we hypothesised that spending money on other people may have a more positive impact on happiness than spending money on oneself".

But is it appropriate to discuss money and happiness here, or should we better consider the effects that minimalism has on its practitioners? Anecdotally, a cluttered home equals a cluttered mind, so what are the mental health benefits of living an *un*cluttered life?

The 2021 article *Minimalism, Voluntary Simplicity, and Well-being: a Systematic Review of the Empirical Literature* suggests there are definitive psychological benefits to opting for simplicity, living the life of a minimalist. Researched and authored by Joshua Hook, Adam Hodge, Hangsong Zhang, Daryl Van Tongeren, and Don Davis, this work explored 23 studies to investigate the relationship between the philosophy of minimalism and human well-being.

Here's an excerpt:

"Research has accumulated over the years to support the adage that 'money can't buy happiness'. As an alternative to the high-consumption lifestyle often found in Western cultures, voluntary simplicity (also referred to as 'minimalism'), involves a lifestyle that is focused on reducing consumption and the excess in one's life so that individuals can focus on prioritising their values. We reviewed the empirical literature for studies that explored the relationship between voluntary simplicity and well-being. Twenty-three empirical studies were identified".

The article adds:

"Overall, the vast majority of studies found a positive relationship between voluntary simplicity and well-being".

Through collating the research and testing the hypothesis, the team actually discovered that over 80 per cent reported a connection between voluntary simplicity and well-being.

Wowsers, this is interesting, is it not? A simple practical utility to practise as part of our unlearning. An invitation for us to consider en masse what it means to apply maximum effort towards a minimalist life. Also, are we ready to explore the notion that our personal relationships with consumerism are not just steered by social drivers but by our psychological pathology and neurosis? If so, how do we feel about marketers manipulating this? Remember the apathy. We permit this and are, thus, by no means victims but willing participants. But is any of this thinking new, or has the idea that less stuff brings more peace, been around for a while?

Dating back as early as 2,900 BCE, the Chinese Yangshao and Hongshan cultures are considered the earliest recorded societies that practised the Taoist philosophy of Feng Shui. What is it? Feng Shui is an ancient Chinese technique that uses the naturally flowing forces of energy (qi) to harmonise environments with their human inhabitants. Feng Shui means "wind-water", summarising the fluidity of the practice and its centring around universal qi. As qi flows similarly to these elements, landscapes and waterways were traditionally believed to direct qi's flow through sites and structures. Hence, Feng Shui specialists can manipulate these flows through minimalistic geomantic design and layout, thus improving wealth, happiness, and life expectancy.

The harmonious nature of Feng Shui leans into the physical and energetic, and peaceful byproducts created by minimalism. Both favour a clutter-free environment that allows the unfettered flow of qi. Feng Shui embodies minimalism yet goes much further, taking time to master it truly. In addition to considering the flow of qi, Feng Shui requires incorporating natural elements (earth, wind, water, wood, metal, fire) and a particular approach to spatial arrangement, thus improving the well-being of the inhabitants of a room, building, or external space.

Beginning a minimalist's journey is simple or challenging depending on your relationship with attachment. For example, it will be significantly more manageable to throw away half of your wardrobe once you've analysed how much space those items consume while realising how little you wear them. There are likely at least three large storage boxes in your home right now containing old school certificates, crayon drawings you did as a child, your favourite childhood stuffed animal, love letters, family photos, and more. How often, if ever, do you open these boxes? What value do you derive from their contents? How attached are you to them? These are the aspects of the process that minimalism invites you to explore. As all good minimalists explain, stuff doesn't hold memories; it's just stuff.

Plotting Your Path to Minimalism

1.   Chuck it

Start with the basics: go through every room (including your garage and storage space) and get rid of all junk.

2.   Use vs Value vs Necessity

Stuck already? Okay, have you used it in the last two years? Nope? Junk. Does it bring value to your life? Nope? Get rid. Do you actually need it? Keep or get rid accordingly.

3.   The Joy Test

Japanese author and "tidying expert" Marie Kondo also invites us to sit with what we're unsure about, hold the item close, and ask: "Does this spark joy?" Apparently, toasters and garden tools share the same fate as jewellery and clothes in this process, so have at it.

4.   The Gift of Giving

"Getting rid" doesn't necessarily mean throwing it away; you can sell or donate things. One person's trash is another's treasure, right? There's a feel-good byproduct to gifting something you no longer need to someone who will find a good use for it.

5.   Stuff's Unseen Cost

How do your purchases impact your micro and macro environments? Are you promoting needless and banal industries out of a perversely innate need to buy stuff? Do you follow a conscious process to ascertain what you want and (crucially) need?

6.   One In, One Out

Get rid of something old every time you buy something new.

7. Scheduled Inspection

Once you've gone through what may be an agonising yet cathartic exercise, set regular calendar dates to carry out a complete inventory so you can keep on top of this. Writing this makes me painfully aware that while I've practised minimalism for almost four years, I'm long overdue a full kit inspection! Consider me put on notice.

Letting go is difficult. But contrary to popular belief, stuff does not make us who we are. Possessions do not define our identity. Never before have we had access to so much. And thanks to social media and the internet, we can now witness what stuff looks like adorned by other folks. Thus, the old adage of *keeping up with the Jones'* has metamorphosised into *keeping up with the Kardashians* (insert your go-to influencer here). Exhaustion piled onto exhaustion

The more things we crave and own, the more cluttered our lives, the greater our distractions and the more we burn through disposable income. Thus, our consumptive habits contribute significantly to our misery. Ironically, what starts as a "Buying this will make me happier" mindset often results in a highly unhealthy energetic connection that can leave us feeling uneasy, thanks to the clutter created by the item's existence. The simplest way to tackle this issue is to buy and own less. Clean the slate and start again, incorporating mindfulness and intention into the process.

We often get into a state where we say, "I'll relax when I get that next thing", but then there are always more things. Life on the hamster wheel is all about keeping eyes on the prize. But if we're always looking down or ahead, when do we pause to look up? How often do we take time to imbibe our surroundings so we might be grateful for what is already ours?

When I got sober, I saw a massive difference in my disposable income as I no longer blew thousands on cigarettes, alcohol, and cocaine every month. Okay, it's not clothes or furniture, but the same methodology applies: did I need it? Nope. Did I want it? Fuck yes, I was an addict. Could I do without it? Yup, I certainly could. And as with so many things in life at Earth School, it starts with a choice. It might feel initially daunting, but I know first-hand what happens to your mind and spirit when you make this shift and take ownership over something you thought owned you. In a ludicrously short time, you can give yourself the gift of financial, physical, mental, and energetic freedom. That's two skips and a jump away from happiness.

If I asked the average person to define self-harm, the question would more than likely conjure images of razor blades cutting limbs. Such an idea is, I assert, limiting one's perspective in these times. Stuff and our addiction to it now actively share a battlefield with peace. Yours. So as and when we succumb to the consumerist mindset, we become our own worst enemy. As such, we must wake up to the myriad subtleties of our self-abuse. We are overworking, exhausting, and breaking ourselves; the stresses of materialistic existence weigh us down more than most know.

CHAPTER TWENTY-FOUR

The Four Noble Truths

You don't have to control your thoughts. You just have to stop letting them control you.
— Dan Millman

The *Four Noble Truths* are practical life utilities that directly address physical and mental suffering. The First Truth identifies the existence of suffering, while the Second explores the cause.

In Buddhism, our wanton nature lies at the root of suffering. We crave pleasure, material things, immortality, and all things external of form. Since such drivers will never be fully satisfied, we are doomed to suffer. Daniel Z. Lieberman and Michael E. Long get into this in the book *Dopamine: The Molecule of More*. This curious chemical we all have ingrained into our DNA, that's always hungry and never satisfied, is rocket fuel for suffering. As if we weren't already handicapped by the nature of our bodies and minds. Our society and technologies are careering headlong into a dark and dystopian future that will seek to control our every move while simultaneously spiking and satiating dopamine fixes on new levels. Our attention is currency for a layer cake of distraction from anything meaningful. And to think: we chose this! What a fascinating time to be alive.

Buddhism also views ignorance as a root of suffering. Ignorance, in this case, is not seeing the world as it actually is. That is living without awareness or any grasp of mindfulness or insight. This is an observation rather than judgement since we either know a thing or we do not. Hence anger, hatred, greed, and envy are not "bad" things; they are merely human traits borne of a limited (yet changeable) perspective.

The Third Noble Truth suggests that we can either end suffering in this life, or spiritually, through achieving Nirvana — a transcendent state free from suffering in the Earthly cycle of birth and rebirth (Samsara). All that is to say that each of us has the power to end suffering through enlightenment. Jeshua said the same thing, by the way. Meanwhile, The Qur'an invites us to accept that suffering tests belief:

"Every soul shall have a taste of death; And we test you by evil and by good, by way of trial. To us must ye return".

Adding to that:

"Be sure we shall test you with something of fear and hunger, some loss in goods, lives and the fruits (of your toil), but give glad tidings to those who patiently persevere, who say, when afflicted with calamity: 'To Allah, we belong, and to Him is our return'".

And so, a true Muslim remains faithful regardless of whatever trials and tribulations life offers. Similarly to Buddhists, our Muslim brothers and sisters agree that suffering is built into the very fabric of existence, and therefore surrendering to this inevitability opens the gateway to enlightenment.

According to the Buddhists, The Four Noble Truths outline the route to end one's suffering as the *Noble Eightfold Path*. These teachings invite us to understand that suffering does exist but arises from attachment to desires. Suffering can therefore end with the cessation of our attachment to desire. So, freedom from suffering is possible through practising the Noble Eightfold Path. This wisdom is absolutely packed with utilities for anyone keen to unlearn, master their emotions and equip themselves to better cope with the ever-present inevitability of suffering.

Right now, you might well be feverishly shouting: "Yes, yes, but what are the steps to this path?!" Okay, take a breath; I've got you.

CHAPTER TWENTY-FIVE

The Noble Eightfold Path

**Just because mindfulness is simple
does not mean that it is easy.
— Geshe Tashi Tsering**

The Buddhists' *Noble Eightfold Path* is a series of practicable steps one can adopt regardless of your spiritual or non-spiritual position. They are a test of how we handle our daily problems and an invitation to unlearn. The steps are as follows:

1. Right View (or understanding).
2. Right Resolve (or intention).
3. Right Speech.
4. Right Action (or conduct).
5. Right Livelihood.
6. Right Effort.
7. Right Mindfulness.
8. Right Concentration (or practice).

The Path is divided into three themes. *Understanding, Thought*, and *Speech* are categorised under good moral conduct. *Action, Livelihood*, and *Effort* under meditation and mental development. While *Mindfulness* and *Concentration* fit snugly into wisdom or insight.

A brief outline of the Noble Eightfold Path is as follows:

1. *Right View* invites us to consider the consequences of our actions in this life and the next.

2. *Right Intention* instructs us to follow the path by renouncing sensuality, ill will, and cruelty, replacing these thoughts with loving kindness and compassion.

3. *Right Speech* reminds us to consider how we communicate, including lying, rudeness, or engaging in gossip. A latter section of this book is dedicated to communication, given our oversight of its importance in a digital world, where words are as disposable as Tinder dates.

4. *Right Conduct (or Action)* relates to how killing or injuring, stealing (materials or another's time), sexual misconduct, and materially-led desire are, in fact, undesirable actions of any person seeking oneness.

5. *Right Livelihood* invites us to consider how we earn our money. What's the energetic result of our labour? What impact does our job have on our community, the environment, and the well-being of humankind?

6. *Right Effort* is a preventative practice to avoid unhealthy conscious states, focusing instead on wholesome states, thus encouraging restraint.

7. *Right Mindfulness* is about training to observe the mind (the Monkey) to eliminate weak mental states, thus being conscious and centred in the now. Here, we are present and aware of our suffering, impermanence, ego, and more.

8. *Right Concentration* ("Samadhi" in Sanskrit) is intense, one-pointed concentration of the mind through meditation. It's an advanced state of mind to which you can work towards.

Tomes have been written of the Noble Eightfold Path, and lifetimes spent devoted to its wisdom. Viewing these instructions through a 21st-century lens is essential, inquiring how they apply to you. These guidelines are as relevant now as they ever were. And in an age where people's physical and emotional well-being have become so frighteningly expendable, I encourage further exploration of these excellent utilities. If the Eightfold Path does not resonate with you for whatever reason, then perhaps at least remember the Golden Rule. If nothing else, we must endeavour, with all our hearts and minds, to do no harm. And if you find yourself debating whether something might be harmful, then best do nothing at all.

Suffice it to say that understanding and practising the Path (without necessarily adopting Buddhism) is a total game-changer. You will find great wisdom here, even as a layperson entirely disassociated from religion or spirituality. This book shares ancient and contemporary knowledge and practical utilities that can help *anyone* - from the downright depressed to the upbeat truth-seekers, from atheists, agnostics, and the spiritually aware. The Noble Eightfold Path is an incredible set of utilities available to those who wish to learn the arts of living and dying. Thus, I recommend that you seek to understand more about these teachings and how to apply them. Twice-daily meditation practice will enhance mindful observation of one's thoughts and actions, expediting unlearning old behaviours.

The Three Marks of Existence

Before ending this chapter, let's introduce one more Buddhist concept: the *Three Marks of Existence.*

As previously discussed, during the early stages of my mental and spiritual "do-over", I studied the Buddhist concept of *Anicca* (Anitya in Sanskrit), meaning impermanence. With some help from Ayahuasca and Psilocybin, understanding this methodology changed my embodiment of grief, profoundly transforming my mental health and perspective on living and dying. Hence my keenness to provide a little more narrative around the subject.

Since stumbling on to my personal development journey, I (being human) felt that accepting impermanence was easier said than done. Learning and practising the Three Marks of Existence changed that forever. So here goes.

Disclaimer: I'm not a Buddhist nor an academic in the field of theology or any other. I actually did relatively poorly at school. However, we can all be scholars when we see there's so much to learn. I didn't read a single self-help book before I was 40. Since then, I've opened my mind to countless concepts, thus collating an eclectic mix of lessons. It just so happens I've found a lot of sense in Buddhist teachings; hence they feature somewhat regularly in this book.

So back to the Three Marks, an underpinning trinity of the core teachings of Buddhism. As with many Buddhist teachings, the concept is paradoxically simple and profound in equal measure. The Three Marks of Existence refer to the characteristics which apply to the natural order of things. Three Universal truths, if you like.

Dukkha (Suffering)

Also translated as "pain", "unsatisfactoriness", or "stress". The teaching here is simple: for us, desire and change bring feelings of being unsatisfied — *we suffer*. The only way to free oneself from the pain of holding on to permanence is to fully accept the inevitability of continual change. You likely already grasped the idea in earlier chapters. Rest assured, we'll bang that drum to the literal end.

Anicca (Impermanence)

Whilst the word "Nicca" refers to the notion of permanence and continuity, "Anicca" refers to its opposite: the absence of the two. Inconstance is a Universal constance. Simply put, nothing is permanent, and all things change. Accept this as fact, and rebuild a mental framework around it.

Anatta (Selflessness)

There is no unchanging, permanent Self. No inherent "I" or "me". Independent enduring existence is an illusion. That is to say that Buddhists believe you have no enduring soul.

Working the trinity, we experience life through perception, form (the body, its five senses, and stuff), and consciousness. Summarising previous discussions, our clinging to stuff anchors us, verifying our existence and identity, keeping us grounded in our story. So form makes up who we are. Or rather, who we think we are. They are all aspects of ego — the things with which we identify as ourselves. However, this presents a rather glaring problem: clinging to something impermanent (as Anicca confirms) can only end in suffering when the state of that thing changes. So fully understanding Dukkha, Anicca, and Anatta is crucial in the path towards enlightenment, life, and living.

Now then, you may have no interest whatsoever in religion — perhaps that's not you. So take what resonates and leave the rest. If you're not aiming for full-on spiritual enlightenment, then simply use these principles to shoot for a significant improvement in your mental health. Truly grasping these concepts, and baking them into your daily practice, will help you unlearn the all-too-human conceptions that have shaped your life to date. Furthermore, these utilities offer the profound ability to observe oneself and one's place in the world. This is how we break down generations of conditioning. This is the road to happiness.

Belly Breathing for Anxiety

Find a comfortable seat, perhaps crosslegged,
or in a chair with your feet flat on the ground.
Sit with your spine straight.
You might like to close your eyes.
Relax your jaw, neck, and shoulders.
Soften your belly.

As you breathe in, let your belly expand naturally.
Inhale through the nose for one, two, three, four.
Hold your breath for one, two, three, four.
Gently exhale through the nose for one, two, three, four.
Hold for one, two, three, four.

Repeat nine times (or more, if you like).

CHAPTER TWENTY-SIX

Ego-A-Go-Go

The identification with thinking becomes ego. Which means
simply that you believe in every
thought that arises, and you
derive your sense of who you are
from what your mind is telling
you who you are.

— Eckhart Tolle

We've introduced ego and egoic traits already. So now feels as good a time as any to embark on a wee journey. Join me on a short yet necessary inquiry into what ego is and does. Understanding how the ego works is a significant step towards comprehending how you are who you currently are, to master this curious and dominant aspect of yourself. And master it, you must. There are multiple ways to come at the subject of ego, and while at risk of patronising, it remains essential to clarify what is meant by the word, "ego".

The word "ego" does not expressly belong to one's ability to "showboat" or "peacock" — both phrases leading to define someone with a very high degree of pomposity. Naturally, this still stands as a definition; however, there is much more to the ego, which, while linked to the former, is an altogether different animal.

In his excellent book, *Ego is the Enemy*, Ryan Holiday analyses this formidable phenomenon of personality, along the way making the following observation:

"The ego we see most commonly goes by a more casual definition: an unhealthy belief in our own importance. Arrogance. Self-centred ambition... It's that petulant child inside every person, the one that chooses getting his or her way over anything or anyone else. The need to be better than, more than, recognised for, far past any reasonable utility — that's ego. It's the sense of superiority and certainty that exceeds the bounds of confidence and talent".

Holiday proposes that ego (the voice in our head "telling us we're better than we really are") is, by definition of its actions, inhibiting us from true success by preventing "honest connection to the world around us". And so, the ego is often our enemy — separating us from reality, inviting us to adopt unrealistic expectations and a sense of entitlement while encouraging us to search for external validation. In this light, it's understandable that we must see ego as an infernal and internal foe.

Carl Jung viewed ego as being at the heart of the field of consciousness, within which a person's sense of identity and conscious awareness of being resides. According to Jung, the ego organises thoughts and feelings, readily utilising access to memories to guide us and our experience. Arising in our stages of early childhood development, the ego defines our personality, devising an emotional blueprint, operating as a utility to help us stay alive on life's rambling journey. Speaking of our relationship to and awareness of ego's function, Jung said: "The first half of life is devoted to forming a healthy ego, the second half is going inward and letting go of it". In his influential work on psychoanalytical theory, Sigmund Freud proposed that we have three main aspects of personality: *id, ego,* and *superego.* Each brings something unique to the personality party, emerging at different life stages. Operating on the pleasure principle, the id is with us from birth and consists of unconscious psychic energy designed to satisfy basic needs, desires, and urges, while also driving our survival instinct. Freud proposed that the id could be distinguished by the exchange of neural energy and primitive thinking. Therefore, the ego's job (as a conscious mind) is to minimise that energy, "bind" it and thus regulate unconscious impulses, ensuring the needs of the id are expressed in an altogether more acceptable way. The superego guides our process of judgement. Learned societal and parental conditioning, superego works to suppress and polish our urges, while acting as our sense of right and wrong.

As if that wasn't all a lot to get your head around (forgive the pun), these three aspects of personality don't act independently. Their fluid and boundless interactions drive our personality and behaviour — it's all going on! With all this in mind (again, with the puns), perhaps it's a wee bit easier to comprehend how and why we find ourselves so easily maladjusted and with a bagful of neuroses. For the uninitiated, balancing the impulses and actions of the id, ego, and superego isn't exactly a walk in the park. Furthermore, it's not on the school syllabus, is it?

So, ego (I now use the word in the broader sense) learns how to react to events based on previous events. All of the aforementioned traits and more are learned behaviours. And while some of us have been lucky enough to learn healthy traits through such life experiences, a boatload of us bimble[1] around Earth School having been educated in an altogether less than healthy way. The brain creates so-called synaptic pathways based on these experiences. So when a similar event comes along, the brain is better prepared. Ego's intention is to have our back — using its experience to help protect us from future harm. Understanding this taught me a thing or two about the ego's function, personality, and how I might begin to unlearn, and, as Jung suggests, "let go of it".

1 *To walk or travel, in no particular rush or direction.*

My childhood and early adulthood included a lot of shouting, smashing, crashing, punching (and being punched), peppered with a cacophony of loud and angry voices. Emotional regulation was not a concept embodied by my tribe. I also spent a lot of time alone. I had plenty of opportunities to be or feel hurt, with no one around qualified to explain these events and my subsequent feelings. So when triggered to move into *fight-or-flight* mode, having already experienced physical violence, my brain would act fast to protect me. But here's the thing: the anterior insula and anterior cingulate cortices inside our noggins are similarly activated by physical and emotional pain. So, while a raised voice in anger, for example, will not necessarily lead to physical violence, our brain doesn't always know the difference and thus prepares accordingly. Harsh words are said, mental injury occurs. Thus, ego learns. An unexpected punch in the face results in physical and psychological injury. Logging the damage, ego's learning continues. The ego is warier through these events, and the synaptic pathways become more ingrained.

Ego learns from the good, the bad, and the ugly. Ego never forgets. Ego never forgives. Unfortunately, at some point in the future, a partner, friend, or total stranger might say or do something relatively harmless, which is almost undoubtedly forgivable. Still, ego's got no time for that kind of thinking. Ego's poised, armed, and in some instances, fully prepared to scorch earth rather than allow us to be hurt again. Poor, poor unsuspecting partner, friend, or stranger. Do you see the paradox? We need ego to live, but ego often makes a hard job of living.

While there's brain circuitry for modulating anxiety, self-doubt, and confidence, in neuroscientific terms, the ego does not exist in the brain. Alongside ego's functions that keep us alive (sometimes avoiding danger), ego also controls self-esteem, pride, self-confidence, and self-worth. We're back to that layer cake, where the byproducts of what ego believes to be entirely helpful activities can cause a whole host of mental health fuckery. Which, in turn, can create a notable (yet avoidable) stink in our interactions with others. All of which are subject to the law of karma, since all actions have consequences — *cause and effect.*

Many believe that ego is all we are, whilst Jung and more know ego to be no more than a learned expression of Self and, therefore, an unlearnable utilitarian aspect of our being. A critical utility, of course, but a utility nonetheless. And since ego develops throughout our lives, it stands to reason that, depending on your age and experience, the ego could be a stubborn driver who's altogether unwilling to hand over the wheel. In fact, it might well be said that when we allow ego to dominate our thoughts, words, and actions, we are demonstrating the most unconscious of behaviour — while paradoxically being awake, operating, and seemingly surviving. The game, therefore, is to recognise and observe this phenomenon in ourselves.

CHAPTER TWENTY-SEVEN

Ego: Friend or Foe?

**The body is just a water bubble.
The mind is like a mad monkey.
Do not follow either the body or
the mind. Follow the Conscience.
It is above the mind. It is permanent. It is the voice of God, the
voice of unchanging truth inside
you.**

— **Sathya Sai Baba**

There is a tendency among those in the epiphanal stages of personal development to see ego as an enemy to be vanquished. I once felt the same. It makes a lot of sense when you think about it. You spend a lump of your life blissfully unaware that Monkey has been taking a long and leisurely joyride in the Earth Rover. And then, for whatever reason, an aspect of you awakens to the shenanigans. It's a bit of a shock. While Monkey is perfectly capable of driving, he learned as he went along — not from a proper driving school, nor does he have a licence. Worse in my case, as one of his teachers was drunk! Alas, this also meant that impulse and emotions played a huge part in his driving style. Monkey would meander, speed, sound his horn, clang, clash, and crash into many an unsuspecting Earth Rover. Moreover, it later transpired that Monkey chalked up a frightening amount of (metaphorical) hit and runs. All this to say that you (and I) knew no different. As far as we were concerned, it was normal; that's life. The Monkey *is* me, is it not?

Ah well, that's where the revelation comes, my friend, because, no, the Monkey is *not* me — or you. Ego is merely a much-needed function of the Self. But you are pure consciousness inside the vibratory distortional complex otherwise known as a human body. Your Earth Rover consists of many complex parts, *including* your ego. You are not the voice in your head; you are the observer of the voice (or voices), and must become aware. And for a great many of us, the early stages of the game must involve teaching Monkey to unlearn, thus allowing our conscious Self to flex to the ultimate point where Monkey retires to the back seat for a much-deserved sabbatical. So, consciousness may finally take the wheel. This is no mean feat! Actually, it's blimmin' hard, but as Eckhart Tolle explains:

"When you recognise that there is a voice in your head that pretends to be you and never stops speaking, you are awakening out of your unconscious identification with the stream of thinking. When you notice that voice, you realise that who you are is not the voice — the thinker — but the one who is aware of it". Tolle is *the* expert on the tug of war between ego and consciousness. Read everything he's written.

So there you have it. Discovering and exploring this new level of awareness of the Self is a very cool thing indeed. This Jedi skill is accessible to all; it just requires work and practice. The essential utility here lies in the common phrase, "Rise above it". When we learn to rise above an unfavourable exchange, we float and thus have clear sight over the cloud of drama below. We can better see and hear what's happening now that we've climbed out of our Monkey suit.

How to float? Breathe. Plain and simple: breathe. Resist the urge to think or do, and instead, do nothing. Breathe in through your nose, and when your lungs are full, sigh through your mouth. This is how to literally rise above it. You may need to do this more than once before Monkey's chattering and scratching subsides. Witness what you say and do with every breath — not with judgement, but by asking yourself: "Where's this going? Who does it serve?" Through this simple action, you are exercising pure awareness, interrupting decades of conditioning, and thus Monkey is auto-relegated to the back seat. You're unlearning.

I did this for the first time during a heated argument with a woman with whom I was emotionally entangled. We were sitting at the dining table in my garden. She was shouting and swearing at me, and despite my initial urge to raise my voice and dive headlong into an endless verbal scrap, I closed my eyes and took a deep breath. On my first out-breath, she stopped mid-shout, and on the second, in absolute disbelief, she asked: "Are you fucking meditating?!" Well, it seemed to me that the best way to respond was to continue doing nothing. So I did. The storm passed while not disturbing my inner peace. I was thus delighted to have risen above it. I can't say the same for her.

Recognising the "witness", "observer", or Higher Self as the transcendent, awake, and aware part of us, we can then learn to activate it. We can do so by incorporating meditation, psychedelics, breathwork, and mindfulness techniques into a regular practice. Start with a single breath and move on from there.

According to a 2020 study, the average person has 6,000 thoughts a day. Activating the observer allows us to elevate our consciousness, rising above the incessant chatter, introspection, and chaotic imagery of the mind. By watching what we are doing, we become aware that we are aware. Alan Watts explains the idea here:

"There was a young man who said, 'Though it seems that I know that I know, but what I would like to see is the I that knows me when I know that I know that I know'".

You may have to read that several times before it settles in. A witty and master wordsmith, was Mr Watts.

Activated awareness has been described by countless ancient cultures over thousands of years. Using this practice, you can transcend anxiety, worry, and other forms of mental stress. Entering this aspect of our consciousness takes us beyond the ordinary level of thinking, providing access to deeper levels of creativity, insights, and intuition. It's Jedi stuff, and it's beautiful.

I've only been practising this for a few years and still regularly become aware that my hairy-handed friend has made another grab for the controls while I'm not looking. But more often than not, that's all he gets to do these days. He snatches, begins his manoeuvre, I notice, and correct the course. Or, he gets away with it entirely, but having observed the event, I can at least rapidly make sincere and wholehearted amends. I was hard on myself in the early days of doing this work, since I was irritated with me for falling from a higher seat of consciousness. But self-criticism is, as I came to learn, just another form of judgement. With proper practice, we can bring ourselves back to being present. When you catch your ego meddling (which you regularly will), try not to be angry or frustrated with it (at yourself). It's natural to feel that way, of course, especially as you begin to work on your self-awareness. But try to be kind to Monkey all the same.

Speaking about ego, Ram Dass said: "The way I would work with the term 'ego', is that it's a structure of mind that organises the Universe, particularly around the relationships of separateness". So he's talking about the ego's role in guiding us through this life in a realm of duality. Which, for the absence of doubt, is not an easy job.

Naturally, we tend to think we must work hard to put our ego down for good. I've been there. Many folks on a so-called "spiritual path" wrangle with this stage of the process as they try desperately hard to shed all aspects of their human self. But is this possible since despite our best efforts to level up, we will remain human? Ram Dass adds: "You don't destroy the ego, you merely turn from identifying with it to instead having it as a functional unit. So, there are two planes, and when you have this type of ego structure for orienting yourself and functioning on this plane, it is still going to be functional where you're not identifying with it. You have the ego and see it as being. As Swami Vivekananda once said, 'a lousy master but a wonderful servant'. The art is to convert it into being a servant".

So, when left in charge, ego *is* the enemy. Thus, on the one hand, Mr Holiday's earlier truth is, of course, absolutely correct. Left unchecked, ego can cause havoc to our lives, ultimately producing nothing healthy, long-lasting, or wholesome. As quickly as ego builds, ego destroys. However, as the Chinese strategist Sun Tzu once advised: "If you know the enemy and know yourself, you need not fear the result of a hundred battles. If you know yourself but not the enemy, for every victory gained you will also suffer a defeat. If you know neither the enemy nor yourself, you will succumb in every battle". Which begs the question: *what if yourself and the enemy are one?*

Knowing your enemy's strength is vital, so in this regard, to know ego, we must make self-inquiry. Your ego is a part of you, and thus, to treat ego as a literal enemy, disregarding it, being angry with it, showing it disdain or even judging it will most likely and ironically create more inner conflict. Thus, the game is to respect and understand it. To, as Sun Tzu suggests, observe its traits, and learn from them. But don't overthink it either because you may find yourself in more ego traps as a result. Ego likes to dress up. Ego likes to hide. The more you learn to observe ego, the more cunning its disguise. Yes, there is an enemy. Acknowledge him, understand her, and ultimately offer them forgiveness and love.

To deny your ego's existence is to deny a natural part of yourself. However, attempting to "kill" one's ego is futile and a pseudo-psycho form of self-harm. The Monkey is here to stay; we need him, her, them. But once you make friends and explain your superior driving qualifications, you can forever change the speed and direction you travel together.

I developed an alternative response that I invite you to try, which amplifies my happiness. When I become aware that I am unaware that I'm thinking a thought or preparing some words that are not *Right Thought* or *Right Speech*, I pause, take one conscious breath, and then smile or even laugh at Monkey, depending on whatever plan the little bastard was hatching. This kind of loving focus of attention instantly diffuses his antics minus any drama or self-judgement. This is a practical utility; it's self-love and forgiveness. It's mindfulness in motion.

Contrary to the popular disenfranchised truths: a leopard can change its spots; you can teach an old dog new tricks. Moreover, an old dog can teach himself new tricks! Consider that an old dog's truth. According to scientists at Stanford University, the Earth Rover replaces most of itself with a new set of cells every seven to ten years, and some of our most vital body parts are upgraded quicker. So every seven to ten years, you are literally a new person. Feel free to pass on that fact next time someone says, "you'll never change", and pay no mind to the haters. Simply smile and nod; perhaps respond with: "Is that so?" And beware your own negative self-talk; that cheeky Monkey's always looking for an "in", so be vigilant. *Everything* is change; ergo, everything can and does change — us included — always. But since there's no magic bullet to healing, the process must begin at the beginning.

Since we're now knee-deep in the weeds of unlearning who we thought we were, it makes sense to make some inquiry into who we are. Or rather, what we are beneath all those layers of identity. Hence, we'll explore *Individuation* and the role of the *Higher Self.*

CHAPTER TWENTY-EIGHT

A Sidenote About The Higher Self

There is only *one* being experiencing the illusion of being many. The One is engaged in an experience of itself as being many.
— Joy-Divine (Zingdad)

Ruminating as I have about what to include in this book, I've realised it's essential to mention the spiritual concept of the "Higher Self". I invite your contemplation regardless of whether or not you choose to identify with spirituality. If you struggle to visualise spiritual concepts, mentally reframe this chapter as a discussion about a higher aspect of the mind with which many of us are disconnected. Labels aside, one's appreciation for one's Higher Self is the gateway to becoming aware that one is aware. The observer of your observer *is* your Higher Self, you see.

Through meditation and extensive psychonautical exploration, I've come to understand a fair bit about the existence, motivations, and location of my Higher Self. However, such tales have no place in this literary venture for reasons that may shortly become apparent. That said, to explore the nature of Self without giving so much as a mention to the Higher Self would be somewhat remiss. So let's get down to brass tacks.

You have a Higher Self, though perhaps you're not yet aware.

Do you know that nagging intuition you have about a thing? That feeling in the pit of your stomach? You don't always trust it, yet, with hindsight, you almost always wish you had. That's right; it's called your "gut instinct". It's an inexplicable knowing which, with practice, you can precisely attune to and thus better hear the whisper of intuition. Or how about those moments when "The Universe" delivers a series of seemingly random opportunities that lead to unexpected good fortune or synchronicity? Using the Unified Field of energy that surrounds and connects us all, your Higher Self has something to do with that too.

The Higher Self isn't a New Age concept; it's as old as humankind and for a good reason. Thus, this premise of an infinite, conscious, and intelligent entity, seemingly separated while also paradoxically being an aspect of each of us, is shared by multiple belief systems. And while said systems have different shapes, sizes, and flavours for the Higher Self, as with most religions, all roads lead to Rome. Come to think of it, since Rome is the home of the Catholic Church, the draconian dogma of which resonates and repels in equal measure, please forgive my misuse of the expression in this case. You doubtless catch my drift, nonetheless.

Certain denominations see the Higher Self as a part of our metaphysical identity, while others see it as a direct connection between us and divinity (our divine nature). Both concepts are correct. So, the Christians, Muslims, Hindus, and so-called "New Agers" all share another fundamental understanding. *Who knew?*

Another way for me to explain it would be to avoid discussing religion at all and instead focus on the concept and existence of multiple dimensions ("planes") outside time and space. There is a version of us that is not of this plane, that has simultaneous visibility of us and other planes beyond the veil of our knowledge and understanding. And to further bake your noodle, we don't all necessarily have an individual Higher Self; many of us share one. Intrinsically connected to us while simultaneously able to multitask at levels incomprehensible to the human mind, our Higher Self is an entity (or perhaps better described as "energy") of a higher dimension, with an entirely otherworldly (other-dimensional) set of capabilities at its disposal. Now, such chatter may well have you questioning my sanity, which is perfectly fine, and your truth, which, as you may have gathered by now, I sincerely respect. As with all my references to the metaphysical in this book, it matters not whether you believe it; merely that you understand its context. Better still, perhaps consider that knowledge and experience, like everything else in this world, are impermanent and thus subject to change. Therefore, I invite you to open your heart and mind to all possibilities and truths, regardless of whether they currently resonate based on your life experience to date. Just because you cannot see, hear, or understand a thing in this time and space does not mean it does not exist.

Zingdad wrote *The Ascension Papers*. I wasn't ready to receive this incredible book's message when first introduced to me. If I recall, it took a couple more years of practice, experience, and understanding before I happened upon it again, at which point its contents resonated deeply. It provides a wonderfully profound explanation of why we inhabit the world as we do and how, with that knowledge, we might better enjoy our time here. When you're ready, perhaps you'll recall this recommendation.

By the way, one does not need psychedelics to connect with one's Higher Self, though I've had many a decent chat with mine in this way. Such communion can be achieved through solo and guided meditation to varying degrees of detail and success. Actually, meditation purists would tell you to avoid using psychedelics altogether, while my truth is that psychedelics are a laser-cut key available for all of us to access altered states of consciousness or planes of existence. With such, we can consciously commune with our Higher Selves, and gain a significantly better understanding of our place, purpose, and intrinsic and beautiful connection to one another. Better still, perhaps, you'll learn to find such a connection by working with plant medicine *and* meditation. Perhaps you're already communing with the help of none of the above. Some folks are just lucky like that.

Now then, as you've likely already gathered, some believe we're bodies with a spirit, while I know we're spirits with a body. Pierre Teilhard de Chardin once famously said: "We are not human beings having a spiritual experience. We are spiritual beings having a human experience". While not necessarily recognising mine and Pierre's shared truth, you might be interested to note that, to varying degrees, scientists and psychologists do recognise the existence of the Higher Self. The kind of therapy that examines all of the mind's characteristics, including unconscious and subconscious, defines the Highest Self (or just the Self) as an inner guide, separate from our personality (ego).

In Jungian psychology, the Higher Self comprises the collective knowledge of all the Jungian Archetypes, thus comprehending the collective unconscious. So while connected to the individual, the Higher Self is also more broadly connected. Advanced as the Higher Self is, it represents the destiny of the human species. Our relationship with this energy is a two-way channel. Unconsciously, we can upload information; consciously, with practice, we can download it. A theory experienced by many meditators and psychonauts[1] states that our individual experiences don't just affect us and those around us. Experiences are uploaded and shared (on a level) by the collective consciousness. All this to say that whether we suffer, feel pleasure, wonder or enlightenment, learning through all provides a rich education for the Higher Self and collective consciousness.

1   *Experienced explorers of no space and no time, using psychedelics.*

Jung called the lifelong process of fulfilling one's potential (being all we can be) "Individuation". Introduced by the nagging soul that yearns to evolve, your Higher Self is instrumental in your Individuation. It's our journey towards self-realisation, discovering and experiencing the meaning and purpose of our life. Such achievement, of course, results in happiness. Hence, this book is intended to support your journey to achieving such a state. Speaking of this not-so-common phenomenon, Jung once said it is "only experienced by those who have gone through the wearisome but indispensable business of coming to terms with the unconscious components of the personality". "Wearisome" indeed, and if you're still set on doing this work, or have already, then take a moment to acknowledge that. Put your hand on your heart and express gratitude to yourself for embarking on this incredible and life-changing adventure.

How does one find oneself if one does not know one is lost?

Anthony Stevens, a Jungian analyst: says: "Individuation is a conscious attempt to bring the Universal programme of human existence to its fullest possible expression in the life of the individual". Jung says: "The aim of individuation is nothing less than to divest the Self of the false wrappings of the persona on the one hand and the suggestive power of primordial images on the other". Therefore, unsurprisingly, Individuation is achieved through self-inquiry and breaking down the illusory facets of our personality propped up by the ego. Along the way, we gather first-hand experience that confirms we are not the voice in our heads. We are far more and are connected thus. To conceive such a thing is to raise one's consciousness. One might even say that through the simple act of asking such questions, we are connecting with our Higher Self.

CHAPTER TWENTY-NINE

Purpose

Do one thing well. It's enough.
— David Hieatt

If you find yourself asking yourself, "Why am I here?" then fret not; you're in good company. However, for some folks, life on the hamster wheel is enough. They care not for big questions, believing the consume, work (pay taxes), sleep, and repeat model is why we exist. "That's life!" they'll declare. "What are we gonna do?" they ask as they nonchalantly throw open hands in the air, discarding all hope in the process.

Is it life? What about potential? Are we really attending Earth School to contribute significant life force energy to a grossly imbalanced system that distracts, drains, and controls us, where peace, mindfulness, and freedom are luxuries rather than fundamental human rights?

The collective consciousness is rising. Unrest spreads like a brushfire of truth on a hillside dense with deceit, and thus we question our purpose more than ever. To many people, "purpose" means "job". Sure, what we do during the day does play a part in defining our purpose because a third of our lives are spent working. And when our purpose is unclear, seeds of unhappiness can quickly flourish. But there are many things to consider as we question our purpose — especially as it's not uncommon to point fingers at people, society, and the cards we've been dealt as we declare why we are where we are and where we may well stay.

Hence, determining one's purpose is far more than defining one's day job. Let's get into this.

Before tackling a well-known practical utility that does a beautiful job in helping define purpose, we must first explore why so many of us struggle to motivate ourselves towards change. Cynicism plays a substantial role when considering achievements and changing our life's direction. And with so many people espousing how we all should embrace a "positive vibes only" mentality, it's no wonder a "fuck your positive vibes" counter-culture shot out of the starting gate with equal speed and vigour. I get it. To crassly dismiss the reality of a person's poor mental health and financial or employment situations by virtually demanding "positive vibes" might well provide ample motivation for people to want to punch other people in the face.

I'm reminded of a podcast interview I did with the accidentally famous YouTuber, author, and meditating farmer, John Butler. John was 86 when I interviewed him. Wise and at peace, and more fond of silence than conversation (perhaps, therefore, an ironic choice for a podcast guest), John has a beautiful view of the world. He basks in gratitude for the simplest of things. On the subject of happy people, John said: "I suppose that's why I'm a bit suspicious of happy people. I suspect they've got a lot to learn. Good luck to them!" John had just finished describing life as "a veil of tears", which was rather a sad thing to say, but then his story had, according to him, had its fair share of painful chapters. So perhaps John's truth was that he couldn't understand people who remained in a constant state of happiness. But then, as we progressively discussed, happiness is not skin deep, nor can it be sustainably connected to form. When one truly understands the anatomy of happiness, one can be happy even while experiencing pain. So this really isn't about "Positive vibes only"; this entire book is stuffed to the stitches with reasons and utilities to help people shift their mindsets while retaining logic, realism, and humanity. While positivity is absolutely required for defining and setting out to achieve one's purpose, it's understood that numerous elements help shape our positive or negative views. To merely decide to exude positivity doesn't work. To make positive changes, we must personally explore and experiment. Thus, we can play with positivity.

Besides cynicism for unnaturally happy folks, negative self-talk can get well and truly in the way of achieving one's dreams. We've already discussed the voice in our heads not being the sum of us, and we do well to remember this daily. In addition, we must remember that words are spells. So consider this a flag raised, as it stands to reason that negative mindsets of any kind are blockers to finding one's purpose.

Fear is, of course, a born enemy of purpose, though we've already dragged its name through the mud, with more to come. Suffice it to say that fear loathes progress, and defining one's purpose is progress incarnate.

Another combination of factors explaining why so many of us are dissatisfied with our lot lies in how we treat our body and mind. Still, even now, with yottabytes of information available at the tap of a tiny screen, great waves of us lackadaisically trudge on through life. We're distracted, divided, lost or crippled by depression, with absolutely no idea that our moods (and therefore attitudes) are drastically affected by all we consume. Likewise, how much or little we move and rest our bodies play massive roles in how we feel from one moment to the next. So be mindful of your capability to stand in your own way. As you can see, such friction comes in many flavours.

If purpose isn't about a job, then what is it? Well, the primary dictionary definition of the word is: "The intention, aim, or function of something; the thing that something is supposed to achieve". Does discovering our purpose, therefore, help us expose the meaning of life? Or is that too high a bar, given the gravitas of the question? Yes and no. It depends entirely on what you feel drives your purpose. Finding purpose doesn't have to be complicated, but it requires practical input and consideration, like much in life. In reality, it boils down to a few simple things.

1. Go Inward

First, go inward. Self-inquiry plays a huge part in defining one's purpose. Ask yourself the questions to understand why you feel lost, misplaced, or dissatisfied. What's jarring in your life that reduces your joy count? Jim Carey once said: "Depression is your avatar telling you it's tired of being the character you're trying to play". What a wonderful validation. *Go inward.*

2. Purpose First

Prioritise purpose before goals. There's often a mismatch between wanting and needing something and finding true meaning. On the journey of discovering one's purpose, goals must align, complement, or lean towards your passion.

3. Gratitude

Practise gratitude, focusing on what you have over what you do not. Gratitude is one of our most potent secret weapons, which we'll discuss in more detail later (Chapter 49). Suffice it to say that the energy in and around the emotion of gratitude transmutes pretty much all negative energies. It's a superpower to wield as we define our purpose.

4. Own it

Take ownership of who you are and where you're going. We often look to others (saviours) to help us get where we want to be. Even in its subtlest form, this mindset is one of a victim. There's a lot of chat about "manifestation" these days, which is an incredible skill. There are those among us who believe that wanting something badly enough will manifest it. Nope. True manifestation requires certain alchemy, a balanced combination of wanting, feeling, *doing*, and sending that vibration out into the Unified Field. We, and we alone, are responsible for our life's direction. Choice and action are the keys. In the movie *Field of Dreams*[1], Kevin Costner's character continuously heard a voice uttering the words: "If you build it, they will come". **Pro tip:** he *built* it.

5. Alchemise Your Suffering

Transmute your pain to purpose. While not simple, this is literally magical. I used my pain and co-created suffering to shape my purpose. Experience is an influential teacher (and driver). Hence this book.

6. Do What You Love

Probe your passions. What do you love doing? Write a list, and dive deeper into them. *Why* do you love the things you love? What is it about them that inspires you?

7. Back to School

Read and learn. When faced with the challenging opportunity of defining or redefining our life's purpose, reality bites. There's a good chance that while we might be passionate about a thing, we might not be anywhere near close to being an expert. We are all teachers and learners and will be through this life story and many more. We must be prepared to learn and be excited about learning. If you're not enthusiastic to learn about a thing, can you genuinely say you're passionate about it?

1 *Field of Dreams (novel by W P Kinsella, screenplay by Phil Alden Robinson)*

8. Do What Makes You Happy

What brings you joy? Cough all that goodness out on to a blank page and review it.

9. Service to Others

Pay it forward. A simple way to generate a sense of meaning and well-being is to help your fellow brothers and sisters (in the broader, non-familial sense) while asking nothing in return. Can you combine that mindset with a passion?

10. Community

Along these lines, joining a cause or community of like-minded people is a beautiful way to get a foot on the purpose ladder.

There are two other things to consider as you play with purpose. The first is to be flexible and realistic, practising self-acceptance. I'd love to be a *Mercury Music Award*-winning singer-songwriter. It's not going to happen. Yes, I can write and sing (and am passionate about both), but countless contributing factors mean I'm unlikely to achieve this goal. Frankly, there are far more talented singer-songwriters out there. So is it realistic to throw everything I have at such a goal?

That said, since I love to write and sing, I write and sing! Often during plant medicine ceremonies, to small circles of people on their healing journey. Sure, the audiences are a lot smaller; but I relish it no less and derive bucketloads of joy, satisfaction, and peace knowing my music is being received while I simultaneously act in service to others.

And finally, be kind to yourself. Exploring the territory of our life's meaning is chunky work and, by its very nature, requires a lot of self-analysis, self-motivation, goal-setting, hoping, wishing, and dreaming. Through all of this, you must be patient and loving with yourself. And avoid attachment and judgement, both of which lead to suffering.

Ultimately, I can't tell you your purpose more than I can insist on what you have for dinner. I can tell you mine, though. For reasons that will become more obvious in a few chapters, it was made clear during my first encounter with my Higher Self that I am here to learn to love. Though, I'll speak of our second meeting here, which occurred in 2020, courtesy of a heroic dose of Psilocybin mushrooms. Some might refer to the encounter as "negotiating a new soul contract". I suppose it was a near-death experience of sorts.

Bimbling around several astral planes on this particular psychedelic journey, I eventually appeared in a new space. I was surrounded by an almost indescribable white aura of stunning luminosity. All was light, even me. Another entity (a light being) occupied the area close by, whom I immediately understood to be my Higher Self. I believe I almost died, though contrary to what one might imagine death to be like, this experience was entirely peaceful; natural, like walking from one room to another. Realising I could choose to die anytime (apparently, we all can), I was thus no longer at the mercy of my attachment, ego, or fear. In this place, outside of time-space, with my collective experiences in hand, I suddenly knew, or perhaps remembered, something I have always known. I.e. amongst its many crucial functions, ego also upholds our existence in this plane. I mean that we are alive (in Third Density) because we see ourselves as alive. Our conscious awareness of being alive is what keeps us alive. Perhaps it's obvious, but in understanding this, I had apparently unlocked a great secret I'd been keeping from myself. The epiphany profoundly affected me; I suddenly felt energised and renewed.

Bemused yet proud, *he* then gestured to his left, where a bridge appeared. He invited me to "cross over". I said: "You're actually inviting me to cross over the Rainbow Bridge and ascend?!" Without so much as a pause, he replied: "Yup". However, as he went to explain, such a journey would come with a cost. As a consequence of embarking on this new direction, the "Martin Story" must come to an end. Upon further inquiry, I understood this to mean that back home, Martin would die. Shocker.

So, after a quick flashback of myriad life events (it turns out that's a thing), further discussion, and a great deal of deliberation, I chose to return to planet Earth in the Third Density. Why? Well, as I outlined to my light-bodied friend: I'd reached a pivotal point where I'd worked out some incredible stuff about life, living, loving, healing, and dying. And rather than accept a bus pass to "the next life" taking this rather useful information with me, my purpose suddenly became crystal clear. Having spent over 40 years more or less serving myself, I would spend whatever remaining days I have left producing, directing, and starring in the Martin Story in service to others.

For over 25 years, I've worked in the communications industry, learning to hone messages and distil and articulate complex concepts and ideas. Whilst I've no particular desire to do that for the remainder of my time, I cannot escape the fact that all of my life lessons and career meanderings have led me to this time and place. Hence everything is perfect. Now, I can write and create other things that might (just might) shine a light on alternative perspectives about life, happiness, attachment, and death. *About living and dying well.*

Naturally, some will say this was nothing but a hallucination; others might theorise it was nought but a cerebrally created complex metaphor representing the death of my ego, chaperoned by a higher (worldly) state of consciousness. All are plausible, of course. All I can do is tell you what I know — as fantastical as it may sound. Regardless, using this direction, combined with a newfound understanding of our intrinsic connection, and putting that learning into action, I now have the bones of a purpose plan.

But what about yours?

I started this chapter by assuming you're likely unsure about your purpose, which is poppycock, of course. There's a grand chance you're all over purpose like white on rice, already dancing in the garden of your own creation. *Bravo (e brava)* if that's the case! I'm chuffed for you. However, for those among us who could use a little assistance, I'd like to introduce the ancient Japanese concept of Ikigai.

The Tranquillifier

Come into a comfortable seat, spine straight.
Relax your jaw.
Relax your neck and shoulders.
Soften your belly.

Place the tip of your tongue behind your upper front teeth.
Keep it there.

Inhale through your nose for one, two, three, four.
Hold your breath for seven, six, five, four, three, two, one.
Slowly exhale through your mouth for
eight, seven, six, five, four, three, two, one.

Repeat.

CHAPTER THIRTY

Find Your Ikigai

Essentials to happiness in this
life are something to do, something to love, and something to
hope for.

— Hector Garcia

Dating back to the Heian period, between 794 to 1185 CE, *Ikigai* plays a significant role in Japanese culture. Interestingly, being a hot-spot cultural ambassador for Ikigai, the island of Okinawa has the highest proportion of people over 100 years old than anywhere else in the world. Coincidence?

Ikigai is defined as one's reason for being, essentially ascertaining the sweet spot between one's personal passions, values, vocation, and beliefs. When one embodies Ikigai, one creates a life-work balance of satisfaction, joy, and a sense of meaning (being). "Iki" in Japanese means "life", "living", and "being alive", while "gai" describes value, worth, and benefit. Finding your Ikigai is to find whatever brings you joy and inspiration; it's your reason for getting out of bed in the morning. You'll also often hear the word "bliss" used in its description. Another wonderful thing about Ikigai is that it's not all about milestones and goals. In fact, the practice of Ikigai encourages one to appreciate and find joy in small day-to-day activities. Thus, it's a beautiful exercise in mindfulness, presence, and gratitude. Three of my favourite words.

So how does it work? Well, it's often said that a picture tells a thousand words, and this occasion most certainly calls for a diagram.

The Japanese Ikigai Model.

With Ikigai, convergence is the key. That is to say, the model invites us to consider four main areas and then focus on their converging points. The four fundamental questions of Ikigai are as follows:

1.   What do you love?
2.   What are you good at?
3.   What does the world need?
4.   For what can you be paid?

Clearly, the latter question is less relevant if you seek to define practices and interests that merely give you joy and you are, therefore, content to keep your day job. Nevertheless, the question is pertinent. As you can see, four relatively simple questions have an undercurrent of order, a symbiotic sense. For example, I can love a thing, but am I good at it? If the answer's yes, move on to the next: does the world need it? And if so, where do I sit among all the other folks doing it? Is my proposition still unique enough to stand alone? Finally, can I make any money doing it? That is, do people want it? Is there sufficient demand? Is the idea sustainable? Observing the nuances of convergence is super crucial here. Hence, applying all the aforementioned in the previous chapter about purpose to passion, mission, profession, and vocation helps you define and distil your Ikigai.

So if you are sensing a niggling feeling about why you're here, or detect a growing dissatisfaction with your place in the world, then taking time to profoundly consider your life's direction is unequivocally worthwhile. Assuming no surprises, we have a few years to kick around on planet Earth. Be sure you spend them doing things you love.

CHAPTER THIRTY-ONE

Woulda, Coulda, Shoulda

The past is a great place
and I don't want to erase it or to
regret it, but I don't want to be its
prisoner either.
— Mick Jagger

If you had a time machine, would you go back to change things? Perhaps you'd like to save a life, turn left instead of right, avoid an accident or talk your younger self out of making a "bad" decision? My mind was once plagued with such ideas. Though, despite what might appear a tragic list of events that devoured great lumps of precious time, I now see all of it was well spent. What should I have done instead of the things I did? Well, there were obviously options. That's the fantastic thing about choice; no matter the direction of our path, we always have the opportunity to leave it for countless other trails. Once upon a time, I knew nothing of self-love, empathy, forgiveness, or acceptance. I walked the course the only way I knew then and learned only when ready.

When we mentally replay past events, we wonder what life might be like had we made alternative choices. Different actions would change our timeline, of course. At a crucial juncture of my journey of acceptance, I realised that I would not be who I am now — grateful for the gift of trauma — without trauma's existence. After all, how can one appreciate the beauty of light having never been immersed in darkness? Hence, while grateful for the lessons,

I am equally thankful to their providers. Is it possible to live free from damage and despair? Would an alternative, unblemished version of me be living and cherishing the life of peace I live now? I think not. Likewise, if you hadn't lived through your many painful experiences, how would you know what bliss feels like whenever it comes around? Therefore, there is bliss in accepting that nothing lasts forever and that all beginnings need endings. Acceptance brings profound peace, after all.

Woulda, coulda, and *shoulda* are all normal responses to adverse events, but serve no purpose but to torture oneself, creating inner conflict with little possibility of a positive outcome. Hence, they must be unlearned. Perhaps a more practical alternative would be to ask: "How can I heal in the present from the traumatic events in my past?" If you're asking this question, you're on a profitable path indeed. And to do so, you must discover and master *nowness*, otherwise known as the art of presence. More of which, we'll discuss later.

They say, "time heals". A platitude offered by many an optimist and often delivered at the worst time imaginable. However, I'm alluding to something entirely different. Imagine if, in the present, we could create a suitable environment, in a quiet space in which to centre. In such a session, we could meditate on the traumatic events of our past. Not running through them all like an audiobook of pain on 2x speed but taking one event at a time, pointing all of our attention, energy, and love to it.

You allow the traumatic memory to arise, bringing whatever feelings come along for the ride. No matter how searingly painful or shameful the memories are, you resist pushing the feelings back down; you avoid erasing or replacing them too. You sit with them. You sit fully immersed in that pain if needs be — free from judgement or being attached to any outcome. Just sit with it and focus on your breathing. Then, knowing what you know now of the transformative power of impermanence, speak to the version of you from then. Offer them love, understanding, and compassion. Without being distracted, what you're looking for through this process, is a change in your emotions. It could be extreme or subtle initially, but you will notice it either way. Remember e-motion; energy in motion.

Change might not come during the first or even the tenth session. But it will come, as change always does. It's a Universal law, remember? Its arrival is the beginning of your transmutation of the painful memory. It's you taking control of that memory, perhaps for the first time in your life. The intention is not to beat the memory but to lovingly observe it and the subsequent change. We can do this work ourselves, but sometimes we need help from others. That's okay. It's a perfectly healthy submission and might even save your life.

Check this for a wild idea: when we mindfully revisit our memories (as the observer), we can alter our experience of past events, editing our emotional timeline. In a sense, we are time-travelling since we can shift energy that's been blocked inside us since that traumatic event. And when doing so in the right conditions, you heal yourself in the present.

Hypnotherapists worldwide heal people's trauma using varying flavours of regression therapy. In Bali, one such respected professional named Kartika helped me purge a bundle of deep-rooted pain. We addressed emotions I assumed had been processed after my mum's death. However, as our session revealed, there was more to do. To my complete surprise, we revisited my childhood and healed profound wounds belonging to five-year-old me.

My mum's mental illness made it difficult for her to offer the parental intimacy so desperately needed by Martin, the child. We never talked adequately about this, and then she was dead. During Kartika's session, however, I was given the rare gift of communicating love and forgiveness to Mum. Previously emotionally unavailable to me, she stood before us — five- and 45-year-old Martin. The child could finally explain how her self-harm was wounding him. Then, in a further shocking transpersonal therapy twist, I "hopped" into my mum, thus experiencing the pain and suffering she bore, instantly gaining a more profound empathy. Mere words cannot come close to expressing the transformative effect this session produced. I sobbed. And with each heaving groan, I felt my heart opening and my spirit lightening — lighter and lighter again. Healing Martin, aged five, impossibly healed the broken heart of Martin, aged 45. An ancient rift was thus mended between him and his mother, enabling him to say unsaid things while seeing her perspective as a poor, lost soul trying her best despite deep depression. It was the very definition of catharsis.

Developed and refined by Dolores Cannon, *Quantum Healing Hypnosis Therapy (QHHT)* takes us into what's known as the somnambulistic state of trance through visualisation. The treatment involves taking participants to "the most appropriate time and place" to address their healing. In my case, this was the upstairs landing of the haunted farmhouse where I lived as a small child. I would skulk here, outside my mum's bedroom, whenever I heard her sobbing or arguing with one of her countless demonic torturers. This therapy enables us to use consciousness to simulate long-term mental and physical well-being. As with so many metaphysical practices, it's been dismissed as pseudoscience. If you're a scientist who can disprove consciousness's healing power, then fair enough, I respect your truth, but it's not a debate I care to have. I experienced profound and seemingly impossible healing in this way, which is the only thing that counts. Interestingly, I've since been able to do the same thing alone, using plant medicine. Though I would only recommend such practice to seasoned psychonauts.

Traditionally, our healing is outsourced, but we should learn more about our minds' inherent ability to heal ourselves. Parapsychology, psychoneuroimmunology, and neuroscience are fascinating territories of which I knew nothing. I still know nothing! The world of the subconscious unconscious is a complex and intriguing space. Though, if we have no interest in understanding it, what does that say about our sovereignty and self-care? These fields and this work can enhance the unlearning process and are thus well worth further investigation.

You can't undo the physics of what has gone before. You can, however, methodically let go of your attachment to it. Without judgement, gently offer it love and send it on its way. The Hindu sage Ramana Maharshi once said: "There is neither past nor future. There is only the present". I've referred to this concept before, and I'll do so again before this book's end because presence is one of the four core pillars of a harmonious and happy life. It's a superpower with the alchemic properties to change everything you know and feel. Shunryu Suzuki once said: "When you sit, everything sits with you". Hence, presence dwells at the very centre of peace.

So, using a form of time travel, or quantum healing, you can forgive yourself and others for things you did or were done to you. Every time you go back to the memory (do this often, applying mindfulness), your experience will change. Eventually, you'll notice a whopping shift as the memory ceases to serve you. Perhaps more crucially, you'll see that it no longer defines you. You can let it go; unlearn. One by one, clear out your negative memories using this process. No further need for *woulda, coulda,* or even *shoulda*. Fully embrace presence. With such a utility, what new reality will you create for yourself today? You don't need a time machine when you've reached this point. The only time worth your time is now.

CHAPTER THIRTY-TWO

A Sidenote About Sovereignty

Sovereignty is not given;
it is taken.
— Mustafa Kemal Atatürk

We must talk about the power of choice because we often believe we have none. That's not necessarily the case. More likely, we're influenced by family, society, our social groups, or the voice in our heads. The missing link between thinking and doing is acting, but to act with conviction, we must recognise and cultivate our sovereignty. Given its vital significance to happiness, we must circle back and briefly explore the gateway to stepping into your power as a reminder that you can always choose to change no matter your age, location, or status.

Dating back to the 14th century, the Anglo-French word "sovereignty" can be defined initially as "authority, rule, the supremacy of power or rank". Thus, many folks interpret sovereignty as something exclusive to an entity with the power of a country. Or perhaps one possessing the power or authority to rule. However, a crucial component of everlasting happiness lies in assuming and embracing our fundamental right to freedom from control or oppression. Free will and its exercise. As such, my use of the word sovereignty relates to your authority and rule over yourself. Your supremacy and power as a creator being currently romping around Earth School in your exquisitely designed, perfectly imperfect Earth Rover. Some would say you are an individuated expression of The One — *All That Is*. You need not agree as long as you concede that you are a sentient expression of something. Even if you believe you are merely an expression of yourself, you are sovereign.

We hand over our sovereignty on a silver platter to ego and others who cannot help but take. Incrementally, we gift tiny slithers of ourselves away to those riding roughshod over our boundaries. As a sovereign being, I assume full responsibility for and ownership of all my thoughts, words, and deeds. For that which I consume, the places I go, the people with whom I interact, and the choices and promises I make. Ergo, you are no one's "subject", victim, instrument, subordinate, or plaything. Nor are you a slave or a child to be spoon-fed or patronised by "highers and betters". And while ego, politics, religion, identity politics, and the ongoing misdistribution of the world's wealth do wonders to keep us apart, we are all equal. *We're all connected.*

Herein lies the conundrum: there's a monumental change occurring in the world, affecting us all and shattering the status quo. The systems guiding how we live are ancient and archaic. What worked for past generations will not work in the future, nor do they now. We, the people, are evolving individually and collectively as we slowly advance to the next level of human evolution. Can you feel it? Can you sense the creaking, jarring growing pains as the draconian system struggles to maintain its white-knuckle grip? The clashes between our collective's demand for sovereignty and the system's inherent desire for control are becoming more frequent and violent. On an individual basis, the same is in flux. As we open our minds to our true potential, unlearning and evolving, we're breaking generational cycles and taking conscious control of our way of life. Many of us already feel this happening, yet we are unsure what to do. Now, more than ever, we must step into our sovereignty to ensure we are not disturbed by whatever rattles the window panes. Whichever illusion seeks to distract or distress should be seen as such.

You must never allow people, thoughts, or events to own you because you are sovereign and the creator of your reality. This crucial point speaks to awareness, self-realisation, ownership, responsibility, and the fundamentals of mindfulness. It's an invitation to develop practices that ensure that you remain on your lilypad, unfettered and at peace, whatever ripples there are across the pond.

Sovereignty isn't just an individual journey; we must walk the path together. Hence we must also seek collective cultivation of awareness, acceptance, and harmony.

Our species has a fantastic future ahead. However, we're at a significant juncture in our collective consciousness journey. What happens in the next few years will determine whether we evolve or spiral into chaos. We are more cognisant and technologically advanced, with access to an infinite abundance of wisdom. However, we must mature collectively and cease squabbling and fighting over illusory nonsense. We must embrace self-inquiry to address unhealed trauma. We must no longer allow internal or external forces to manipulate or control. We must adopt personal practices that bulletproof us from bullshit, *including our own*, empowering us to master our emotions, so that separation may no longer determine our direction.

While I invite you to consider how our connection to any entity or system affects your happiness, this is a reminder that you are sovereign. No one has the right to control you. While perhaps an extreme metaphor, how content would you be to consciously allow a vampire to drink your blood? Likely not at all. Vampires come in many shapes and sizes. Read that again.

The Chinese *Yin* represents femininity, passivity, and the darkness of the moon. *Yang* is masculine, light, and active. The game of sovereignty is to become masters of our fate. To achieve this, we must learn the balance between Yin and Yang. We must find peace even when all around us is chaos. This is an expression of self-love. It's sovereignty in action.

Buddhist Prayer of Forgiveness

If I have harmed anyone in any way, either knowingly
or unknowingly through my own confusions,
I ask their forgiveness.

If anyone has harmed me in any way, either knowingly or
unknowingly through their own confusions, I forgive them.

And if there is a situation I am not yet ready to forgive,
I forgive myself for that.

For all the ways that I harm myself, negate, doubt,
belittle myself, judge, or be unkind to myself
through my own confusion, I forgive myself.

CHAPTER THIRTY-THREE

Forgiving the Unforgivable

An eye for an eye makes
the whole world blind.
— Mahatma Gandhi

Revenge, spite, anger, and fear. With a vice-like grip, these emotions drag us kicking and screaming up Memory Lane whenever the mind feels. We hold on to past traumas where we played victim to another's thoughtless or deliberate actions. Some of us can forgive, while others are unwilling or incapable. Angry and hopeless, we say, "I can never forgive this", or we'll "never heal from that". We want to hold on to our trauma, demanding to know: "Why should I forgive them anyway?!" Fuelled by such feelings, I once thought the same way. My suffering was part of my story, and I wore it like a badge begging people to see and hear me. Learning to forgive was a significant stepping stone on my journey towards self-love. Much forgiveness was up for grabs, and I held grudges like hot coals. High on my list was the incident of my blinding.

Shortly after meeting James for the first time in the summer of 2015, he struck me in the face. The unexpected sucker punch landed like a sledgehammer, immediately shutting down my left eye and fracturing my orbital socket. The damage transpired to be somewhat severe, as the impact had crushed the front of my eyeball, misshaping the iris and dislocating the lens, which no longer sat snugly inside what ought to have been a perfectly circular pupillary sphincter.

About a year after the assault, my lens was usurped from its comfortable seat of 42 years. It moved into the less familiar neighbourhood of the middle of my eyeball. I had a cataract and was in the unenviable position of needing two surgeries: the first to fish out the lens and the second to implant an artificial one over the iris (just under the cornea). Sadly, a few months after the second operation, the lens became dislodged and began chaffing against my iris, causing acute discomfort for rather more than the blink of an eye.

James was angry. I had begun seeing his ex-girlfriend, with our affair overlapping their relationship's end. Our coupling had not gone down all that well with him despite their breakup having nothing to do with me. He'd sought me out at my local bar to exact revenge and presumably alleviate the pain of his recent loss. And that he did. "You reap what you sow, Martin", he said. James was arrested and charged with my grievous assault and eventually found guilty, though he never saw the inside of a cell. I later learned he was grieving following a family tragedy, although heartbreak is no defence for harming another. All that said, I have a lot of love for him. Though it took me some time and practice to feel this way.

I'll Never Forgive Them

We cannot achieve everlasting happiness without fully embracing forgiveness. Hence, this miraculous mental health gift is the next stage in the Anatomy of Happy. It's common to declare the memory of past painful events as inescapable. While an entirely valid truth, such declarations are a highly effective form of self-programming. Some folks are intent on unhappiness and content drowning in despair. Unhappy and traumatic memories can provide sharable stories that make us more interesting. We love our suffering even though we know it burns. It may remind us of our capacity to feel pain, or subconsciously, we like that it adds flavour to our story. Do they deserve our forgiveness for what they did? That's a fair question, but without forgiveness, there can be no healing. When using the word "forgiveness", we often forget its true definition.

Forgive: to stop feeling angry with someone who has done something to harm, annoy, or upset you; to stop feeling angry with yourself; forgive somebody/yourself (for something/for doing something).

Contemplate this definition for a moment. Trauma is not the event, but our feelings of the event. Ergo, *forgiveness is not about them.*

As previously discussed, Eckhart Tolle speaks at length about how our ego creates stories to convince us that we cannot be at peace. He muses that hanging on to emotion strengthens our identity. So, consciously or subconsciously, we suffer as our emotional pain develops as an intrinsic part of us. It's a part of our story, as are the feelings to which to cling.

So what of judgement? I reached a point where toxic thoughts about my assault contributed as much to my poor mental health as my physical injuries. I judged this man for his actions, despite sharing culpability and having committed heinous violence against others in my past. Jeshua once said: "He that is without sin among you; let him first cast a stone". Remember that old adage about rocks and glass houses? There's solid gold wisdom right here — far beyond what you might initially comprehend. Think about this. Do people deserve our forgiveness as we deserve theirs? How can we judge another when we've done our fair share of damage on the rocky road to learning to love? And do we always treat others how we hope to be treated? When we forgive, who does it serve? Considering these questions helps us learn to let go.

We all have a fair claim to suffering, don't we? Everyone's played victim to someone or other. Subsequently, we can cultivate our own illness by mentally projecting the past that's passed or a future that hasn't yet happened. It's exhausting. Yet, likely, our perpetrators couldn't care less whether we've forgiven them or not. The more heinous the trauma, the less interested the persecutor may be. I do not write these words to shame those who refuse to forgive or seek forgiveness. Merely to say that choosing not to forgive is to opt for self-harm. Hence, letting go of suffering changed my life forever, and I've no doubt you can experience the same.

I Forgive You

Revenge and resentment are commonplace, and I was angry for a long time. I often fantasised about blinding or maiming my assailant. My sick mind was a bile-filled washing machine, while my story served to gain attention and pity from my audience. Paradoxically, sympathy would somehow alleviate and fuel my suffering story. Eventually, the time came to release this negativity stored in my body and mind. I had to process the trauma. So in a Psilocybin-assisted deep meditative journey, I sought out and forgave James with all my heart and soul. Whether he got the message is broadly irrelevant; the crucial component was my fully and profoundly letting go, sending unconditional love and light to the man who blinded me. And in doing so, I healed.

After that, I should take whatever lessons were evident and discard the rest. I suddenly understood that clinging is how we choose to feel about an event. It has nothing to do with the other person. To forgive is to stop feeling angry and upset; stop feeling annoyed. *Let go.* Not to fall directionless into some abyss and not because it's a cliché, because it isn't. When we let go of white-hot coals, we cease self-harm, and our healing can begin. We are free.

Happiness cannot come without forgiveness. Hence, learning

to make peace with the past using the power of the present will change how you feel in future. A crucial component of the anatomy of happiness, forgiveness equips us with utilities we'll need later down the road.

In asking, "How can I forgive?" you should see that the past cannot hurt you. It's only our conscious and unconscious thoughts that torture us so. And whether we know it or not, such memorial storage is self-harm. How to tackle that dark passenger? Become aware of the whirring thought machine and your feelings. Become aware that thoughts belong to your ego *(Monkey)* and that you are not your mind. Become aware that you are aware. Take the helm, steady the waters, and plot a new course using pure awareness.

Forgiveness requires the tradecraft of acceptance. It's hard work that no one will force you to do — offering many milestones along the hero's journey. Learning to forgive makes us the heroes of our own stories. It allowed me to rewrite mine, making me happier and healthier. And the pain in my eye? It dissipated right around the same time.

CHAPTER THIRTY-FOUR

Learning to Love

Silence is the sleep
that nourishes wisdom.
 — Francis Bacon

We're a funny bunch comprising countless personalities, beliefs, and truths. While often frustrating, should we choose to see our intrinsic connection, this undeniable fact also offers a profoundly rich learning landscape. Thus, we can learn a great deal about ourselves from one another. On the other hand, we can learn about ourselves from ourselves. And so, we move into the next Anatomy of Happy territory of self-love.

Many in our eclectic human tapestry view introspection as a waste of time and effort. For them, such nonsense is unnecessary; they can't change, don't want to change; they are who they are, and that's all there is to it. I respect that truth. However, it's safe to assume that as you're reading this book, you are open to introspection and the power of self-love. Going inward is the most challenging yet rewarding story writing we can do on this plane. So if you are in the process or have already done this work, you have my respect and admiration. Regardless of how well it's going, the fact that you are willing to face your shadow deserves all due deference and praise. I salute the adventurer in you. Never forget to express gratitude to yourself for this work. It is brave, vulnerable, and highly progressive; whatever happens, growth will come from it.

Introspection, self-reflection, self-examination, Shadow Work — whatever you wish to call it — embodies many methodologies. The short story I'm about to tell curiously combines meditation, guided meditation, and what is commonly known as the attendance of a silent retreat. The latter drew a beautiful line under months of ugly yet wholly rewarding work.

Around six months after moving to Bali, I embarked on a crucial phase of my healing journey: to deepen my meditation practice. So one morning, I packed a modest bag, mounted my motorbike, and charged into Bali's green countryside. I eventually arrived at a plot of land surrounded entirely by a steep-sided valley. The natural, moat-like bamboo perimeter was so thick and high that the stream at the ravine's base barely saw the light. The bike descended the valley side, over a bridge, then uphill again. Quitting the darkness, I rode into the bright green and serene camp of *Forest Island*, a modest, land-locked plot surrounded by a bamboo-lined ravine. It was time to embark on a prolonged period with no tech, speech, reading, or writing. This would be serious work for my mind, spirit, and body. And every minute and hour would be spent in silence for seven days.

The master's name is Pak Merta Ada, and his training is the *Tapa Brata*. It's an intensive retreat where one cannot fail but go inwards. We train the mind and body through meditation to achieve peace and happiness. By definition, the process involves a deep journey into Self, spiritualism, and healing past traumas — no matter how small — buried and stored inside the subconscious, unconscious. The retreat typically includes fasting and meditation and can be aimed at various personal intentions. The objective is to redefine one's concentration, consciousness, calmness, gentleness, and compassion. While this accurate description is an indication, it cannot fully articulate the life-changing nature of such an experience.

I did no research before my trip. During this phase, I deliberately leapt into every new healing experience, setting fear aside and following my heart. Expectation-free, I would embrace these new modalities with an open mind. And so, during our introduction, I could do nought but give a (silent) chuckle to myself as I learnt that every day would begin at 04:30 sharp, courtesy of a gong.

Our first evening was hosted by a kind and gentle woman named Eva — a learned and gracious healer of many years. On occasions he was absent, Pak Merta's younger video version of this jolliest man would assist Eva in introducing the nitty-gritty of our programme. This would include talks, ancient Far-Eastern chi exercises, and a significant amount of meditation. Eva expertly guided us throughout the process. I watched my 32 fellow students — united in this most magical of ways. These people from the far corners of the planet were of all ages, creeds, and religions. Surreptitiously, we observed each other that first evening — listening, meditating, assimilating, and eventually drinking hot ginger tea. Who were we? Where were we from? What drew us to this time and place?

As the first evening closed and we stumbled wearily to our beds, we slumped and slept in short order. I quickly learned that the early morning alarm clock would be a walk in the park compared to my roommate Ken's snoring. It's an odd thing to spend a week in the middle of the jungle, sharing a bedroom with two strangers with whom you've never spoken, nor will you for several days, despite your close proximity. As I drifted off with surprising peace and stillness, I realised I was judging based solely on actions and body language. Our Monkey mind loves to fill in the blanks. And when nobody's talking, Monkey's chatter can be incessant, to say the least.

My teacher is a most beloved and blessed man — an internationally respected and renowned Balinese healer whose practices have been examined and applauded by countless physicians worldwide. He lectures on a rare blend of science, spirituality, and what Westerners might call "mysticism". For me, Pak Merta Ada is a cross between Yoda, Gandhi, and a lovely man you got chatting with in a cafe or park. You would gladly imbibe his wisdom for hours, blissfully unaware you'd missed lunch or your train. As I consider his gift to me, my heart still sings with love and gratitude for him. Whenever I stop to mindfully breathe, I can hear his thick northern Balinese accent, speaking in detail about the human body, cheerfully declaring, "May all beings be happy!"

As a young man, Pak Merta was naturally drawn to healing. One could even say that at every corner he turned, the Universe planted a string of clear and present signposts for him — inevitably directing his life purpose as a healer. His early years were spent in the garment trade, in which he was highly successful. Regardless of having around 2,000 employees, to this day, he splits his time between running his business interests and as head of the Bali Usada Institute and Bali Usada Foundation. In addition to the work he does teaching his students during the week-long and daily retreats in Bali and Java, he also holds weekly healing sessions for people in various centres in Bali and beyond — helping those who cannot help themselves. When he's not doing live-streaming events and managing regular radio broadcasts, he works with countless WhatsApp groups, continuing to mentor students from the 800+ silent retreats he's overseen in the past 29 years. Pak Merta Ada has taught meditation face-to-face to more than 127,000 people. I'm conscious of writing about the man this way, as he is humble and unassuming. He would rather share cheeky jokes or access his ludicrously vast memory bank of inter-faith stories and parables than speak of himself grandiosely. With this in mind, I'll avoid any seemingly sycophantic description and simply say this: Pak Merta Ada and his incredible devotees have changed the lives of millions, no doubt with millions more to come.

There will be readers meditating as part of a daily ritual and others who know the Tapa Brata. You may also know of the *Vipassana* — the oldest of silent Buddhist practices singularly pointed at meditation. As a regular meditator, already practising one to two hours daily, the Tapa Brata was still challenging for my mind and body. That being said, it's also one of the most rewarding things I have done in this less-than-dull visit to Earth School.

An essential part of Pak Merta Ada's teachings relates to our understanding and ability to observe Anicca, the meaning of which we've already discussed. We were invited to consider the impermanence of everything and that everything changes faster or slower and sooner or later. Cheerfully and often, Pak Merta would blurt the words, "Anicca. Anicca. Aniiiiicca!"

I'd just had a real lesson in Anicca when Macy went missing three months before. Still, the technique we learned during the retreat — understanding how to sit with that pain, free from attachment, and let it go with loving-kindness — was a real game-changer for how I now react to the events in my life.

Focused meditation can be challenging. Sitting in multiple daily sessions for up to 45 minutes takes perseverance and attention. My knees complained about being cross-legged, and my back of no support. I angered myself and lost concentration. Though, the deep meditation presented random faces, long-lost songs, and forgotten events. Mundane and human thoughts endangered my mission, yet something magical was happening that I dared not miss.

As any meditation practitioner will know, these early pains are far from harmonious, though they are a necessary part of an enriching journey inward. Training the mind is like teaching any other body part. It is hard work and requires regular practice, but it does get easier. Primarily because you ultimately realise that meditating requires no work. In fact, the whole point of meditation is to learn how to do nothing at all.

We worked hard every day on the exercises. We learned how to discover what Pak Merta calls the "Harmonious Mind". The key lies in developing a feeling of love, gentleness, and kindness. First, it's felt inside our body, then radiated from our hearts. Every one of Pak Merta's meditations begins with the internal declaration, "May all beings be happy", which we offer to every living being on the planet and beyond. As I later discovered, the words derive from the Sanskrit prayer, "Lokah samastah sukhino bhavantu". The selfless purity of this mantra resonated with me deeply and immediately. The meditation is pure and beautiful chakra activation; it's the stuff of magic and transferrable and sharable. This practice cultivates love.

The first few days were tough. A trapped shoulder nerve distracted me constantly from successfully clearing my mind. Halfway through the second full day, I got close to throwing in the towel. Eva's invitation to "trust in the process" helped me press on.

On the afternoon of the penultimate day, our "noble silence" was broken. We were allowed to speak to each other for the first time. This was such a beautiful moment. We had all learned and meditated in silence, passing each other on the grounds, eating side by side at every meal. And now we could speak. The group embraced this moment wildly and enthusiastically. And as we dined together for the first time without silence, I remember thinking I'd not heard so many people laugh together like that for such a long time.

I lived in an unreasonably haunted house aged five and six. Aged ten, I summoned the ghost of a nun. My first profound spiritual experience, however, was aged 24. The interaction occurred during a deep, guided meditation with a wonderfully kind soul named Amanda. The session would be a journey inwards. Once in this place, she invited me to seek my "Higher Self". While the process was entirely alien, I remained open-minded, transmitting a thought, suggesting I should like to meet this entity. A classical crazy white-haired character appeared. He floated in an armchair capable of reaching incredible speeds. It could move in any direction while evidently bypassing the laws of physics. The entity, as it transpired, was my Higher Self.

At that time, I had no idea what a Higher Self was, and by that rationale, I was somewhat surprised by this ethereal turn of events. Amanda suggested I ask him something, so I mentally blurted: "Why am I here?" He said: "You are here to learn to love". As remedial as this instruction might sound to some, I thought it profound. Notwithstanding the fact I'd never before meditated, the entire interaction was surreal. And while I was technically talking to myself, I *wasn't* talking to myself. Had I known then that I was having a lucid and unfettered conversation with my consciousness, perhaps my life would've been very different. But then, I would not have learnt the perfectly painful lessons that led me to this here and now.

Of course, as previously alluded, as an emotionally impaired young man, broken in so many ways, I developed anger and various modes of detachment. So, despite this profound spiritual experience in my twenties, Monkey and I quickly diverted our attention back to drinking, drugs, womanising and work. And womanising at work — just to add a little spice and drama. As the years and people came and left, I created a large and complex psychological structure with battlements, shark-filled moats, with lasers, and CCTV for good measure. Such psychological devices ensured nothing would get in or out. Self-love was an impossibility.

On the retreat's final day, those willing could share stories with the rest of the group. So I told them what had brought me to that place, of my near-suicide, and my journey towards self-awareness. I spoke of my transformational experiences and my healing process. Mainly I wished to talk about something that had happened to me the previous day.

Day six had been dedicated to developing our ability to channel loving-kindness towards each other, to friends, family, and complete strangers. During a later guided session, Pak Merta had invited us to turn the loving-kindness on ourselves, mentally chanting the words "May *I* be happy". The moment I did so, my heart filled with a warm energy I'd never felt before. The feeling burst and rippled throughout my body, taking me entirely by surprise. After this rush of radiance, I began to sob uncontrollably. At first, I was confused. Was I unhappy? But as the sobs shook me, I felt my chest well with love, forgiveness, and gratitude. The tears streamed down my face, and I knew right then that this beautiful journey I was on had come to a critical point. Once wholly broken and staring down the barrels of a loaded gun: here I was, in my mid-40s, single, reinventing, *and alive*. Despite the trail of destruction and unconscious behaviour in my wake, I finally learned to love. *To love me* in the best way possible.

I sat quietly with this exquisite feeling. The tears continued as I rode grateful and happy waves. I was struck with the acceptance that for years I'd mistreated myself. And as I consciously breathed through this changing process, any fleeting feelings of regret and sadness were replaced with unilateral forgiveness. Then suddenly came a profound sense of serenity. Shortly after that, Pak Merta again invited us to extend our loving-kindness to family, friends, and even enemies. To people who may dislike us. Or folks we hardly know or never met. Perhaps you felt it. I sent it loud and fast your way. I'll send it every day I'm alive.

Pak Merta must've said, "May all beings be happy!" a thousand times during that week. Every time he dispatched this Universal invitation of loving-kindness, I would smile, my heart brimming with love.

As the retreat closed, I said farewell to my new teacher, his colleagues, and my new friends. I jump-started my sleepy bike down the driveway. Over the bridge and through the bamboo canopy, I gained enough momentum to wake up the engine. I shot from the dark into the light, back into the "real" world. School was out, and the kids were everywhere, in their clean ceremonial whites. As I adapted to Bali traffic's organised chaos, 50 shades of green, countless small warungs (shops and canteens), and smiling dark faces whizzed past. I rode up behind a three-vehicle convoy of vans. Stuffed so full of kids, feet trailed from half-open rear doors. Our eyes met, and beaming white smiles filled the back of the vehicle, their "Hallo!" heartily greeting this foreigner on a bike. I let out a loud and happy laugh as I responded in kind — gleefully offering a thumbs-up to them all. Overtaking, I chanted the mantra, "May all beings be happy, may all beings be happy, may *all* beings be happy!" while my face and heart smiled as one.

The healing secrets of Bali and its people continue to surprise and delight. When I think I could fall no further in love, I fall deeper into her arms. She's cradled my damaged body and soothed my busted mind. She gave freely and willingly all which I needed to heal. And then, on a land-locked island, surrounded by a bamboo forest, she repaired my broken heart, so I might share it with the world. I'll never forget my first Tapa Brata and the wonderful souls I met there. They're a part of my healing journey, the moment when I learned to love.

Pure Love

Rambling from one drama to the next, as we often do, we can spend our whole lives focused on anything but our true Self. As Rumi once said: "Maybe you are searching among the branches for what only appears in the roots". We might give love with frequency and volume or fill our days with unhealthy distractions. But what of our intrinsic needs? What of connection, purpose, a full heart, and a healthy mind and body?

When offering ourselves the mantra, "May I be happy", what shall we do to manifest this exquisite aspiration? How much time do we dedicate to self-care? How much attention and energy do we invest in personal growth? If the stark truth is that we don't exercise healthy self-love, then how can we expect anyone else to understand or love us? In learning to love in a world of separation, even in ourselves, we can achieve the goal of all goals, of remembering our true nature. Therefore, our relationship with love must begin within. The prize at the end of this inward journey is the revelation that you are enough. That, in fact, you are the Universe and pure love, with boundless opportunities ahead.

CHAPTER THIRTY-FIVE

Zen and the Art of Earth Rover Maintenance

**Enjoy your body;
use it every way you can.
Don't be afraid of it or what other
people think of it. It's the greatest
instrument you'll ever own.**
                                        — Baz Lurhmann

Zen: neither religion nor philosophy, Zen is a form of Buddhism that concentrates on embracing what it is to be human while living in the present moment. Zen is peace.

Earth Rover: the super-intelligent biotechnology suit our consciousness wears while manifesting upon and romping around Earth School.

Maintenance: the proactive process of preserving someone or something or the state of being maintained.

You know that expression, "Your body is a temple"? Well, it took me four and a half decades to see one of life's greatest truisms in these words. Shying from sports, I enjoyed the typically less-than-healthy diet of an 80s kid. I had flirtatious relationships with the gym and long-distance running in my 20s and 30s. Still, I heavily drank, used cocaine, and picked up a sexually transmitted infection or two. With regular check-ups, my prolifically profane lifestyle involved many sexual partners. Alcoholism and cocaine addiction have you missing one, maybe two or three nights' sleep in a row, perhaps chain-smoking 60 cigarettes during such carnivals. We don't sleep well, if at all, drunk or high. Booze suppresses rapid eye movement, and REM sleep is when we process memories and emotional experiences; it's when we dream. It's also the point at which healthy brain development and repair happens. Evidently, one doesn't sleep at all thanks to cocaine — hence we cannot even rest our bodies. That poor heart pounds at 135 bpm, rocketing towards cancer or other sleep-deprivation-linked illnesses.

Being drunk invites countless bumps and scrapes, unhealthy eating, or no food at all. By "bumps and scrapes", I mean fights, falls, and all manner of bizarre injuries only curatable by shit-faced someones. Temporarily, they feel little to no pain alongside immortality. *They know not what they do.* In those days, I thought I was invincible. More to the point, my investment in self-harm outweighed any distant aspiration to live a long life. My poor old body was desecrated for years. Propped up by a complex of rickety, rusty scaffolding, the Earth Rover required rambunctious renovation.

During my first Ayahuasca ceremony, "The Grandmother" told me, under no uncertain terms, that unless I began to love myself and change my life's direction, the short time I had left was destined for misery. Doctors, media, friends, intuition, and outright commonsense had offered the same warning for years. However, when a goddess outside of time-space tells you during the most profoundly life-changing experience you've ever had... Let's say I got the message.

Perhaps under the circumstances, one didn't need an inter-dimensional entity's surmise that my body required desperate repair. While I'd been alcohol-free for almost 12 months and worked out regularly, my body still bore countless signs of ill-treatment. I had not long had surgery on my left eye, whereby they'd fished out and replaced the collapsed lens following James' well-placed sucker punch. Besides leaving me blind, the injury bore much long-lasting physical and mental trauma that decorated me in ways that took years to fully understand. The stitches had come out of my cornea five days earlier: I could at least see again with the help of ocular prosthetics. My right knee was still in severe pain due to a torn meniscus from a drunken injury a year earlier. My right shoulder had chronic discomfort having snapped the Coracoacromial ligament while snowboarding drunk in an English park. The inventory went on. Sadly, not one of the injuries listed was contracted purely by accident. All were linked to my excessive consumption of alcohol and cocaine — cohorts with determined self-harm. And as I would later discover at a Balinese hospital in 2021, my heady and extended career as a high-functioning alcoholic had also resulted in liver cirrhosis.

The air is currently thick with irony. Of all my self-inflicted injuries, the most significant manifested last week. The fertility clinic informed me I could not conceive children. For the first time in my life, I'm in a healthy, loving, and nourishing relationship, engaged to marry the woman of my dreams who wants nothing more than to bear my children. Aged 47, I'm finally ready to be a conscious and loving parent. I can share the little I've learned about choice and love while simultaneously breaking the traumatic cycles of my ancestral line. Yet, with all the creations within my power, I can no longer create life.

Meanwhile, with all her heart, this divine goddess craves the natural birth of a child or children. No doubt you've already seen the conundrum? What treatment is there? Could we adopt? Might she leave if I cannot co-create her lifelong dream? She would be well within her rights. And as much as I am pained, I could see and respect that truth. *Isn't that a trip?* A real-time collection of obstacles encompassing content from previous pages. Lessons are being presented right now as this book is almost complete. Wild.

It was my lifestyle, of course. My disdain for my existence and a woeful lack of self-love. The STIs and cocaine, the "toxic agent", as the Andrologist called it. Processing this will take work. Last night, we had a tough conversation that ended in a fallout because Monkey appeared, dressed as my wounded inner child already preparing for the worst. Later, I had to sit and self-inquire to see whether there was a risk I might drink again to dissolve the pain in my heart. And if she leaves, how will I grieve the loss of this great love who contributed to my happiness? Could I ever put my heart on the line again for love, knowing it would not last forever?

Oh, woe is me! Martin v1.0 would've tackled this event differently. He'd ask all the above while leaping from a moving wagon, pity-party-bound with a bottle of booze and a big bag of Peruvian Marching Powder[1]. It actually didn't even occur to me to drink or use; how far we have come. The irony is not lost, though. If he hadn't done the things he did, we would not be in this current medical predicament, devoid of the gift of life. But then, we would not be who we are now — grateful, mindful, happy, and free.

Here's the big question: would I do it all again despite knowing its effect on my power to create? Yes, I suppose I would. These lessons have been painful yet priceless for my growth. They helped create a new me. Can I be human while simultaneously maintaining presence? How may I achieve this harmony, and could that practice one day become the very best of my creations? All I can do is try.

My care for and adherence to Earth Rover maintenance has been a woefully and often willfully ignored priority for years. My method of self-love had been purely narcissistic; thus, I had not

1 *One of the many excellent euphemisms for cocaine.*

loved myself nor cared for my body or mind. What a strange thing to concede. In hindsight, it seems utterly preposterous that I did not care for myself. Why do these things that I knew would hinder and shorten my Earth School experience? When we say: "What doesn't kill you makes you stronger", and "I'll sleep when I'm dead", we conceal destructive behaviour with jest. But why do we do it? Sure, we're societally conditioned and even actively encouraged to treat ourselves so. We may even feel we don't deserve to be happy. But there's more to it — an inherent apathy and a belief we cannot change.

Observing such disdain for oneself can be genuinely heartbreaking. Forgiving oneself can take years of concentrated practice. Even now, writing about Martin v1.0's treatment of our body, I'm tickled to think of how careless he was of the legacy he would leave behind. It was *his* truth, though, valid to him at that time. Bless his heart. Yet here I am now, in November 2022, having just celebrated my birthday with the best party in the history of the Martin Story. It was a gorgeous Balinese water blessing, with singing, feasting, and laughing in the company of a collection of beautiful souls. Sober, content, and with a full heart, I fell asleep before midnight. How far we have come from that day with the gun.

Following The Grandmother's stark warning, I pointed the Earth Rover towards unlearning previous consumption habits and developing new ways to look after myself. My approach would evaluate three areas as follows:

1. Consumption.
2. Movement.
3. Rest.

You'll forgive me if this all appears remedial, but much was new in my eyes. I was keen to learn how to better look after my body. Moreover, my first plant medicine ceremonies were a total reset, a rebirthing if you like. I considered my reinvention and the unexpected gifts a life within a life would bring. I came away set alight by the exciting prospect of living, a flaming torch of opportunity burning bright within. That journey continues to unfold and will persist until the day my ever-so-loyal Earth Rover packs in for good.

I can't come close to offering meaningful guidelines for looking after the human body in one book, let alone a chapter. And frankly, it would be fraudulent of me to even attempt to profess expertise in nutrition, physical training, or practices like yoga, breathwork, or sound healing. Having only embraced these modalities a few years ago, I'm a layman in such discussions — a man on the mend. Perhaps the only expertise to which I lay claim is suffering and how *not* to suffer.

Anyway, many incredible books have been published in this field, including Matthew Walker's *Why We Sleep: Unlocking the Power of Sleep and Dreams, How Not To Die*, by Michael Greger MD and Gene Stone, *Lifespan: Why We Age and Why We Don't Have To*, by Dr David Sinclair, *Beyond Training*, by Ben Greenfield, *The Body Keeps The Score*, by Bessell van der Kolk, MD, and *Becoming Supernatural*, by Dr Joe Dispenza. The latter two focus on how our thoughts and emotions directly affect physical well-being. All these books belong on the reading list of one caring for one's Earth Rover maintenance. And many more, of course.

As each moment passes, we're a breath closer to one of many conceivable and inconceivable deaths. Therefore, this chapter serves merely as a reminder that our bodies are as impermanent as everything else. They need regular maintenance to function correctly, avoiding injury, pain, and disease. Thus, reducing unnecessary suffering while providing more time to learn myriad arts of living well. *Thank you*, Earth Rover. I mean that from the bottom of your heart.

Sleep, sunshine, laughing, clean-eating, breathing, meditation, exercise, nature, and self-love are the best medicines. But there are many other ways to cleanse and optimise our Earth Rovers. It's called self-care, and we must care enough to learn. As we work to heal hearts and minds, we should know how to maintain our bodies. This comes easy for some, while others find patterns harder to unlearn. The same goes for forming new routines and habits. I'm one of the others. While I took to the mental and spiritual work and wholesale changes in my consumption, excuses come all too easily as to why I don't commit to regular physical exercise. But now, here I am, just turned 47, with a whole host of injuries that could be reduced or eradicated if I commit to a new regime of regular movement and strength training. So that's my new challenge to myself. It's time to commence serious work on the Earth Rover because I'm finally enjoying a happy, healthy life, which will be prematurely curtailed without a similarly wholesome body.

Move, sleep, and seriously consider what you're putting on and in your body. These words are deceivingly simple. Their associated actions, however, require a wholesale personal audit and a great deal of hard work. How much do you love yourself? Enough to show humility and reverence to the meaty vehicle that keeps you here?

As Mr Luhrmann reminds us: it's your body, your choice. It is your body, so how long do you want to stay in it? And how preferable would it be if the body was sick less, hurt less, and rested more, giving you a shot at a long and happy life? What will you choose?

CHAPTER THIRTY-SIX

Teacher Plants

> Psychedelics are not suppressed because they are dangerous to users; they're suppressed because they provoke unconventional thought, which threatens any number of elites and institutions that would rather do our thinking for us.
>
> — Dennis McKenna

Throughout this book, we've discussed the illusory layers of identity, built over time by conditioning and personal experience. For some (myself included), this isn't a regular head-height dry stone wall but an elaborate structure similar to *Fort Knox's* design. Whilst it is imperative that we acknowledge there is no hack to everlasting happiness, it was never my intention to present the removal of such complexities as an impossible mission to achieve through mindful practice.

However, you may intuitively feel that time is not on your side. Perhaps you sense your ego to be exceptionally robust and equally stubborn. Thus, you would prefer a laser-guided head-start that allows rapid and profound changes to your egoic state. In this case, consider working with psychedelics. A common report from people in their early work with these medicines is what some refer to as an "ego death". I.e. the shattering of the illusory layers of identity and the bright white presentation of your true Self. For many, the layers are stripped away in short order.

Now then, two common misconceptions surround psychedelic use as follows:

1. Because you once had a "bad trip" using mushrooms at a full moon party on a Thai beach (or any party anywhere for that matter), psychedelics are "dangerous".

2. Only people with genuine mental illness engage in psychedelic therapy.

Firstly, using psychedelics in recreational settings, mixing them with alcohol and other drugs alongside total strangers while wandering around in an unsafe space, is a totally shit idea. It's like hating clowns; going to the circus, and then being surprised and upset there was a clown show. Hence, what is known as "bad trips" are typical results of disregard for these potent healing medicines.

Secondly, everyone has a mental illness; the only question is: to what degree? When we observe the typical human traits of unhealthy phone usage, status craving, miscommunication, short tempers, over-eating, alcohol, and drug use, violent language, narcissism, or low self-esteem as legitimate forms of neuroses, then we see mental illness everywhere. Perhaps such normalisation is partly thanks to drama-filled news feeds. Or ever-present on-demand TV, the writers of which know all too well that a great script must contain authentic, idiosyncratic characters and conflict in every scene. Hence, our collective neuroses are accepted as standard as they are re-presented to us in an always-on audiovisual echo chamber.

On a more fundamental level, our egoic layers are not our essence but imprints of countless other individual and collective egos piled on alongside our memorially stored responses to events and interactions. Beneath this dense layer cake of emotional interpretation lies an altogether more peaceful, knowing, loving, Universal, and connected being — buried alive by experience, waiting patiently for the chance of excavation. Psychedelics will undoubtedly provide a rapid and stealthy exfiltration for your consciousness, presenting the opportunity for a new life within a life. Though, you absolutely *must* respect the magnitude of their power.

Psychedelic plants and compounds are as old as time. Growing in fields, jungles, deserts, and even on the backs of toads, these ethnomedicines are in abundance worldwide. Ancient advanced civilisations like the Mayans, Inca, Africans, Native American Indians, the druids, and ancient Egyptians were all working with Psilocybin, Mescaline, DMT, or other healing plant medicines. Societies have worked in harmony with psychedelics for aeons.

Plant medicines' (perfectly natural) existence was attacked in the 1960s by authorities terrified of the collective's rapid revolution in consciousness that might have entire generations drop out of a societal system propped up on the unnecessary toil and suffering of others. The result was a so-called Western "War on Drugs". Despite research in the 50s and 60s proving that psychedelics could heal many of the mental illnesses we suffer today, research was abolished, and the medicines have been labelled "drugs" and primarily misunderstood by the wider world ever since.

The psychiatrist-turned-psychonaut activist and philosopher Timothy Leary coined the counter-culture phrase "Turn on, tune in, drop out" as an invitation to awaken from the failing dream spell of centralised bureaucracy and instead connect with community and divinity. Governments and media outlets spat the "drop-out" label at those courageous enough to work with these medicines, implying idleness and a lack of direction. In reality, all the majority wanted was to drop out of what they knew to be an entirely unhealthy and illusory system of consumption, distraction, and control. They wanted to create a *New Earth*.

You may find it bizarre that I, a recovered addict, would use so-called "drugs" as a route to sobriety. But if you understand that, unlike other drugs, psychedelics are in no way addictive, you might better comprehend my choice. Moreover, after his first LSD experience in August 1956, AA co-founder Bill Wilson declared that acid could cure alcoholism. He went so far as to credit the drug with aiding his recovery from often debilitating depression (and thus, his addiction) by (among other things) saying: "I find myself with a heightened colour perception and an appreciation of beauty almost destroyed by my years of depression".

Interestingly, the second of the 12 Steps says: "[We] Came to believe that a Power greater than ourselves could restore us to sanity". Wilson clearly met that "Higher Power" through his psychedelic experience. Following his own rules to the letter (and beyond), his sanity was most certainly improved. Apparently, when the AA fellowship heard of his newfound support for psychedelics, they were none too pleased, and he was thus encouraged to pipe down. Of course, he wasn't the only one in those days to be silenced by the establishment.

Now that mainstream science is finally accepting the profoundly transformative connection between psychedelics and various mental illnesses, it's widely accepted that these medicines will launch a new era in psychiatric treatment. Thanks to the work of the *Multidisciplinary Association for Psychedelic Studies (MAPS)* movement and the recent Michael Pollan book and docu-series, *How To Change Your Mind*, and many more, there's been an enormous upsurge in applications for psychedelic-assisted therapy training. Still, according to a 2021 survey, 75 per cent of therapists reported they would be unlikely to provide psychedelic therapy if it meant a reduction in income.

Factoid: just one psychedelic therapy session could heal one's neuroses to the point where one could end their counselling in weeks or days. It's a game-changer for humanity and will shake the world of psychotherapy to its very core.

Since the first 1950 report about the therapeutic effects of LSD, psychedelic treatments have shown great promise in tackling mood disorders and alcohol dependence. Since the 1990s, although still ludicrously regulated, a resurgence in research has slowly grown. According to *The Therapeutic Potential of Psychedelic Drugs: Past, Present, and Future* report by Robin L. Carhart-Harris and Guy M. Goodwin, lo and behold, countless neuropsychopharmacological studies have proven the power of psychedelics as an effective treatment for mental illness. These include:

2006 (Moreno et al.).

In treating obsessive compulsive disorder (using Psilocybin), all patients showed improvements within 24 hours of treatment.

2011 (Grob et al.).

Psilocybin treatment of anxiety and depression in end-stage cancer patients showed significant reductions in anxiety at three months and depression at six months.

2014 (Johnson et al.).

Long-term chronic smoking was studied using Psilocybin. 80 per cent of the group remained abstinent after six months.

2014 (Gasser et al.).

Anxiety linked to a life-threatening disease was studied using LSD, resulting in significant decreases at two months, sustained for twelve months.

2015 (Bogenschutz et al.).

Treating alcohol dependence using Psilocybin showed a significant decrease in drinking behaviours for up to nine months.

2015 (Osorio Fde et al.) and 2016 (Sanches et al.).

Major depressive disorder was studied using Ayahuasca and showed significant decreases in depressive symptoms for up to 21 days.

The list goes on.

These medicines, criminalised and vilified for decades, are indisputably crucial to healing human trauma and addiction on a level that will forever change the psychiatric, pharmaceutical, and mental health arenas, enabling millions of people to heal themselves and end generations of inherited trauma. Imagine the future for these people's kids and their kids to follow. Imagine a society of people whose words and deeds are not governed by ego or fear but by oneness and love. Psychedelics can do that for us, but not if we continue to fear these medicines, largely thanks to propaganda. Nor if we hand over our sovereign right to explore human consciousness to governments and the medical-industrial complex. Contemplate how they fit into the utopian future I've just presented. If 75 per cent of psychotherapists don't want you to try psychedelic therapy because it'll put them out of business, how will Big Pharma or the hospitals or authorities feel about a happier, healthier society? A lot less profit in that, isn't there. And far fewer opportunities for control.

There are horror stories surrounding psychedelics, though there are mitigating reasons too. Psychedelics are best put to use in therapeutic rather than recreational settings. When engaging with these medicines, we must consider our mindset and the proper setting while ensuring our guide's unequivocal credibility. Far from being used mindlessly or excessively at social gatherings, we must work with them in the ancient ceremonial environments channelled, practised, and protected for thousands of years by the indigenous tribes and masters.

These medicines changed my worldview and beyond. The plants eradicated my addiction. Rather than treating my symptoms, they reached into my subconscious unconscious. They re-presented countless earlier incidents of damage, offering fresh perspectives devoid of conditioning. They allowed me to see, beyond all doubt, trauma's impermanence and thus let it go. Free from trauma's grip, addiction no longer served me. Nor did depression, anxiety, or suicidal tendencies. I do not call these gifts "drugs", as they are medicines with profound healing properties. *Plant medicines.*

Without psychedelics, I would not have written this book. Perhaps I would not be breathing, either. Plant medicines are a divine gift, and their existence is no coincidence. Unless you work with them yourself, you can never hope to comprehend the life-changing lessons they offer. Nor can you provide a meaningful contrary view. As Chris Bache, PhD, put it best: "All psychedelic practice is, in essence, purification". I have seen the realities of life, love, death, and life beyond death with the help of these plants. So here, I give thanks to Grandmother Ayahuasca and Grandfather Huachuma. And gratitude in abundance to "the flesh of God", also known as the Psilocybin mushrooms.

Psychedelics are laser-cut keys to doors you could never imagine existed. They are one of many ways to remember the truth. Meditation, breathwork, yoga, and practices like Qi Gong and Tai Chi similarly create higher states of consciousness.

However, psychedelics commonly have a more immediate and profound effect. One is not better or worse than the other; all are valid. The choice of which route is entirely ours, just as we might not choose any route at all.

A psychedelic renaissance is happening right now. But it's coming with a land grab as governments and pharmaceutical companies hustle to patent and control the synthesisation of natural plant medicines. It is absurd that one can criminalise nature any more than privatise it. And the notion that such profound healing will come with a premium price tag is utterly abhorrent. We must be mindful of what lies ahead when a byproduct black market saturates our cities. A dangerous future looms that blatantly discards the shamanistic process, which assuredly will not be healthy for any of us.

The Vine of the Soul

Ayahuasca medicine is quantum biotechnology that aligns perfectly with human physiology. The alliance between medicine and the human body allows us to transcend the plane of existence in which we live. Free from the material confines of this plane, we can take a metaphysical journey to the past, present, elsewhere in the future, and alternative realms or planes of existence. In such arenas, what we understand to be time and space do not exist. In this limitless field of knowledge and love, we can explore entirely new facets of ourselves. Our experiences and those of the collective consciousness receive profound lessons regarding the nature of humanity. We can also receive and give quantum healing.

Ayahuasca is not the only medicine that facilitates such expansive journeys. It is DMT, *Dimethyltryptamine* — also produced in the human body by the pineal gland and lungs. Many forms of DMT, Mescaline and Psilocybin, provide equally profound psychedelic experiences when appropriately used.

Psychedelics and "Spirituality"

I was an atheist for many years despite my earlier metaphysical exploration. Then I discovered psychedelics. It's safe to say that I am no longer on the spiritual fence. Following countless psychonautical experiences, I have suspended all beliefs and judgement of what I knew to be "reality". I approach such exploration with an open heart and mind to all possibilities. Having witnessed these sights and planes, I know humans are not what we believe.

Our plane of existence is not as it seems. Our separation from one another and from nature is an illusion. Our identities are fantasies. Our disconnection from everything and Self is detrimental to every one of us. We must address these territories with agency and reverence for humanity to evolve and flourish.

I will write more about psychedelics and their profound effect on mental illness, but not in this book. I'll leave you with two thoughts:

1. It should be mandatory for every world leader and entourage to attend at least ten Ayahuasca ceremonies before taking office.
2. If the world attended a plant medicine ceremony simultaneously, we would be well on our way to achieving world peace.

Used appropriately, psychedelics are medicines. They heal what we mistakenly think cannot be healed, sicknesses that many cannot even see.

CHAPTER THIRTY-SEVEN

What We Have Here
is a Failure to Communicate

**Much unhappiness has come into
the world because of bewilderment,
and things left unsaid.**
— Fyodor Dostoevsky

The lion's share of our past and future anguish likely links to interpersonal exchanges — be they family, friends, co-workers, or even total strangers. Can you think of a relationship where you constantly feel patronised? Is there someone in your life who continually complains while expressing disdain for positive change? Perhaps you find yourself people-pleasing so as not to rock another's boat, despite yours being scuppered while avoiding the collision. Or do you simply struggle to express your truth? Learning how to connect profoundly impacts our well-being and that of others. It's a dance for which we are ill-prepared, an underrated art form primarily discovered and developed through self-mastery.

As a youngster, I was never taught the finer arts of communicating my feelings, listening, or holding space for others. Nor was I trained on our penchant for drama or how empathy cultivates healthy relationships. Who is? It's ludicrous that we are sent to school to learn a long list of things we'll never need, yet the absolute basics — how to regulate emotions — how to interact

— are frequently kicked to the curb. At least we learn how to do as we're told. And what of parenting? What if their parents, and parents of parents, imprinted their generational trauma and perverse perspectives? They can only teach us what they know, which is learned by example — toxic or otherwise.

We're all having a human experience. Though a variety of flavours, our thoughts and deeds are much the same, which renders our judgement of one another somewhat paradoxical. We can adopt many personalities in one lifetime. Therefore, changing one's persona coat, or at least trying the odd one on from time to time, helps us experience humanity's facets, thus stimulating growth. So, when interacting with others, we would do well to consider their experience and feelings. Why and what are they? How are they? How often do we ask ourselves, "What emotions is this person experiencing?" before, during, or even after our exchange? And if we did, how would that affect the outcome? As Carl Jung once said: "Everything that irritates us about others can lead us to an understanding of ourselves". Empathy for behavioural traits offers mirrored lessons. We can alchemise this combined learning to reapply it to more interpersonal exchanges, thus levelling up. This is growth through observation, self-education, and applied harmonious interaction.

How often do we break or set aside relationships because of poor communication? Whether it be an incorrect assumption, misaligned expectation, lacking empathy, or incendiary words shot in anger, we all recall unpleasant interactions that could've gone better with an alternative approach. Much of our discontent comes from our dissonance with others, and, despite the tools at our disposal, our communication skills are often derailed by innate egoic responses.

As for happiness, said status is drastically enhanced when we all get along. Hence harmony is a wonder to seek and behold, and thus our time together can be drastically improved through closer understanding and more mindful communication. But we must acknowledge our shortcomings here and care enough to want to express and receive feelings better. We can all improve our communication since this art form relies on presence. Few of us can say that we're always truly present.

So the game is to alter the outcome of our interactions by equipping ourselves with the right tools to communicate maturely and effectively. We are to treat others as we would hope to be treated ourselves. Such mastery requires a combined understanding of mindfulness, psychology, authenticity, and responsibility. The latter, because, despite our best intentions, we can still fuck it all up, and in such moments, the ability to own that is priceless. We utilise awareness and presence in our communications, where emotions would otherwise have us knee-deep in shit in less than a heartbeat. So what follows in the next few chapters are wisdom and utilities to help tango with others while stepping on fewer toes.

Alternate Nostril Breathing

Come into a comfortable seat, spine straight.
Perhaps close your eyes.
Relax your jaw.
Relax your neck and shoulders.
Soften your belly.

Position your right hand in front of your face.
Rest your middle and index finger between your eyebrows.

Inhale.
Close your right nostril with your thumb.
Exhale through the left nostril completely.
Inhale through the left nostril for one, two, three, four.
Close the left nostril with you index finger.
Exhale through the right for four, three, two, one.

Inhale thought the right for one, two, three, four.
Close the right.
Exhale through the left for four, three, two, one.

Repeat ten rounds of this breathing pattern.

If you feel lightheaded, release both nostrils,
and breathe regularly before returning to the practice.

CHAPTER THIRTY-EIGHT

The Truth About Truths

We are never so much disposed
to quarrel with others as when we
are dissatisfied with ourselves.
— William Hazlitt

One thing humans do is believe we know other humans just because we're, well, human. However, if we're still working out who we are, might we know less about others than we lead ourselves to believe? We may think we know people, but our opinion of them is highly subjective — it's *our truth* about them; ergo, it is flawed. Why? Because how we form opinions is heavily influenced by our conditioning and psychological history. It comes down to personal preference. *We judge.* And thus, the more dysfunctional our psyche, the more exaggerated our judgement will be. Your perspective and my perspective of the same person are distinct and driven by internal values, experiences, and how we view the world.

So one person's truth about another can be wildly "false" in comparison. Ergo, while there may be common themes, no one shares the exact same opinions about you. So, by that rationale, there are many versions of you. Not to mention how the Observer Effect likely creates subtle (or exaggerated) changes in your behaviour depending on with whom you interact. So our judgement of each other is not healthy for our relationships. When we judge, we project our values, morals, experiences, and expectations on to others. As the saying goes, what we see in others, is a reflection of ourselves. For example, if a friend continually expects your judgement, pre-empting your words, they front-load their defensive position with mitigation. Perhaps you had no intention of speaking because it never occurred to you to judge them. Yet, they continue. In all likelihood, this friend judges others and, therefore, themselves harshly — hence they anticipate the same attitude from us, whether deserved or not. And it likely follows that they were judged, perhaps often berated, by parents who eroded their self-esteem.

What of our projection? How crucial is mindfulness as we project our persona on to others? Well, that depends entirely on our authenticity. Life is straightforward for those with the confidence to simply be. They are who they are to anyone and everyone. They — we have no inclination to be someone we're not. Others' opinion of us is not our business, provided we've shown them respect. Such a philosophy requires the mindful navigation of our subtle differences to optimise our exchanges. It's a conscious approach to cultivating harmony, and it's easier said than done. If, on the other hand, we project inauthenticity by design, such mentally exhausting activity is more likely manipulation. Perhaps this is a carefully constructed pretence designed to protect one's true feelings. Often these are the actions of the broken-hearted. While it may not be entirely apparent, their inauthenticity is not malicious, but a mechanism for self-preservation. Be the change you want to see in them. *Show them love.*

Where are our role models? To whom should we look for pointers on how to communicate? As we've discussed, family members create an imprint in our early childhood years, though their example might not be altogether healthy. Teachers do their best, but can only share what they know. Spiritual leaders follow doctrine, offering the sage advice of a religious organisation.

This is good if driven by unconditional love. But when tutelage comes with conditions, laws, dogma, and intolerance, is this wholesome? What about the leaders of our communities? Are these individuals really the best of us?

All one can wish for is that all people take a journey of introspection so they might heal their trauma, embodying wellness and becoming better role models to those they represent. Doing the best we can for ourselves and others is all we can do, but are we *really* doing the best we can? Or is there room for improvement? After the events of recent years, perhaps we can agree that we could all use some world peace in our macro- and micro-communities right about now. Who will lead the way?

Ultimately, we are sovereign beings with minds of our own, unaware of the power we wield when working on ourselves and standing in unity. So, what are we doing to cultivate harmonious community relationships? We have a mental illness problem that goes right to the top of the societal food chain. If our commanders and chiefs can't put peace, love, and collaboration at the forefront of their agendas, how will we, the people, choose to lead by example?

As much as a world free from conflict and judgement would be a wonderful place, such an ideal is only possible once we grow as a collective, and there's a lot of room to grow. I spend a lot of time writing in eateries because I enjoy the change in environment. The way people treat cafe staff is a thing to behold — entitled strangers meeting hospitable servers with outright disdain. Wrapped in self-importance, they talk down to people as if they are inferior. Is this kind? Is it necessary? How we treat those with nothing obvious to offer says a lot about us.

In our dualistic realm, one hand can create while the other destroys. *And we do* — lashing out with words and opposing opinions. What starts as healthy debate often snowballs into a toxic battle, with brutal finishing moves for good measure. Have you ever dropped into a social media thread around a contentious topic? Via smartphones and desktop computers, so-called "keyboard warriors" spend lunch breaks or entire evenings tearing lumps off one another over petty disagreements. Our mutual mistreatment is heartbreaking yet commonplace. And what about our treatment of family, friends, neighbours, and the rest of our Earth School-attending humanoids? Perhaps it is time for an audit.

Never before has our global community been so divided, with so many options to express our differences in the vilest ways imaginable. From race and gender politics to vaccinated versus unvaccinated, sick versus healthy, red versus blue, abortion, climate control, religion, sports fandom, you name it! Somewhere in the world, at least two strangers are verbally abusing each other's mothers via a social media thread because one is adamant that Idris Elba should never play *James Bond*. The more imaginative ways we create to separate ourselves, the more reasons there are to fight like rabid dogs. And the digital platforms to launch our attack are aplenty. What are we learning? Confucius once said: "Without feelings of respect, what is there to distinguish men from beasts?" I wonder what the Chinese master would make of today's human interactions. While effortlessly, the Taoists would promote harmony through a smile.

Despite being the most sophisticated spirit, mind, and body complex on this planet, we remain shamefully primitive. We've lost sight of our infinite potential, seemingly content to consume, judge, fuck, and brawl while further driving wedges of difference between us. Perhaps, the illusion of separation has never felt so potent. Why do we conceive more ways to fall out rather than to connect, collaborate, and co-create? Is this what we want? Of course, I say "we" while fully appreciating this might not be you.

You may be doing all you can to shine a light, share, and cultivate love. And if so, thank you for the gifts you bring.

So, how can we seek to better understand another's truth? Simple. We avoid our default mode of interjecting with our own thoughts, pause, and simply hear them out. Then pause again. Even if it's a criticism of us, is there some truth in it? When heard from a place of peace, with Monkey safely secured on the back seat, do their words resonate, or not? Either way, they are truths nonetheless. If we all spent less time arguing for one truth or the other, offering ours to take or leave while respecting the opposition, we'd all get along much better. So next time your partner, sibling, friend, or even a total stranger says something that triggers you to disagree or attempt to change their view, ask yourself whether it might indeed be the case that their truth is absolute to them and with good reason. It's the very definition of being able to "agree to disagree". Not with malice nor resentment or to make forced peace. You simply observe such situations as phenomena and let them go.

The time has come for us to take a cold, hard stare at humanity's inability to rise above noise and ego. Perhaps this is too simple a utility, but all I can do to change the world is work on myself. So I try with all my heart to openly accept another's argument should they oppose me. "I respect your truth", I say. It's their truth, even if it's not mine. You do not have to agree or disagree. You can move on to another conversation. And if it's abundantly clear that you cannot share common ground, then smile, collect your things, bow your head, and say your goodbyes. Part ways conflict-free, and wish them all the best on their journey. This may be common sense, but it's not commonplace. I was a people-pleaser for years, as many folks are. The need for approval and accord runs as deep as the desire to win, so we dig in like truth ticks, ready for the long haul. Don't do it. Smile, walk away, and observe the pleasure in peace.

Respecting the Truth

If ranters and ravers could develop a mindfulness practice, they'd witness the futility of pouring energy into discord's negative void. Imagine if, instead of endless vitriolic exchange, people paused and simply replied, "I respect your truth", or some such variation. Try it on for size; see how calming it feels to accept that there's always a story behind another's opinions and that their view of you is not your business. It's interesting to watch the reaction. Nine times out of ten, it'll take the wind out of their sails. The rest of the time, they'll attack your passivity. Some folks just want to fight. It's always worth remembering that's nothing to do with us, and the best course of action is to leave the building, being mindful not to throw a hand grenade over one's shoulder on the way out.

Try as we might to improve our situation, there will always be tyrants. Showing them your back while retaining peace and composure is exceptionally good for your health. Moreover, removing your attention and energy from them erodes their power. It's all about boundaries. Perhaps you dislike confrontation as much as me. I once thrived on it, perverse as that may sound. Now, I relish stillness and love, knowing as I do that arguing with you is equivalent to clashing with myself.

Humans bring a boatload of conditioning to the table, and few of us are incorruptible. Hence, the utilities for avoiding all the aforementioned lie in self-realisation and unlearning old communication styles. Adopt presence and awareness of our behaviour and the common themes during each exchange. Look and listen. Remember, everyone's behaviour is driven by a hidden something. In practising this work, try to avoid judgement — of yourself and others. There's a difference between judging and observing, as one is done with love.

Looking to others for a clear direction on how we should behave and communicate is a mistake and, consciously or unconsciously, is an abrogation of one's responsibilities. Though objective observation can teach us much, working on ourselves is the key to improving our exchanges with others. We can transform the way we communicate, often avoiding conflict. And if conflict comes knocking regardless of our best efforts, then walk away. Walking away is healthy. If you must, then respond to a quarrel with silence. We can say much when we say nothing. And there's less to retract later as the dark clouds disappear.

CHAPTER THIRTY-NINE

The Jungian Archetypes

I don't like that man.
I must get to know him better.
— Abraham Lincoln

The primary reason we fall out is miscommunication. We clash because we assume what people are thinking rather than simply asking. Or we expect them to be like us and are disappointed when they are themselves. We regularly fail to appreciate our differences. How do we fix this? Understanding others' values and motivations means we can better comprehend their feelings and actions alongside our own.

Through observation, we seek resonance. Given our intrinsic connection and the occasionally inconvenient necessity for us to interact, we do well to adopt the study of humans and their personality traits. We can embody and share multiple personas at any time in this life or the next. So whether you're on a mission to become someone or no one, there's an argument for learning more about everyone. Friction comes easily in this age of separation, while harmony is borne from empathy.

This is where profiling, like the *Myers-Briggs, DISC*, or *Personality Shapes*, and the more esoteric *Human Design* models come in handy. Some might give off a faint corporate whiff. Still, they're legitimately practical tools to help us better understand the various facets of humanity.

We've already discussed C. G. Jung's concept of Individuation.

For this chapter, we'll focus on the *Jungian Archetypes*, thus dipping our toe in the collective unconscious. The twelve Archetypes represent milestones in our personal development journey. Brand strategists still use them today, instrumental as they are for isolating and humanising a brand's personality. It's not uncommon to see a combination of two or possibly even three Archetypes in one individual. For example, the Jedi Master Obi-Wan Kenobi displays blended traits of the Hero, Magician, and Sage.

Jung's Archetypes were partially inspired by Pluto's Forms, and you can lose days, even weeks diving into the tomes of psychobabble written on this thinking. I'm keen to keep my observations breezy in comparison. Similarly to Jung's assertion that our substantial appreciation for the Hero's Journey is genetically inherent, the Archetypes belong to our collective unconscious as an imprinted, inherited aspect of the human psyche.

Perhaps the Creator's brief to Self went like this:

"I'm making a multi-generational holographic game of learning in a giant, round, green and blue school designed to last for aeons. I'll leave subtle trace code in the game players' collective unconscious psyche. Every time they find the Easter eggs inside the game, they unlock special abilities and level up".

The Archetypes comprise knowledge and experiences shared by humans, personified by twelve characters collectively representing us and our various personas. So if this stuff is hard-coded into our DNA, one has to wonder how and to what end?

Jung created the original Archetypes, but they saw a renaissance in 2001 when Margaret Mark and Carol Pearson published *The Hero and The Outlaw: Building Extraordinary Brands Through the Power of Archetypes*. Here, the Archetypes had a 21st-century overhaul, making them altogether more accessible to the layperson.

Associated with the Archetypes are four cardinal orientations, essentially four drivers underlying three archetypes each. The drivers are:

Ego (to be seen, heard, admired). *Order* (to maintain structure within societal situations). *Social* (to cultivate meaningful connections). *Freedom* (yearning unrestriction from one's limits).

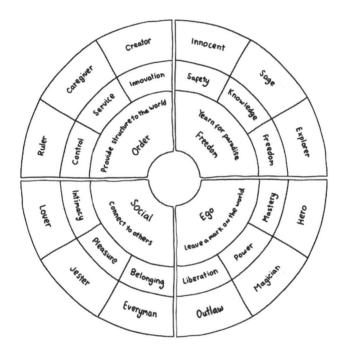

The Jungian Archetypes.

As you can see, three Archetypes are driven by *Ego*, three by *Order,* three by *Social*, and three by *Freedom.*

A brief summary of the twelve looks like this:

1. Innocent *(Freedom)*.
2. Sage *(Freedom)*.
3. Explorer *(Freedom)*.
4. Outlaw *(Ego)*.
5. Magician *(Ego)*.
6. Hero *(Ego)*.
7. Lover *(Social)*.
8. Jester *(Social)*.
9. Everyman *(Social)*.
10. Ruler *(Order)*.
11. Caregiver *(Order)*.
12. Creator *(Order)*.

Innocent

A mystic, romantic dreamer, the Innocent seeks happiness through rose-tinted glasses. Oblivious to the world's dangers, they float through life with a delightful sense of naivety. Optimistic and understanding right and wrong, they're keen to avoid punishment on the road to utopia. However, overindulgence can distract them from society's realities and dangers.

Sage

The Sage knows there is freedom in truth. Valuing knowledge, peace, and wisdom in equal measure, the Sage welcomes learning to help make sense of the world. Objective and thoughtful, the Sage researches, plans, philosophises, and mentors. They may study forever without putting learning into action. The Sage can appear to lack empathy, perhaps due to their evolved love of logic and an established understanding of suffering.

Explorer

The Explorer is always on the lookout for the next adventure. The Explorer searches far and wide for fulfilment but can be aimless and ungrounded. Fiercely independent autonomists, staying true to themselves, can appear self-centred. They remain ever keen to escape feeling dissatisfied or forced to conform. As Explorers seek to understand themselves through travel and experience, freedom is their everything.

Outlaw

Fearing powerlessness, the Outlaw is a misfit who shuns conformity in favour of chaos and occasional destruction. A reinventor of wheels, the Outlaw spits in the eye of rules and regulations that suit them not. Disruptive and inventive, the Outlaw challenges the status quo, inciting a riot to create meaningful change. Wild as they are, we agree with their ideas yet lack the courage to express this.

Magician

Magicians are visionaries, inventors, and healers. Alchemists by nature, they create beautiful connections through charisma and conversation. The Magician understands the mind and the world's ways and thus can make things happen. They seek transformation in themselves and others. Magicians strategise and stick to their vision, constantly keen to find an accord. With this skill set comes the risk of deception and manipulation to meet their goals.

Hero

Crystal clear on what's "right" and "wrong", the Hero defends, beating injustice with a stick. Obstacles and challenges are welcome ways for the Hero to define their character. Heroes often become rescuers, focused on helping others, whether requested or not. Thus, the Hero can also be controlling — narcissistic even, as their accomplishments feed the ego in real-time. Strength, competence, courage, and arrogance play a tug of war in the Hero's head. This warrior and winner likely fears vulnerability; gutsy or not, such uncharted territory is unwelcome.

Lover

The flames of passion, romance, and lust are fanned daily by the Lover as they seek to imbibe the associated emotions of bliss and adoration. Though flinging themselves into love as they do, the Lover often objectifies others while having little understanding of true intimacy. Keen for affection, the Lover may also struggle with silence or solitude. Their inclination towards people-pleasing may mean they lose their sense of Self. Though they seek romance, a Lover can make an enthusiastic friend.

Jester

Hedonistic, full of beans, often silly and fun, the Jester lives from one moment to the next and will sleep when they die. The Jester is the breeze in a stuffy room, capable of raising the energy of the flattest crowd. Boundless enjoyment drives them, but their lacking self-control can cause chaos, and they rarely accept responsibility. Prone as they are to distraction and feast, a Jester can often fall foul to addiction. Burning bright as the Jester does, they risk exhaustion and depression. Who will be present for this event? What lies behind their energetic mask of frivolity?

Everyman

Fitting in to feel secure drives the Everyman to seek loyalty, tradition, and the safety of the comfort zone. The Everyman is happiest as a crowd member, made anxious by compulsion and spontaneity. Frictionless societal membership works very well (thank you) for the Everyman. No need for revolution if things work "just fine". Connection and belonging are as crucial as realism and simplicity. In their effort to conform, the silent majority risks missing out — keen as they are to blend in.

Ruler

Order is the order of the day for the Ruler, which they seek to impose with rigidity and control. Structure is vital, supporting much productivity. A Ruler fears chaos or losing power while nurturing responsibility and leadership. While a Ruler's heart may be in the right place, their communication skills and authoritarian nature can often cause unnecessary friction. Controllers and expert planners, spontaneity is not the Ruler's way.

Caregiver

Driven by self-sacrifice, the altruistic Caregiver is inclusive and compassionate. Generous and dedicated, they give seemingly not to receive. Codependency often motivates Caregivers; thus, they tend not to protect their boundaries. Caregivers can often be rescuers, likely to become victims of another's Drama Triangle[1]. Therefore, exploitation usually follows. Helpful, supportive, and loving, the Caregiver puts everyone else first.

Creator

Ideas and projects are the Creator's lifeblood. Natural generators, they manifest dreams with drive and determination. Though, with so many ideas, resistance is the Creator's number one enemy. Creators have multiple projects in play. Hence often, their projects never see fruition. Creators are masters of expression through a selection of mediums. While their perfectionism is often exhausting, their creativity and imagination inspire.

---

1 *Karpman's Drama Triangle (see Chapter 41).*

Heroes on Journeys

All great stories contain characters like this; they are inherently relatable. Who, from your life, could you immediately see as one or a mix of these personalities? And since this book is all about self-inquiry, which are you? As with all personality profiling, there's a danger of pigeonholing, and it's worth noting also that our characters can change as we grow. Martin v1.0 was part Jester, part Magician, part Outlaw, with a wounded subset slice of the Innocent child. Not anymore. We wanted to change, so we did.

Imagine combining adventure with innocence, selflessness with love and a lust for life, courage, alchemy, and more. We can become every one of these Archetypes. In choosing to do so, we invite the most fulfilling life experience. Many dare not dream of the gift of collective learning in a single lifetime, yet it remains a possibility.

The Hero's Journey follows a long and winding road, so collision avoidance is advantageous. Suppose you recognise personality traits linked to an individual's needs. In that case, you can more appropriately engage with them on their level, softening, elaborating, or trimming your communication style, to better suit theirs. As same as we are, we're not all the same. So, we must learn to look past someone's surface-level behaviours. Consider them an iceberg, with us often only seeing the tip. What mass of experience and emotions lies in their depths? What trauma steers their words and deeds, perhaps beyond their control? Why are we the way we are? There's always a reason — a pathology — and taking the extra step to consider it puts us in good stead to better interact with more depth and meaning, empathy, and compassion.

As we plough headlong into a future of screen and VR-based relationships hiding behind avatars in a virtual world, human communication as we know it might become a lost art. Though ironically, an avatar in itself, ego already stands between us and breaking this down to find common goals is challenging enough for many. Whether digital or mental facade, underneath, we remain humans with trauma, vulnerability, feelings, and beautiful idiosyncrasies to be observed, navigated, and enjoyed.

CHAPTER FORTY

Berne's Transactional Analysis

A word to the wise is infuriating.
— Hunter S. Thompson

Eric Berne was a renowned psychiatrist, author, and significant influence on the world of psychoanalysis. It's his work in the territories of multifaceted personalities and collision on which I wish to focus this chapter. My discovery of his work changed my approach to communication. Although I'm still a work in progress, I regularly practise embodying these utilities.

Berne spent years formulating theories centred around human interaction, which he referred to as a transaction. All part of his deeper exploration into the dynamics of human relationships. Berne was fascinated with human behaviour and influenced by Freud's work on the *id, ego,* and *superego*. Berne's work was different from traditional psychological observations on interaction. According to him, much could be learned through transactions. In the early 1950s, Berne counselled hundreds of patients at his California practice. Through these sessions, he detected three ego states present in all. So after much study and consideration, in the late 50s, he introduced *Parent, Adult,* and *Child* to the world — the core players in his model, dubbed *Transactional Analysis.*

Far from matching the traditional dictionary definitions of the words, Berne's three ego states represent underlying personality drivers that might influence our behaviour during a transaction. Berne was keen to point out that Freud's id, ego, and superego, as well as the Jungian constructs, were concepts. On the other hand, his ego states were "phenomenological realities" since these behaviours had been legitimately observed.

Transactional Analysis provides a powerful utility to help better interact, specifically but not exclusively, as a tool to avoid conflict. Before diving into the model, we've to understand these ego states.

Parent

The *Parent* state represents our early childhood developmental experience, perception, and mental recollection of the actions of our parents and adults close to us during the same period. Our mental recordings are often of these people providing instruction (as a parent would). This kind of basic provision of life advice is rather more imposed than the child's choice.

Child

The *Child* state is our internalised account of external events perceived as a tiny human. It's our mental store of emotions and feelings attached to specific events. Our mental recordings, therefore, comprise experienced events and their associated feelings.

Adult

The third ego state represents our ability to witness feelings alternative to those felt in the Parent or Child states. The *Adult* is a data-crunching state of evaluation, providing pause, observation, and the ability to raise one's consciousness before transacting. The Adult can therefore become *the witness.*

The Adult is matter-of-fact and comparatively Zen. Berne says this state is "principally concerned with transforming stimuli into pieces of information, and processing and filing that information on the basis of previous experience". Imagine if this was our go-to state, rather than spraying the room with a word gun after a dose of triggered trauma. Keep in mind that as we demonstrate how transactions work, I'm giving you the breezy outline of this incredible tool of human analysis. Think *stimulus and response.*

According to Berne, the Adult state invites the least friction; thus, if we regularly communicated Adult to Adult, we would have a very cordial and respectful relationship. Wouldn't that be doozy? Sadly, that's not how things roll around here, so there are a few options for how each state might communicate and the opposing state's triggered response.

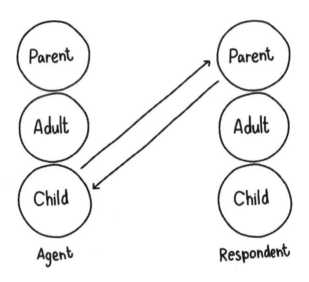

Example Complementary Transaction.

An individual (the Agent) assumes the Child state and communicates something to the Respondent (stimulus), who readily adopts the Parent role, responding accordingly. What happens next? Well, that would depend on the response. If the

Parent responded by hearing and addressing a need, there would be no friction. These so-called *complementary transactions* are, perhaps unsurprisingly, considered healthy.

The unhealthy alternative is a *crossed transaction*. There might be friction if the Child responded as if triggered by emotions. Perhaps Parent castigated Child or responded with condescendence. And so it goes.

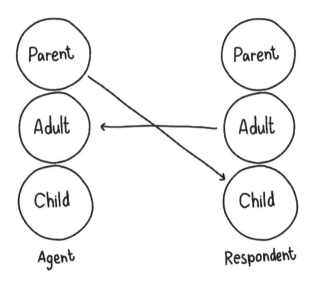

Example Crossed Transaction.

One example of a crossed transaction could be when an individual (the Agent) has sent several text messages to the Respondent and received no reply. Triggered by their childhood neglect, the Agent seeks a response (validation) from the Respondent (Child to Parent). Choosing not to enable this behaviour, the Respondent instead communicates Adult to Adult, respectfully suggesting that, for reasons of self-care, they are not available 24/7. This encourages healthy boundaries.

You can see how Child to Parent, Parent to Child transactions can play out and the complications arising from crossed transactions. Following the example above, despite the Respondent offering Adult to Adult interaction, the triggered Agent might refuse to play along, keen to continue communication from the Child state. At this point, there's a good chance that the Respondent might lose patience, thus patronising the Agent (Parent to Child). Next, they're struck by the toys thrown from the Agent's metaphorical pram. All this unnecessary drama because the Respondent did not instantly address the Agent's needy behaviour.

Human transactions are highly sophisticated regardless of how exciting or dull the stimuli and responses are. Delivery is as paramount to observe as the content. What's their face doing? How about volume, intonation, and body language? The science says we focus less on words than delivery styles and facial expressions. There's a lot to look out for. It's a beautiful game. Or so Berne thought. Check out his book, *Games People Play*, for more from the man's extraordinary mind. Meanwhile, next time you transact with someone, observe the role you assume and their chosen role to respond. All of a sudden, your communication can become a lot more conscious.

CHAPTER FORTY-ONE

Karpman's Drama Triangle

> You can lie down for people
> to walk on you, and they will
> still complain that you're not flat
> enough.
> — Mature Gambino

People either radiate energy or absorb it. Sometimes it's conscious, sometimes not. And in instances where one who radiates falls foul to another who absorbs, theft takes place on an altogether unpleasant and unnecessary level. This phenomenon is more complex than it might seem since an energy-absorbent person might not always intend such behaviour. It's a phenomenon nonetheless.

Studying under Eric Berne, inspired by his work, psychologist Stephen Karpman developed another model to add to the Transactional Analysis utility kit. Karpman's model is called the *Drama Triangle*. This practical utility can drastically improve communication — it's an excellent way to protect your energy. Perhaps you've already heard of it since coaches, therapists, and corporate mentors use it to garner better personal and working relationships. The model might not be new to you, but perhaps my interpretation will serve as a welcome refresher. If, on the other hand, you've never heard of the Drama Triangle, I'm happy to share this fantastic and pragmatic communication tool.

The Drama Triangle centres around unhealthy transactions.

With its help, we can learn how to spot the warning signs of harmful interactions in our short- and long-term relationships. I'll warn you now that mastering the Drama Triangle requires brutal pragmatism. To protect ourselves from drama, we must be prepared to accept that not all people in our lives should necessarily be allowed a place at the table. Just because they are a friend, partner, family member, employer, colleague, religious mentor, or any other conceivable role does not oblige you to keep them in your life.

Thanks to our conditioning and the pressure of others, we tend to feel dutiful — a sense of responsibility for people's actions and feelings. Because, for instance, they are family or close friends, we believe we must stick together, no matter what. But relationships, just like everything else, are impermanent. Moreover, in many cases, maintaining toxic affinities through obligation alone can invite a great deal of self-harm. So how do we spot drama?

The three personas in Karpman's model are:

1. Victim

Victims choose or fail to see their inherent ability to help themselves. With feelings of powerlessness and weakness, Victims are stuck in a cycle of causality, playing injured parties, which they often enjoy. Victims are exhausted and exhausting because they regularly host or attend "pity parties", and misery loves company. Victims seek saviours or, in extreme cases, wish not to be rescued at all. An energetic feed will instead suffice.

2. Rescuer

Every Victim needs a *Rescuer*. Adopting the saviour role, while possibly noble, doubles down on the Victim's disempowered status — pouring petrol on a fire, or boosting a pity party's attendance numbers. Similarly to Jung's Hero, the Rescuer might also seek validation through their actions. Regardless of their intention, the Rescuer's actions enable the Victim to continue fulfilling their role rather than helping themselves. Thus, encouraging a perpetual behavioural loop.

3.   Persecutor

Passive-aggressive or just plain aggressive, *Persecutors* can bully or criticise without offering guidance or alternatives. Aware or entirely ignorant, they attack and blame others, abrogating responsibility to avoid facing their imperfections and weaknesses.

When we step up to the plate, we activate the Drama Triangle. It usually initiates with the Persecutor or the Victim, though an uninvited Rescuer can cause havoc too. Alas, no siren or buzzer forewarns us of our impending pain. We have only our wits and awareness to protect us.

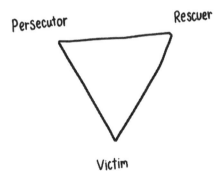

Karpman's Drama Triangle.

Conflicts can be very subtle; you might not even realise you're in a dramatic confrontation — at least not in the early stages. So, understanding each role shows us how easily conflict can arise. According to Karpman's model, the drama begins with two individuals occupying the triangle. They are pushed towards their "preferred" role when the inevitable conflict occurs. Often unbeknownst to them, their interactions in the triangle undergo transformation. For example, a Victim might lure a Rescuer using a well-crafted tale of woe. The Rescuer inevitably falls foul of the transaction as the Victim's manipulation of the Rescuer becomes, in essence, persecutional. Thus the Rescuer becomes the Victim. Bewildered, they wonder, "What happened?!"

These dynamics can play out in a few different ways. Perhaps it's as straightforward as *Individual (A)* assumes the role of Persecutor, constantly dismissing *Individual (B)'s* opinion; making them a Victim through general mistreatment. Striving to see the best in *(A)* or optimistically believing change is possible, *(B)* sticks it out, switching roles to Rescuer. Lured into a false sense of security by *(A)* responding favourably for a while, *(B)* is shocked back into the role of Victim, when *(A)* returns to the familiar role of Persecutor. And so on.

If any of this sounds familiar, then you're unnecessarily involved with someone with a penchant for drama. We're all capable of creating Drama Triangles, some of us are more prone than others. Thanks to digital communications, we don't even need physical contact. A simple social media post could embody one of Karpman's personas — inviting a global audience to interact and play in a triangular sandbox of inevitable misery.

A classic example of this would be when *Individual (A)* writes another one of many posts about how hard their life is: "Why does the Universe always shit on me?!" they ask (Victim). Despite awareness of the frequency of such posts by *(A)*, *Individual (B)* offers their advice (Rescuer). Two things can happen next:

1. *(A)* now has *(B)* on the hook. The invisible invitation sent and blindly received reads, "There's a pity party and you're invited. Please come, bring your own drinks and snacks. P.S. Nobody

loves me".

2. *(A)* mows *(B)* down with a metaphorical machine gun, saying something along the lines of, "I don't need your advice, thanks!" Or, "Easier said than done, though, isn't it!".

We all know a pity-party planner or two. Of course, at times like this, we must discern the Victims with no desire to change from someone making a genuine cry for help. Beware of the difference between rescuing and enabling. The latter can utilise a hands-off approach. Plant the seeds for them, but draw the line at watering the garden.

Utilising this model will help you evaluate your drama-intense relationship transactions and the connection between your personal responsibility and conflict power dynamics. It also highlights our destructive and shifting roles in moments of conflict. Perhaps stating the obvious, none of these roles cultivates healthy relationships. They're part of a toxic dynamic that's commonplace in our interactions. Drama allures us because it offers control of another — either invited or uninvited. Ego likes control for safety's sake and to reinforce one's sense of identity. Desirable as such transactions may be, they massively drain our life force and mental health; hence, they're perhaps best described as energetic vampirism.

So what to do? Get out of there. Wherever the exchange is, with whomever, regarding whatever, it matters not. *Get out.* That is to say: assuming you're 100 per cent confident it's not your own conditioning that's triggering intolerance. If you see a way, invite the opposing individual to step out too, though to do so, they must agree to leave their assumed role behind as you do. From there, remember Dr Berne's model: invite an Adult-to-Adult exchange. Watch out for their Child state coming into play. Be mindful of banana skins that would have you lose your Adult footing.

My suggestion that you surgically remove another from your life might seem contrary to the themes of love and empathy conveyed throughout this book. However, consider the wholly pragmatic notion that we all exist on a broad spectrum of emotional maturity. Some people might be atavistic compared to others and thus simply do not have our best interests at heart. Depending on the circumstances, pruning people can be an incredible demonstration of self-love. Only you can know if such action is necessary, but you must dive deep for the answer. At the very least, the practical application of the Drama Triangle allows us to evaluate our relationships more objectively and formulate an action plan.

Before my addiction recovery and healing process, I regularly played Persecutor or Victim, wielding a hefty and well-tended dramatic portfolio, wreaking havoc for any well-meaning individual who made efforts to rescue me. Pre- and post-recovery, I loved to play the Rescuer — which hilariously almost always resulted in me becoming a Victim. Hence nowadays, I avoid drama like a Wuhan research facility.

Consider your current relationships. Who's radiating, and who's absorbing? Who deliberately or unknowingly leaves you feeling drained after your interactions, and do you want that to change? I've left the following two pages blank. Write a list on one, draw triangles on the other, and observe your dynamics. From there, you can invite offenders to discuss your observations (how these people make you feel). You can prepare to transform the dynamic the next time you transact or simply get busy pruning. Choices.

People in my life regularly inviting drama

My current Drama Triangles

Despite your best efforts, certain relationships will never improve. In that case, the next time you're in a Drama Triangle with a repeat offender, hold up your hands, stop them in their tracks. Make a loud "beep-beep" noise and begin reversing like a truck. This is you giving notice that, for the sake of your own mental health, you're setting healthy boundaries. You can explain why later if you think they'll listen, but try not to expel much more energy in that process. Removing yourself from the equation is the best way to avoid being pinned and pummelled in the far-from-fun Drama Triangle arena. And, of course, the beeping is optional. You might feel this approach to be brutal. Don't mix a lack of compassion with setting healthy boundaries that protect you from emotional harm and unhappiness. This is a critical exercise in self-love.

It all boils down to what you want from your relationships and understanding their profound effect on your happiness. Which would you prefer? A shorter list of close contacts who treat you equally, respect and value you, with no judgement or unreasonable demands on your time and energy? Or a long list who thrive on dragging you into their energetically draining dramas whenever opportunity knocks?

(Beep-beep…)

CHAPTER FORTY-TWO

Rumi's Three Gates

Words have the power to destroy
or heal. When words are both
true and kind, they can change
our world.

— Buddha

While the old adage about sticks and stones is wonderfully Zen, words can and often do hurt us. Words can lift our spirits or smash us on the rocks; leave us hanging from a cliff or drowning in an ocean of sorrow. Even though what others think of us really is none of our business, words can be laser-guided missiles for the heart.

Words are magical; it's "spelling" for a reason. Thanks to the dark miracle of the smartphone, we can send intense love or hatred directly to someone's pocket, or even their bedside to make a morning or ruin a night. All too often, without properly engaging our awareness, we say something we regret.

And so here is a simple utility courtesy of Rumi:

> "Before we speak, let our words
> pass through three gates:
> At the first gate, ask yourself, 'Is it
> true?'
> At the second gate, ask, 'Is it nec-
> essary?'
> At the third gate, ask, 'Is it kind?'"

This wisdom applies to words and thoughts alike. Better it should apply to the latter since, with such use, we could avoid ever thinking ill. *Right Speech, Right Thought.*

Words. We must be mindful of their might. Many a harsh word are avoided when Rumi's wisdom is practically applied. Once through those gates, there's no taking them back. Kindness costs nothing, yet it's paradoxically priceless. Everyone you meet fights a battle you know nothing about, yet your words can transform their day.

CHAPTER FORTY-THREE

The Beauty of Boundaries

"No" is a complete sentence.
— Megan LeBoutillier

I'll keep this brief.

Most of the time, most of us try to be nice. So we say "yes" to people. Some of the time, some of the people exploit this and they take from us. "Give them an inch, and they'll take a mile, Martin", my mum used to say. That's some ancient wisdom right there. So, consciously, this is bullying; unconsciously, it's self-centred ignorance. Either way, the onus to change this arrangement lies solely with us.

What's missing? Healthy boundaries. Why are they important? Failure to exercise boundaries invites folks to mistreat us, leaving us feeling used and questioning our worth. Without boundaries, we become victims who might wind up feeling helpless, fearing rejection, or seeking approval through people-pleasing, which can harm our mental health. It compromises our values and may lead to a profound sense of personal uncertainty, enhancing low self-esteem. Perhaps, thanks to our early childhood development, we're already prone to these traits. Maybe they're learned behaviours from parents, or they result from trauma. Regardless, they make us a magnet for Boundary-Riders. And we're destined for a life filled with exchanges like this until someone breaks the cycle and fucks off.

Boundary-Riders possess a brazen ability to ride roughshod

over another's feelings and wishes. Often, their behaviour is so fla-
grant that it would be funny if it didn't result in a Persecutor to
Victim dynamic. They simply cannot help themselves. They'll use
you as a stool if you stay on your hands and knees long enough.
They behave like this for many reasons we should not judge, and
their psychology isn't pertinent now. This chapter concerns taking
charge of such situations and becoming aware of the perpetrators.
The result will be that you can step into your sovereignty and push
back firmly against those who would take from you.

When we say "yes" to everyone, we're also saying "no" to ourselves and likely to something we would prefer — something more
important to us. So here's the most straightforward utility I have to
offer: learn how to say "no". Repeat after me:

"No, I don't have time to do this".
"No, I don't want to do that".
"Dude, I already told you, 'no'".
"Which part of 'no' did you not get?"

And so on.

It took me an extraordinarily long time to discover the power
of "no". Honestly, this superpower changes the game. You don't
even have to provide mitigation! No need to back it up with a
"because", or an "I would, but..." Just say "no". Remember, inches
and miles. *Give them nothing.* It may not feel like it at the time, but
in setting healthy boundaries, we're actually helping other people
evolve in their own healing journey. Everyone feels more comfortable when they know the boundaries with which they have to
operate, whether their own or others. So get used to seeing your
boundaries as a gift to others.

It takes some practice, and there are nuances to its use, but in simple terms: you either want to do a thing or you don't. I'm assuming you've got a good heart and good intentions, so it's not like you're inherently disinterested in helping people. So if you don't want to — or perhaps cannot — do a thing, tell them straight: "Nope, sorry, no".

Saying "no" to strangers is easy because they'll take it as your first answer most of the time. It's the friends, family, and co-workers who push boundaries; they'll need telling a few times in a few ways before you'll notice the shift in dynamic. But boy oh boy, you feel lighter and freer when that shift takes place. And so you should. Setting healthy boundaries cuts toxic energetic ties. It draws a line in the sand. And there's a sign by your handiwork. It says, "Respectfully and with all the love in the world, don't fuck with this line". With boundaries, you're setting out your stall to define who you are and who you most certainly are not. Some of you might think, "I dare not do this", or "*X* would be unhappy with me if I did that". Whose contentment is more important? Whose mental health takes a jab or a kick each time we bow to the pressure of others?

Setting boundaries is a healthy expression of authenticity. Boundaries are brilliant. They're beautiful. By their nature, they're yours. And so the only person qualified to design and execute them is you. Only you can answer this stuff because it's your happiness — your mental health. It's your family, colleagues, and friends who need to hear and feel your resounding "no".

CHAPTER FORTY-FOUR

Mea Culpa

**Never ruin an apology
with an excuse.**
— Benjamin Franklin

After a disagreement where we're aware or not that our actions or words caused harm, we have a choice: double down, shuffle off, or bow in humility. Emotional latency and hubris are typical drivers behind our failure to apologise. Relationships flourish or flounder based on how, if at all, we accept responsibility. And so we must learn how to say *sorry*.

An apology's immediacy is not as crucial as its sincerity. Thus, repeat after me:

> "I've had time to consider our
> exchange.
> I said some things I regret.
> I respect your truth.
> I realise I was wrong.
> I want you always to feel heard.
> I want to make amends.
> I love you.
> I'm sorry".

With the folks you really love — the ones whose death will undoubtedly break you — tell them this, or a variation, now. Put this book down, seek them out, and tell them right now. Because in ten minutes, they might be dead. And speaking from personal experience, you don't want that kind of regret churning inside you.

For some of us, such vulnerable expression is like a walk in the park, while others would rather eat a shoe, thus making a meal of apologising. However, a sign of emotional maturity is accepting fault without the need to score points. Moreover, offering to make things right is to lay ourselves bare and reopen what was closed or perhaps even slammed shut. Therefore, an apology devoid of mitigation while loaded with sincerity will go a long way. It is a reflection of one's real-time awareness and self-realisation.

Whether or not your apology is accepted has no bearing on your obligation to provide one, and real growth starts when you own your shit. Besides, once you become accustomed to delivering heartfelt apologies, there's a cathartic alchemy that leaves all parties feeling rather warm and fuzzy. Then, along the way, the harmony you create renders less need for apologies at all.

CHAPTER FORTY-FIVE

Surrender

*Doing nothing often leads
to the very best of something.*
— Winnie the Pooh

What do you feel when you see or hear people using the expression "Surrender to the flow"? Some consider this advice sage, while others think it an empty and overused cliché. As it goes, emptiness is vital to this powerful life advice. We talked about surrender early on, but in this chapter, I'd like to dive deeper into its significance. On the journey to finding long-lasting happiness, we do well to interrogate this alleged flippant guidance to fully understand how crucial the art of surrender is to maintaining balance and peace in our ever-increasing chaotic world.

William Earnest Henley wrote this stunning and poignant poem, to which many can relate and which has become a mantra of sorts for those determined not to fall foul of life's obstacles:

Invictus
Out of the night that covers me,
Black as the pit from pole to pole,
I thank whatever gods may be
For my unconquerable soul.
In the fell clutch of circumstance,
I have not winced nor cried aloud.
Under the bludgeonings of chance,

My head is bloody but unbowed.
Beyond this place of wrath and
tears
Looms but the horror of the shade,
And yet the menace of the years
Finds and shall find me unafraid.
It matters not how strait the gate,
How charged with punishments
the scroll,
I am the master of my fate,
I am the captain of my soul.

Rousing words, indeed. Henley's poem once resonated powerfully with my conflict-addicted approach to living — my somewhat perverse enjoyment of the "hustle". Life is hard. So, battling through it, regardless of the "bludgeoning", naturally instils a sense of pride. I once saw all adversity as a challenge, and thus Invictus reminded me of our incredible capacity for gumption and tenacity. However, what results from "hustle and grind" are not always what we have in mind. There's a fine line between resilience and belligerence, and forcing situations causes friction, which in turn can cause pressure, often resulting in stress.

Many coaches, mentors, and business leaders use the language of "the hustle". Yet, few bother to explain that hustling and grinding can crush your physical and mental health like a hammer meeting a peanut. Any entrepreneur worth listening to will tell you that self-care and mindfulness are equally crucial to achieving so-called "success". I'm not a millionaire, nor am I interested in coaching anyone. Not that there's anything wrong with coaching. We all need mentors we can trust. I do know a thing or two about burnout, though, and of the transformational power of surrendering.

Wu Wei means "inexertion", "effortless action", or "inaction". It's "non-doing" or "doing nothing". This ancient Chinese philosophy emerged from Confucianism, adopted by Taoism. Early on, it was used in reference to government and an emperor's behaviour, depicting a condition of personal harmony, free-flowing and spontaneous behaviour, devoid of conflict. More generally, Wu Wei signifies a state of mind.

The curious thing about this ancient wisdom is that there is no thing to do to achieve Wu Wei other than letting go. It's in the *not* doing and the *being* where the mastery happens. There is no singular verb for *letting go* in the Wu Wei. One must simply be.

As the Tao Te Ching advises, "The Way never acts, yet nothing is left undone". So, far from suggesting we sit around and do nothing to the point of laziness, we're invited to maintain peace and optimal efficiency, no matter how feverishly immersed we are in a task, thought, or situation. Is this surrender? Yes and no. Hence the paradox. In Wu Wei, we're in flow, or "in the zone", as they say. So Wu Wei is to be present and practise a one-pointed focus. However, the principle also dictates that one should live spontaneously, surrendering to the natural flow of the Tao. And in doing so, one does not "go against the grain" nor nature's order or rhythm.

Michael Singer wrote an excellent book called *The Surrender Experiment*, which greatly inspired me to fall into the arms of surrender and further explore its alchemy. Singer's wisdom, which I thoroughly recommend you examine further, invites us to mind the subtle possibilities presented by events and people in our proximity. We must observe opportunities, no matter how convoluted they first may appear. And we surrender to them, regardless of our personal preferences. This counter-intuitive approach often results in something quite magical. We cease to fight a situation; instead, we flow with it. "Be like water making its way through the cracks", Bruce Lee said. "Do not be assertive, but adjust to the object, and you shall find a way around or through it. If nothing within you stays rigid, outward things will disclose themselves". He knew a thing or three, did Bruce Lee.

Surrendering, therefore, has nothing and everything to do with doing nothing — and everything to do with acceptance. Because when we accept a thing, we let go — we cease to "cling", as the Buddhists might say. And in this freeing act, tension slackens, and anxiety shows signs of relief. We shall no longer suffer when we learn how not to force a thing, not go against the grain, nor fight with the natural order of events. Now then, this line of thinking should not be confused with being downtrodden or adopting the role of victim or sloth. One must fight for what's right, but then one must also make adequate self-inquiry as to who (or what) is defining what's "right", and what will the fighting cost? Furthermore, a great many fights are best won by walking away.

One can have and know nothing, yet be the happiest person in the world. You cannot honestly know the catharsis this philosophy provides without putting it into practice. Suffice it to say that I was once a prolific fighter — standing up against so-called perpetrators, righting any wrongs that Monkey would blindly identify as wholly necessary. But when I learned of the not-so-subtle nuances that ride along with our *fight, flight,* or *freeze* modes, it became abundantly clear that our subconscious application of these preventative, defensive, and survivalist egoic facets often do us more harm than good. These traits are, after all, our most primordial drivers — designed to keep us physically safe and sound — *alive.* Though they're not always helpful when inappropriately applied to social, personal, or professional situations.

It's not other people or events that cause friction; it's our mind, troubling itself with typically human concerns. Attachment, expectancy, judgement, impatience, intolerance, greed, and more. Going against the grain causes tension. This manifests as anxiety, worry, sleeplessness, short tempers, substance abuse, and mistreatment of our bodies and minds. Not to mention those unfortunate enough to be nearby.

Acceptance is mastery of the highest order. It is not necessarily about succumbing to defeat; rather, exercising pure awareness to observe discord in one's life journey. Mindfully plot a new course of avoidance by simply flowing through or past whatever phenomenon stands before you. Far from being subservient, if you can swipe Monkey and then switch directions, your surrender to the torrent might offer the precious time needed to take stock.

If a thing is out of your hands, then it deserves to be out of your mind too. This is acceptance. It takes practice, and, as with many mental obstacles, breath and meditation are transformational utilities one can use as resolution. I know, right? Who would've thought the power to overcome the crushing weight of anxiety could be uncovered by simply slowing down and emptying our minds? By doing nothing.

Box Breaths

Come into a comfortable seat, spine straight.
Perhaps close your eyes.
Relax your jaw.
Relax your neck and shoulders.
Soften your belly.

Inhale.
Exhale for four, three, two, one.
Hold your lungs empty for one, two, three, four.

Inhale for one, two, three, four.
Gently hold your full lungs for one, two, three, four.
Exhale for four, three, two, one.

Repeat until Zen.

CHAPTER FORTY-SIX

Pure Awareness

**What is necessary to change
a person is to change his
awareness of himself.**
— Abraham Maslow

Many alcoholics don't know they're alcoholics — especially if they're high-functioning. They drink every day, sure, but hard drinking quickly creates tolerance. In the US, 20 per cent of alcoholics are high-functioning, meaning they hold down a job and relationships while drinking heavily — publicly and privately. So while chaos may occur in the dark or behind closed doors, the drinker and their friends and family — used to the heavy drinking — are often apathetic. Alcoholics drink to get drunk because being drunk does something for them that they believe cannot be done sober. Sometimes it makes them happy; every time, it helps them forget whatever fear or traumatic memories their addiction seeks to eradicate.

People with narcissistic personality disorder do not see their broken hearts and minds seeking solace through environmental control. Unaware of their exaggerated sense of self-importance, they use complex forms of manipulation, often employing rage as a tool to rule, confused about their private feelings of low self-worth and shame. The emotionally immature can bring a boatload of bad weather. They unconsciously sneeze negative energy, clueless of its effect on others. Hapless witnesses to their mood swings, ego leads them from one Drama Triangle to the next, with almost no ability to be present. Each and every time, they sidestep culpability, abrogate responsibility, firing the finger of blame like an AR15.

The world is full of people doing their best yet falling short of being able to love themselves or others. They are unaware that their thoughts, words, and deeds cause substantial and sometimes irreparable harm. And they will not be told — not without another bust-up or drama. People like this are a total pain. They're self-centred, arrogant, self-destructive, and not deserving our energy, attention, or love. Right? I used to think that way. Perhaps more amusingly, all the traits I've just mentioned once belonged to me. And so I can never judge another's mental illness. Observe it, though, I may.

My lack of awareness was probably more of an issue due to the extremity of my behaviour. I recycled friends and business associates while romping wildly from woman to woman like a chimp on a monkey bar. One minute I walked the line; the next, I snorted it. Other times, I leapt off it in whichever direction the wind would take me. Such erratic behaviour was typical and concealed my true nature from me and everyone else. I held down a successful career and was highly sociable and popular. Though as the years ground on, a mist began to clear.

So what happened? As Samuel L. Jackson's character in *Pulp Fiction*[1] says, "I had what alcoholics refer to as a moment of clarity". My moment of awareness wasn't one, but a string of them. Suddenly I saw that, despite my best efforts to blame the world for my problems, the common denominator amidst all the blood, shit, and tears was me.

What? Likeable, fun-loving me? The generous, popular, and ever so charming me is co-responsible for all my misfortune? How could this

1 *The feature film, Pulp Fiction, written by Quentin Tarantino.*

be?

Bless my cotton socks. Yes, Martin, it's you. It's always been you. And sure, your perverse behaviour has been learned through familial trauma and social conditioning, so there's no doubt you were a victim. However, it is *your* responsibility to take stock, unlearn, seek forgiveness, and learn to love. You must take yourself back to life school, and start again. Not everyone's prepared to do that, though, are they?

We're not all emotional extremists; thus, "rock-bottom" moments are only sometimes needed to launchpad personal change. The rest are blessed with only mild neuroses with which to contend. However, a common trait amongst the masses is a distinct lack of self-awareness. *Awareness* is one of the four components to maintaining happiness. So work on it, we must.

Just as one can awaken from a nightmare, one can pull oneself from unconscious thoughts and deeds. *Remember the Noble Eightfold Path.*

Words like *mindfulness, awareness,* and *awakening* all refer to conditions of consciousness. They're lofty by nature, but somewhat ironically, the premise is mindbogglingly simple. Awareness provides clarity. With 6,000 daily thoughts ping-ponging around the inside of our heads, it's no wonder awareness can be a challenge. The game is to be mindful of succumbing to a full mind. Awakening is at the core of all meditation practices. We must ladle consciousness from our cerebral soup, draining the mental broth until something transcendental occurs. In this conscious act, we pave a new emotional and spiritual path, awakening our potential and slowly uncovering capabilities we did not know existed.

To master our application of awareness in the moment, one must have successfully tackled the early stages of the Anatomy of

Happy. You've already done the Shadow Work of self-realisation; a welcome moment of clarity brought you to your knees and helped you own and unlearn your previous bullshit. You've forgiven yourself and thus uncovered the gift you give to yourself when you forgive others.

The byproduct of your trauma rewarded you with self-love; you now see the infinite nature of that gift. And with the help of utilities to connect and better understand another's truth, you have all the tools you need to deftly apply awareness whenever and wherever necessary. What more could one wish for? The ability to be aware that you are aware. And the prize of unfettered peace.

CHAPTER FORTY-SEVEN

The Gift of Presence

The present moment is filled
with joy and happiness. If you are
attentive, you will see it.
— Thich Nhat Hanh

Regarding death, Eastern philosophers are perhaps more interested in the benefits of living presently than in the afterlife. For people in the East, living well removes karma, thus reducing the likelihood of reincarnation; ascension could be just one lifetime away. Stoics share these ideals, with much wisdom to imbibe on how to live wisely, justly, courageously, and in moderation. The ancient Stoics, however, are agnostic — indifferent of an afterlife apparently out of our control.

Similarly, with Buddhism and Taoism, there is rich wisdom for agnostics, Omnists, and new-age spiritualists. It is, therefore, not uncommon for mindfulness practitioners to utilise a wide selection of techniques and philosophies. You need only look at meditation apps like *Headspace*[1] and *Calm* to experience a contemporised spin on ancient teachings.

Ultimately, a Universal and crucial goal for those adopting these values is to live a "meaningful life". The invitation is to develop and exercise moral and social obligations while constantly minding one's ability to live in the present moment. Furthermore, to consider our place in and contribution to the broader system of humanity.

1 *Founded by Andy Puddicombe, a former Buddhist monk.*

So what does living in the present mean?

Mindfulness is learning to observe oneself from a higher seat of consciousness. More simply, it's an invitation to move, speak, think, and act mindfully. To step back from the canvas to better see the painting. To take regular pauses to remind ourselves that the *now* is all, while past and future do not exist. In this practice, we affirm that the only thing we can do to keep check of our feelings is to centre, do our best to observe — without judgement — whatever is happening in and around us. This simple act places us centrally within the now — the present moment. In his book *The Power of Now,* Eckhart Tolle has written wise words of inspiration on this subject, which I exuberantly encourage you to read if you haven't already.

Practising presence eventually results in the cessation of expectations of any kind. You're neither focusing on success (wealth, Heaven, ascension) nor failure (poverty, Purgatory, Hell, or reincarnation). More simply, your attention and energy are directed towards observance, gratitude, and living fully because, well, it's just the best way to live. The Greek philosopher Epicurus once said: "The art of living well and dying well are one". Just as life and death are twin flames, we prepare ourselves for a beautiful death by mastering the art of living. Thus, the secret to the art of dying begins and ends in a life well-lived.

Once we've developed the ability to "switch" presence on, we don't stop; we have to work at it daily, training the mind and body with self-awareness, breath, and meditation. Hence, shifting to a state of presence is a lifelong practice, and now more than ever, Earth School's design distracts us from training at every sugar-coated, oil-saturated, substance-stuffed, and pixelated turn. Being present in the present day guarantees an interstellar gold star for all active participants, from whichever galactic federation leaders are watching us play the barmy game of life on Earth. So kudos to anyone willing to try.

Courage is fear's arch-nemesis. Both reside in us all. I imagine them socialising when they're not at war. Constant companions locked within the complex maze of our psyche. It's as normal for us to fear as to have courage. Though the latter is more challenging to find thanks to ego's role as our internal head of counter-terrorism, counter-espionage, and every other possible assumed preemptive and protective role. All the same, courage is there — ready and waiting to step up to the plate and face down fear with a breath-filled chest and furrowed brow.

The British Army's Yorkshire Regiment motto is one close to my heart — not to celebrate war or violence, but courage. "Fortune favours the bold", it says. Fortune can be many things more than financial success, so perhaps, paradoxically, I see fortune to mean peace. And what of the bold? I do not see loud or brash. Bold, to me, is brave. Ergo, peace favours the brave.

Fear and anxiety socialise too. They play squash twice a week and watch football together on Saturdays. So when one hogs the spotlight, seeking to be the primary voice in your head, the other stands backstage. Glibly, it prepares a complementary set that will knock courage right out of your mind and into the cheap seats where ego believes peace belongs. Be under no illusion; fear and anxiety are merely Monkey in drag, and knowing this means you can master them both. Whichever headlines the gig, their game seeks to ensure we find no peace at all. They clog our minds with noise, our breath shallows, and butterflies play snare drum solos in the depths of our bellies. How on earth can we stop such a force? Two words: breath and meditation.

The first and simplest thing to do when anxiety symptoms arise is to stop what you're doing. Close your eyes. Listen to the sounds around you before tuning into the rise and fall of your chest. Relax your belly; breathe slowly and deeply through your nose, filling your lungs almost to capacity. Hold, then through your open mouth, let out a long, loud sigh. Pause and repeat twice before allowing your breath to return to normal. Continue to observe the rise and fall of your chest.

You just meditated. You just took Monkey's hands off the wheel, and regardless of whether it was one breath or ten, with presence, you made space for peace.

You know what made me write this section? I was in the bath, thinking about this book, two documentaries I want to make, and my lacking funds and followers to support it all. *When will I find the time to finish this book? How will it be published and promoted? Will anyone buy it? Will anyone enjoy it?! Argh!*

I suddenly realised that I wasn't feeling great thanks to this thinking. So I tuned into myself, rose above the increasing cacophony, and observed Monkey in a speed boat, erratically tearing up the peaceful canal I'd been idly floating along just 30 minutes earlier. Monkey doesn't do presence. Not the kind of presence we need to cultivate peace. The closest Monkey comes to being present is during disaster aversion or planning our next meal. We need him for that, but not for peace. Certainly not for peace.

While this book demands it, my quantification of the power of presence will fall short despite my best efforts. Learning to attain and maintain the ability to be fully present is the third of four principal components to meaningful happiness. As I've made clear, while there are numerous ways to create instant presence, breath and meditation are two primary weapons at your disposal. We'll talk a little more about these next.

CHAPTER FORTY-EIGHT

Weapons of Mass Tranquillification

**The quieter the mind,
the louder the soul.**
— Matshona Dhliwayo

Plant medicine can permanently heal trauma and its symptoms, but as we've discussed, there is no magic bullet to long-lasting happiness. Such a mindset relies on hacks and quick fixes, not dissimilar to the reliance on material things to mask and distract us from our inherent feelings of dissatisfaction. You need it to work? You do the work.

Meaningful neurogenesis comes with applied practices, diet changes, around eight hours of sleep, and regular exercise. To maintain peace, we must be willing to work every day. In my case, meditation and breathwork help me maintain inner tranquillity, gratitude, love, and composure. These are my daily practices — *my tools* to regulate my emotions. The more you practise these methodologies, the easier things become because, through these techniques, we retrain our brains and bodies. Never forget that our brains will likely require much reconditioning unless we've been lucky enough to learn mindfulness practices from a young age. We must also beware of not becoming frustrated when Monkey gets a hold of the wheel. The point of regular practice is to help us quickly observe when our egos step in, take appropriate action, own our mistakes or triggered responses, and remedy the course within a relatively short time. This newfound response to our interactions shows vulnerability while accepting full responsibility for our words or actions. It's reprogramming.

Throughout this book, I've alluded to two core ideas. Firstly, we can all choose to change at any time; there's no such thing as "too late". Secondly, raising one's consciousness is a critical life skill for anyone keen to grow and cultivate healthy interactions. Far from being a lofty or "spiritual" practice, the latter ability trains us to pause in any event and observe our thoughts or deeds — to real-time tranquillify ourselves and those around us. Think about the Transactional Analysis utilities, both requiring awareness and presence (raised consciousness) to be actionable.

So how does one battle the worldly and mental noise so prevalent in everyday life? There are, of course, many ways. For this chapter, I wish to focus on those available to us free of charge, at a moment's notice and requiring nothing but self-love and the combined power of awareness and presence. Namely, breathing, meditating, and sonic healing.

How to Breathe

On breathwork, my wonderful friend, Jonny, once joked: "How the fuck can anyone teach me how to breathe when I've been doing it all my life?" Jonny is also bemused by my love for coconut water. Well, he had a point. About breathing, I mean. They're his lungs, after all. However, whether we accept it or not, most of us don't breathe properly simply because we're under constant pressure in this day and age.

We breathe in and out about 22,000 times a day, yet we constantly use shallow or what's known as *chest breathing*, almost always unaware we're not engaging our diaphragm to breathe. Conscious breathing allows quick physical and mental pause, which reduces our stress levels while enabling us to rise up from the sea of thoughts and actions which unknowingly drown any chance of peace or clarity. Diaphragmatic breathing uses long, slow, and full belly breaths to relax the nervous system. When we use this method or any of the myriad breathwork techniques, we activate the breath to "check in", calming the nervous system. And in doing so, we can check out — in an entirely healthy way.

Try it now.

Relax your face, jaw, and shoulders. Take a slow, deep, fulfilling in-breath through your nose for five seconds, allowing your belly to push out. Hold your breath for the same period with your lungs full, then slowly release it until empty. Close your eyes and do it again. Your exhale is where the magic happens, where you have the most control. That's breathwork.

Yogis and masters worldwide have been practising this art daily since the dawn of humanity. Regardless of culture, geography, or era, breathwork is the common practice of all these masters. As Eckhart Tolle says: "One conscious breath is a meditation". The benefits of breathwork are innumerable, from increasing your respiratory function to balancing your blood pressure. Breathing properly improves your immune system, allowing the body's release of stress hormones. Conscious, diaphragmatic breathing also stimulates your vagus nerve. This, in turn, reduces anxiety while increasing the parasympathetic nervous system response, thus instantly calming you down. Have you ever seen someone offer a paper bag to a hyperventilator? Well, it's like that, but prevents hyperventilation and anxiety through self-regulation. Hence, you can use it for prevention and reaction. While as old as time, breathwork has seen a massive renaissance thanks to pioneers like Wim Hof and James Nestor. Nestor's book *Breath:*

The New Science of a Lost Art is an excellent guide connecting the ancient science of breathing with a newfound understanding of its transformative physiological effects.

When you realise the long list of improvements introduced by learning how to breathe, you'll never go back to *fight-or-flight* chest breathing again. Or rather, as soon as you realise you're doing it, you'll be able to modulate it immediately. So, regular breathwork offers access to inner tranquillity and a broad selection of benefits that improve the health of numerous systems and internal organs.

How Not to Think

The Tibetans say: "If you take care of the minutes, the years will take care of themselves". This beautifully simple observation of the *Law of Little Things* reminds us of the long-term benefits of being mindful and present. Conversely, a full mind busies us with past regrets or worries over futures that might never come. This chaotic mental preoccupation causes a great deal of unrest, poor health, hindering our ability to focus. Hence, with practice, meditation demonstrates we can simultaneously feel unwelcome emotions alongside deep inner peace.

So how does one master one's thoughts when the noise becomes too much to bear? By now, you've likely noticed this book is littered with invitations to pause and check in with yourself. With any luck, some of them resonated, and you were able, even if for a short time, to meditate. Perhaps they served as welcome aids to those who find it challenging to quieten the mind. That's okay; it's perfectly normal — the struggle is real. Gurdjieff said: "If you're meditating and the devil comes, make the devil meditate", for this very reason. I remember the first time I tried to meditate. I was in the bath, straining for such a long time, eventually becoming immensely angry with myself because I couldn't *not* think. It was the opposite of relaxing.

Four monks agreed to meditate together in silence for two weeks. By nightfall of the first day, the candle flickered and went out. The first monk said: "Oh, the candle went out!" The second said: "Aren't we meant to remain silent?" The third said, "Why must you two break the silence?" Laughing, the fourth monk declared: "I'm the only one who didn't speak!"

Our blessed monks experienced common obstacles to meditation. Some of us are distracted by sights or sounds. Others worry about perceived rules. Some become angry, as I did in the bath, with their inability to settle in silence. As for the fourth monk's message: suddenly impressed with oneself having attained stillness, one's meditation is derailed by ego.

The trick to meditation is that there is no trick. Nor is there anything to do. Though in the business of doing nothing, many are frustrated. Now that sucks for several reasons — the main one being that practising daily meditation is a platinum-plated tool to access a higher seat of consciousness and live well.

Another wonderful thing is that once you've mastered the basics, you can check out of the madness and into pure, blissful peace at a minute's notice, all thanks to your breath. Approach meditation with no expectations whatsoever. Try not to think about not thinking. It's about *being* rather than doing.

There are countless types and styles of meditation — all valid and activated for different purposes. But the most fundamental reason is to free yourself from chaotic and anxious thoughts. The easiest way to begin that process is to find a quiet place and focus solely on your breath. As you relax your body, observe the breath as it enters and leaves your lungs. Witness the space between breaths. Witness the space between the space. Then, after a couple more breaths, witness the triple-whammy space between the space between the space. Whatever you witness during meditation, notice it, but don't get involved.

Breathe, observe, repeat. Do all of this without judgement or internal commentary. If you're distracted, pay it no mind, there's always the next breath or the one after that. Now, you're meditating, even if you manage this just once. Anything else is a bonus; everything else is practice. More learning and practising the art of nothing.

Another technique is to use mantras. Mantras originated from the Buddhists and Hindus. These prayers, used to still the mind or connect with a higher power, are as old as humanity. The (often) short, repeated verses come in many languages and forms. They affirm our hopes, dreams, and devotion to the divine. More than that: some believe mantras are spells, with specific words and melodies acting as inter-dimensional portals. Others think that when conveyed with an open heart and the right intention, we send resonance out into the Unified Field, calling energy in through the power of vibration. I know all of the above to be accurate. Focusing on your breath and the mantra's repetition cultivates transcendence and peace.

To suggest that one cannot or does not have time to meditate might be a convenient truth, but it's not mine. Everyone can and should meditate daily, because the benefits are truly transformative. It will bring you peace, rewire your brain, calm your nervous system, energise you, and extend your life. Ultimately, meditation provides a profound and constantly available utility enabling you to step out of your way and become the observer of your body, thoughts, words, and actions. And when you get better at it, you don't even need silence. All you need is awareness and breath.

During my podcast interview with the meditating farmer, John Butler, I recited his poem about meditation, which I'd like to share:

Clouds

Unmistakably — up in the sky,
The sun is obscured when clouds pass by;
With this natural fact, I'll endeavour to show
How problems of life can diminish and go.
For problems arise when we take by mistake,
Changing scenes for our permanent state.
Within each of us shines a similar sun
Dependant on nothing, beholden to none.
In all things sufficient, with freedom and bliss,
It's there from our birth, and it's what a man is.
Now that you may query, but look, and you'll find
How your sun gets hidden by clouds of the mind.

Such beautiful lines and an apt description of the illusory power of impermanent thoughts. I recommend you read more of John's work and check out his *Spiritual Unfoldment* YouTube channel. His voice and words are medicine for the mind.

Buddha was once asked: "What have you gained from meditation?" He replied: "*Nothing!* However, let me tell you what I have lost: anger, anxiety, depression, insecurity, and fear of old age and death".

Then he dropped the mic.

We've spoken much of our involuntary subservience to emotions. The key to their control lies in our lungs. Through the utility of meditation, we master our feelings, creating space for consciousness to further expand. The ability to meditate is inherent within us all but involves learning to observe arising thoughts while avoiding being caught up in them. Eventually, unnoticed, the clouds will pass by, and the sky empties of colour and sound. Here, we find peace and divine connection. That's meditating.

Observe your feelings come and go, rise above the flurry of thoughts, and notice when your old traits are triggered in new situations. These are all benefits of regular meditation. They're proof of emotional development through mindfulness. The sweet spot where self-awareness meets presence for a picnic in the park.

How to Tune in

The sounds we consume can profoundly affect our mental health and tranquillity. Similarly to meditation and breathwork, the science of sound healing is as old as time. It explores our integration with resonance to realign our physical and mental states. We are, after all, made of atoms comprising 99.9999999 per cent space. Thus, we are a complex arrangement of vibrations on a sub-atomic level. We are resonance, the "Om". Hence why most Sanskrit and Vedic mantras begin with "Om". Om ("Aum") is the universal sound for All That Is — the sound of love. Chanting or listening to "Om" fills us with peace and a warm and inexplicable sense of being home. And so, in this way, all frequencies can transform how we feel — calming or discombobulating. There's a rich science in what's known as isochronic and binaural beats, showing us that certain frequencies activate specific brainwave states as follows:

Delta provides access to the unconscious mind, cultivating deep sleep while also providing pain relief (0.1-4 Hz).

Theta stimulates REM sleep and deep relaxation, cultivating creativity and inner peace, enabling meditation and altered states of consciousness (4-8 Hz).

Alpha enhances relaxed focus, accelerated learning, self-introspection, and stress reduction, creating a natural flow state (8-14 Hz).

Beta makes us more alert, providing focused attention, analytical thinking, and problem-solving (14-30 Hz).

Gamma is our peak awareness wave for information processing, memory recall, and transcendental states (30-100 Hz).

If this topic piques your interest, you might also be intrigued by the science of *Cymatics*. Here, you'll witness water molecules' inexplicably geometrical and magical transformation when exposed to specific frequencies. Then, consider that the average adult human body contains between 55 and 60 per cent water. Welcome to the fascinating world of sound healing.

Of course, we don't need music for sonic healing. Step outside and find a place quiet enough where the birds, insects, or the psithurism of wind in the trees can help you blend into a state of stillness.

The incredible utility of sound is often overlooked (or under-heard). It can envelop us in peace and tranquillity, providing unimaginable healing. Using sound and vibration, we can enter deep states of altered consciousness. Most nights, I meditate, listening to specific frequencies designed to activate lucid dream states and astral travel. These tones continually offer the most luscious nights of sleep.

The mind is a motorway packed bumper-to-bumper with thoughts on their way to somewhere or nowhere. We are not our minds any more than the thoughts in our heads. However, perhaps paradoxically, those thoughts can and do consume us, grind us down, and eventually bury us. So we must learn whichever techniques work best to cultivate inner peace. We can thus step out of the illusory and often conflicting nature of existence, checking in to our true essence. This is the gateway to serenity, stillness, and silence. You'll hear the most exquisite music in this place. All you need do is listen.

CHAPTER FORTY-NINE

Your Number One Superpower

We can only be said to be alive in those moments when our hearts are conscious of our treasures.
— Thornton Wilder

What can we be grateful for when there's so much injustice, pain, and suffering? No matter where you are in the world, you face untold challenges from your past, present, or future, and often the combination of events and emotions can bring you to your knees. Sometimes, it's all just too much to bear. Earth School can be a real drag.

When I first heard people discussing "gratitude practice", I recall being irritated. It seemed like a "woo-woo" idea, rather pointless and naive. With the benefit of hindsight, however, I see that much miracle and wonder had yet to reveal itself to me. I had not suffered enough to appreciate the true beauty of life; focused as I was on the "bad", I failed to see my myriad and proximal gifts.

Evidently, there was a time I couldn't muster gratitude. People pointing loaded guns at their faces have likely lost sight of sentiments surrounding the giving of thanks. However, not a day goes by now without my grateful heart bursting with love for this incredible experience we share. I used to think life on Earth was a curse; now, I see it's a Universal gift.

What's a "Gratitude Practice"?

There are several ways to cultivate gratitude. One of the easiest things is a daily self-inquiry of three things for which you are grateful. Alternatively, tell it to someone you love. Keep a gratitude journal that you update as and when you feel genuine appreciation for something. Go outside and walk on the earth barefoot. Observe the beauty in nature, or if you live in a concrete jungle, take a hike through the streets and observe the diverse characters that pass you by.

If you're struggling to find anything for which to be grateful, get outside and move. If you can run, run. If you can walk, keep going until you've bested 8,000 steps. If you're in a wheelchair or mobility scooter, ride like the wind! And if your arms don't work, bug your carer to suit up and introduce you to some fresh air.

If nothing stimulates you, simply note that your homeostatic lungs suck air into your body without prompt — pumping life force energy around your Earth Rover. It's a veritable miracle. *Everyone* has something to be grateful for — even if it's the mere fact that you are alive. At this point, the folks suffering from depression are rolling their eyes while declaring, "I've got nothing to live for!" Yes, I've heard that one before. And so even that truth has an alternative viewpoint. If you are at rock bottom, and your life feels utterly joyless — pointless, even, and you cannot find anything worth celebrating — then change your life. Yes, you read that right. What you're not changing, you're choosing. Likely if you are feeling this low, the first thing you might wish to consider is a consumption audit.

Are you eating a lot of red or processed meat? **Factoid:** in 2015, the WHO classified both as carcinogenic for humans. What about refined grains, high-fat dairy products, sweets, excessive consumption of potatoes or butter? How's your alcohol intake? Cigarettes, weed, coke? Painkillers? Antidepressants? **Factoid:**

two common side effects of SSRIs and SNRIs (antidepressant drugs) are feeling agitated, shaky or anxious, insomnia, or even sleepy. Understating the obvious, all these side effects severely dampen one's mood. How about caffeine? What music are you listening to? What's your daily screen time? Social media usage? What are you watching on TV?

Contrastingly, how much sunlight and exercise are you getting? Fresh organic fruit and vegetables? Home-cooked foods? How much sleep do you gift yourself every night? Are you meditating? Socialising with kind, loving, healthy, and positive people? How much time do you spend in parks or in nature, sober?

Sadly, due to the enormous pressure on general practising doctors, added to financial incentives from pharmaceutical companies, such questions will only be occasionally forthcoming from your GP. So like I said: what *you're* not changing, you are choosing. Take action. It's your Earth Rover, your mental health. It's your life. And ultimately, the first and last person to help you should and will be you. *Remember, you are sovereign.*

This is Samsara; it's a playground of pain. Hell (and Heaven) on Earth. I know you've suffered terribly. You were abused as a child, or your drunken husband beats you. The accident disfigured or maimed you, you were raped, you were bullied, your whole family's dead, you accidentally killed someone, you're bankrupt, homeless, or dying. Perhaps a loved one is dying, you're going to prison, or your child recently passed. Or worse still, they fell victim to abuse. Our limits are tested by unspeakable horrors or a simple twist of fate. It is natural to be brought to one's knees.

You are not unique in your suffering, though; no one is. No matter how dark the situation, we can seek the chance to heal, learn, grow, and move on. Not like robots, devoid of emotion. We've already discussed how to embrace the pain, and we're human, after all. While suffering might not make us unique, how we rise from the skin-peeling flames can and will.

Gratitude is a superpower, a total game-changer, heart-powered and alchemic beyond understanding. Once you claw and clamber out of that dark pit you thought impossible to leave, looking back into the abyss through gleaming eyes, you will feel gratitude well inside you like you've never felt anything before. It will eclipse your fear, regret, and hopelessness. Remember that feeling; cultivate it every day — twice a day, even. And watch your life change forever.

What's There to Feel Grateful For?

How often do we focus on the things we don't have rather than the things we do? The Stoic, Seneca, once said: "Being poor is not having too little; it is wanting more". Can we be happy with less? The Minimalists would argue so, as would the Balinese workers whose smiles regularly light up my day. It's not uncommon to take things for granted; thus, it's only when we lose them that they are missed, much like a mother or an eye. A daily gratitude practice reminds us of the magic we hold in our hands and our beautiful connection with others. Tell them every chance you get. Loss can inspire gratitude — wise teacher that it is. Our challenge (should we choose to accept it) is to embrace the lessons.

So, why is gratitude so transformational? Because, through a simple choice, we can override our negative self-talking emotions and tales of woe. Instead, we fill our hearts with the warm milk and honey of loving thanks. Gratitude transforms what we have into enough. There's an alchemy to such wholehearted expressions of appreciation that's difficult to comprehend. There's a wonderful guided meditation by Dr Joe Dispenza called *Morning Meditation*, in which he says: "Now, have compassion and care, and kindness towards your beautiful self, giving thanks".

Every morning that I listen to this meditation, I am energised with gratitude and self-love. There are many such meditations available, should you seek them out.

What Am I Grateful For?

Not that you asked, but these days I'm grateful for everything. The sun on my face and the wind in the trees. The sand between my toes, my sobriety, my love, my freedom, my dad, my brothers, my nieces, and my two beautiful dogs. Thanks to the beautiful souls at Moorfields Hospital, I have two eyes to see and a healthy and active mind, ever-keen to create. Lest I forget my hands — that I might write so fervently about gratitude!

In the corners of cafes, from which I watch folks — each of them glorious expressions of consciousness, creating and experiencing amazing stories I know nothing about. Observing them, I contemplate the absolute wonder of life at Earth School, our connection to one another, and Earth's consciousness. Countless stories unfold before our eyes in this way, all incredibly interwoven with the phenomenon of love — the *Om*. Denis Waitley once said: "Happiness cannot be travelled to, owned, earned, worn, or consumed. Happiness is the spiritual experience of living every minute with love, grace, and gratitude". As we've learned through these pages, happiness is not one thing but the attainment of a delicate balance between many magical yet achievable states of mind.

My new life, the sight of boundless possibilities, and the incredible souls with whom I've come into contact have taught me how to be grateful. Their lessons, good or bad, have led me to this time and place, where I use awareness, presence, acceptance, *and* gratitude as homegrown superpowers to guide me.

CHAPTER FIFTY

The Anatomy of Happy

There should be a balance between spiritual and material progress, a balance achieved through
the principles based on love and
compassion.

— The Dalai Lama

Zen training initially discourages intellectualisation because, as Alan Watts explains, it creates a "lack of rapport between you and your life". Elaborating, he adds: "You think about things so much that you get into the state where you're eating the menu instead of dinner". Naturally, as we progress, we intellectualise. Without such, this book should not exist. How else might I share these lessons, save that we sit together in silence? Watts' observations remind us that thinking is doing, yet we are *beings*. Words and thoughts can distract and attract to the point of attachment. So you must engage in a seamless waltz of doing and being. The string quartet of awareness, presence, acceptance, and gratitude will serenade as you move with the flow.

My exploration of the deepest trenches of depression and contrasting heights of delight has convinced me that one can fol-low a method to find happiness. And wherever you are on your journey, you can hop on board to suit your level of understanding. In structuring this book, I've guided you through the stages of this process while deliberately, only subtly, drawing attention to it. Having laid the foundations, we're at the point of putting the lessons together. So it's time to circle back and provide a proper introduction to the *Anatomy of Happy.*

As you can see, there's a hill to climb. And like the classic game of *Snakes and Ladders,* there are plenty of points where one might falter and fall. But since conscious change is not a linear process, one can also skip up and around the spiralled hill of learning, using the same shortcuts.

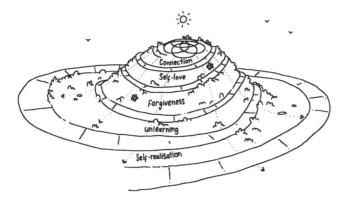

The Anatomy of Happy.

Self-Realisation

As materialism has marched across the planet, the life of the mindful mystic has been relegated to the fringes. Thus, ancient ideas and practices are perceived as whimsy and barriers to progress. Suppose we could see past the aeons of religious and social conditioning that have muddied the waters of spiritual experience. In that case, our collective consciousness can rise to new planes. It's already happening, whether you know it or not. As individuals learn and share, more of us begin to understand. This simple, beautiful idea was on Ram Dass's mind when he said: "I can do nothing for you but work on myself; you can do nothing for me but work on yourself". And so the cycle goes, and our knowledge evolves, personally and collectively. All roads lead to Rome, so to speak.

In this case, they lead back to Greece and the challenge set forth at the Temple of Apollo: "Know thyself". Since you're reading this book, perhaps you ponder, as I once did, whether there is more to life on Earth than the daily grind? If so, I invite you to take on the challenge. Conclude that it's time to take your inquiries inwards — *to the roots*. Sustainable happiness lies ahead should you choose to embark on this journey. The incredible expedition into knowing oneself is endless, yet never without reward. The deeper one dives, the wider one's inquiries, and the more layers of understanding unfold.

I am here to learn to love; that is my realisation. Such simple words hide a construct of infinite complexity. Ironically, yet deliciously, such a journey might take an entire lifetime. If I die tomorrow, then it *will* have done just that! I cannot think of a more worthwhile goal than to dedicate life to understanding, accepting, and loving ourselves. What possibilities could such exploration create for us, those around us, and those yet to cross our path? It's a gift, my friend, a vast reward offering endless wonders of bittersweet delight. Perhaps despite my best efforts, I cannot convey the gravitas of such a bright and beautiful blessing save to suggest that all you can do for me is work on yourself, and I on me, for you.

Unlearning

So open that door and begin to explore the foundations of you. There's an expansive Universe inside. Your story made you who you are. Yet contrary to popular belief, it's not over nor set to autopilot on a path you cannot alter. With every breath, we can choose to change our life's direction. Though as Hippocrates reminds us, "Before you heal someone, ask him if he is willing to give up the things that made him sick". The price of happiness requires wholesale changes as you unlearn everything you thought to be true about who you are. Stare that Monkey down, give him, her, or them a hug, and explain the new rules of engagement.

Unlearning will change your life and, with this, dominion over the circumstances of your death. And knowing that and sharing it makes my heart sing for what might lie ahead for humanity. Pure magic happens in the process — *alchemy*. You alchemise your mental processes and prioritise what's truly important. Forget possessions and status; instead, focus on the fundamental and beautiful aspects of loving and living. You may not be able to hold them in your hands, mount them on a wall or lock them in a safe, but they carry immeasurably more value. I know this because I've done it. To think that I almost checked out early and missed all the fun.

Forgiveness

Whatever the event, it's in the past and thus does not exist. You carry the emotion in body and mind, and to move on, you must forgive. Remember the word's true meaning and ask: "Who does it serve for me to hold on to this?"

A silent war wages inside us, and Monkey, in all forms, is a master strategist. She will try to convince you that you need your grudges and loathing because it makes you who you are. "What doesn't kill you makes you stronger", he'll say. "Use your hatred as fuel to move forward", they'll suggest. And so on. Hatred, anger, condemnation, and the desire to punish are not inherent but learnt.

Unlearning these emotions is like removing a millstone from one's neck. Learning to forgive, to let go — *to accept* — creates light and space in your life. Make room for miracles and wonder as you rise from the ashes of suffering that serve you no more.

We can forgive others by learning to forgive ourselves; there's magic in understanding that we're all in this together. As a wise man once said: "We're all just walking one another home".

Self-Love

Our pursuit of happiness often results in self-harm. We do untold damage to body and mind through consumption, distraction, work, internal conflict, an addiction to suffering, and the need to please others. Where is our healthy love for ourselves?

Make self-care your number one priority. Audit your behavioural traits, your internal dialogues, and the relationships where you come second place. Judge not yourself, and readily accept the gift of a daily mindfulness practice, regardless of where you are and what you're doing in the world.

Love yourself.

Connection

See that you are not alone, and in fact, through a complex energetic field, you are connected to everything, and everything is connected to you. See yourself through new eyes — get out of your own way. Use the numerous tools at your disposal to observe your interactions without attachment.

Acceptance is a golden key to mental and spiritual freedom. Realising our affinity changes the game. Learning to deeply connect with yourself and others is a truly transformative gift. Your radiance will be noticed by everyone with whom you come into contact. And those seeking light will wish to know you better. Though be mindful of to whom you give your energy. Drama seeks peace like a moth does a flame.

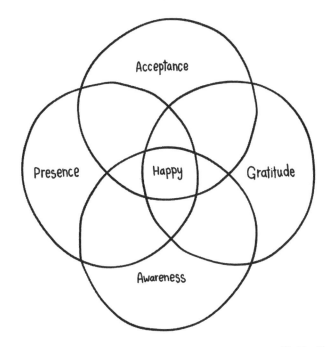

The Zen Venn.

The Den of Zen

Atop the happy hill lies the proverbial golden fleece, situated in the centre of the earnestly dubbed *Zen Venn*.

Finding happiness is a mission, but retaining it is another story altogether, and in a world of impermanence, retention is no more than an illusion. We must practise and play in the Zen Venn den. So, remember the Taoist Wu Wei of effortless action and the Buddhist's Anicca. Accepting the changeable flow of all things removes friction from our daily existence. If we've done the work of self-realisation, unlearning, forgiveness, self-love, and connection, we are well-equipped to dance naked in the exquisite garden of our creation. And so the game is no longer about fighting yourself or others, blindly flailing with fists and feet. The contest has evolved alongside us, thus drawing our focus to maintaining a balance between *acceptance, awareness, presence,* and *gratitude.*

When we open our hearts and minds, we uncover the secrets to living well. Less fretting about futures, free from the past, we enjoy the peace of a mindful and connected life. Happiness becomes the norm by blending the Zen Venn components into a daily routine. So, when the inevitable time comes, your Earth Rover hits a wall, careers off a cliff, or runs out of gas, you stand a solid gold chance of dying happy.

The Gift of Lessons

Events come around us, you see. Lessons in camouflage, returning over and over again. They pass in a circular orbit yet move further away as we learn to discern their true meaning. Imagine yourself at the centre of a series of orbiting lessons, all passing at different times. The eventual outward trajectory is the natural course for Universal lessons. Early in our evolution, events come hard and fast; the closer, the more intense. They burn.

As we discover how to transmute events into lessons, recognising the Trojan Horses they undoubtedly are, we master acceptance and the secrets of our mistakes. We no longer embody the trauma. *We suffer less.* Thus, subconsciously and consciously, we indicate to the Universe that we require fewer such lessons. And since the Universe is us, the Universe concedes. Hence, the lessons become few and far between. Still orbiting, they possess a lower intensity as they travel to outlying regions. Now, far from being immersed in the torrent of emotional experience, we witness them with less attachment, less suffering, and more gratitude and love.

Thank you for the gift of trauma.

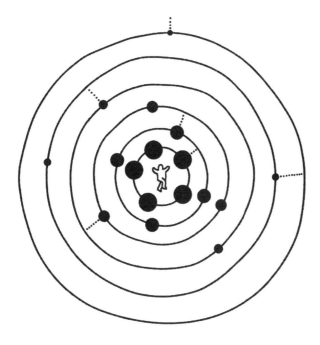

Lessons in Orbit.

Playing the Game

For each of us, attaining and maintaining mental-spiritual equilibrium will vastly vary depending on work, home life, and our general environment. And whether you make meaningful changes as outlined in this book's previous pages while being sure not to skip your Shadow Work. As with much of the advice I've laid down, all I can say for sure is that this worked for me — a man on the mend. And armed with these powerful tools, knowing myself as I now do, I can lovingly observe the gentle play and tussle between my spirituality and humanity.

At a certain point in his career, Ram Dass realised that he was working so hard on the path towards enlightenment that he resented his humanness. Such inner acrimony is typical for people seeking personal truth and growth. We work tirelessly to become someone (or something) else, often at the cost of forgetting our roots. And at the root of those roots is a simple truth: we attend Earth School to learn to love in a simulation designed to make such a phenomenon a worthwhile challenge. And playing the game as conscious and proactive participants, we learn more of our myriad wondrous facets. Thus, to wish we were not human — to seek ascension on Earth and rise above our fellow brothers and sisters is another sneaky trick residing up the hairy sleeves of the Monkey. Perhaps he's protecting us from the pain of facing unhealed trauma. Maybe he's gotten carried away with the airs and graces of his new identity. To wear one's spirituality as a form of identification is ego in drag. Military-grade stealth drag, but drag all the same. So keep a mindful eye on those hairy hands.

While doing this work, you must hold love for yourself at all times. That means avoiding self-judging or scolding over your personal development expectations. Hell, try not to have any expectations, as they're just another form of attachment, which, as we've learned, will lead to more suffering.

Remember, we're not necessarily trying to be gurus or ascended beings. We're here for a human experience. If we're pushing to be even five per cent better, that's beautiful. It's awareness in action, a higher state of consciousness exploring its potential. To do this work is to ask oneself, "Who am I?" So kudos to you for whatever you're doing, wherever you are on the path. You are leaning into your creator being nature; you are awake. Just as I know nothing, you are imperfectly perfect. When we practise, we enhance our human experience, so never think ill of yourself if you falter. Your practice might take an entire life cycle. This is an excellent use of time. This is the mission.

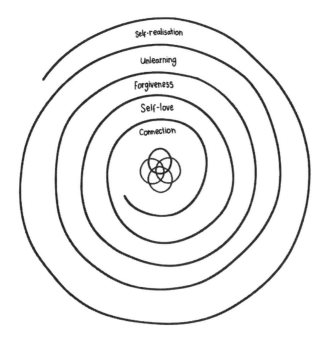

Aerial Anatomy of Happy.

The game is to know and be yourself, to take what you've learned, roll with the punches, and use breath and gratitude as your weapons of mass tranquillification. In this place, we're no longer looking down; we're looking around the expansive sky and landscape of learning and love. From this vantage point, we can see others playing at various game stages, all with their own hills to climb. And we want the same for them as that which we've learned. So, rather than looking down at them, we use those short-cuts to pop over and visit. How might we help without rescuing? How might we enable them without losing sight of ourselves? Exercising compassion, armed with healthy boundaries, means we can do just that. And in service to others, in helping them heal, we mend another tiny fracture of ourselves.

There are many ways to work on your mind, spirit, and body — enough teachings to fill a library. In *How To Die Happy*, I've introduced a mere handful to provide inspiration. Follow the process, using whatever methods and practices work for you. Regardless of your chosen techniques, be mindful of the cruciality of embracing your Shadow Self. Also, observe the non-linear nature of the Anatomy of Happy. Grasping this process and a subsequent daily practice will transform your mastery of the art of living. So set aside the banality of doing, and get busy with the business of being.

CHAPTER FIFTY-ONE

Write Your Own Eulogy

**Only in the agony of parting
do we look into the depths of love.
— George Eliot**

Anyone who's been to a Western funeral has likely heard or given a eulogy. The point of the address is to observe and celebrate the deceased's life. Anyone who knew the dead person can read the eulogy, be they family, close friends, a priest, or cleric.

I've heard some downright miserable eulogies; poorly written and poorly delivered through snot and tears. I've also witnessed a couple of absolute belters — the best was about my friend Bob, who, thanks to terminal cancer, had time to plan his funeral. And plan he did. Bob's was one of the rare ones, as most of the other funerals I've attended were sombre affairs, missing the whole point of the get-together, failing in the main to celebrate the dead folks' life.

Life is a ritual; a celebration.

So, I thought it might be a worthwhile exercise to invite you to write your own eulogy — here and now — still living the fantasy that you've only five minutes left to live. Not to say you have minutes left to live and write this eulogy (the pressure); the point is to continue the fiction that you are not long off kicking the bucket. The twist? You can't write it from you. Remember: it'll be a family member or friend, or if you're really unpopular, a cleric who didn't even know you. The double twist? Don't hold back. Assume this eulogy can be delivered as unfiltered brutal truth and with the gloves off — the way eulogies ought to be written.

What will they say at your funeral? Perhaps more important-ly, what won't they say? Were you loving and compassionate? Or always too busy to visit? Were you fearless, living your wildest dreams? Or were you famous for holding a grudge? Did you wear your heart on your sleeve? Or did folks find it challenging to connect with you? Were you love incarnate?

I don't believe there's a hard and fast rule about how long a eulogy ought to be, but the internet says that twenty minutes is too long. Also according to the internet, a typical eulogy should be between two and ten minutes. It's really up to you how much you write; it's your funeral.

Now then, somewhere in this book, I've already said that what others think of you is none of your business. Suspend that concept for this exercise. When you write it, assume your eulogy will be a collective of opinions and feelings from all your nearest and dearest. Try to put yourself in their shoes. And remember that on this rare occasion, your eulogy will be beyond brutally honest and pull no punches whatsoever. Gloves off.

The brutally honest eulogy they'll deliver at my funeral

In following this exercise, you've just written some solid gold truths about yourself — perhaps even your shadow Self. Kudos for your unfettered self-reflection and vulnerability. Depending on what you've written, there might be a nugget or two in that speech. Perhaps it uncovered some opportunities for growth or a new perspective. Some issues you now have time to address before they become end-of-life regrets. If you're game, combine it with the regrets you wrote at the beginning of this book. It's a place to start, at least. I've left another blank page for you.

Opportunities for my growth

CHAPTER FIFTY-TWO

Beginnings Need Endings

In the end, these things
matter most: how well did you
love? How fully did you live?
How deeply did you let go?
> — Buddha

Perhaps it's befitting that I'm writing the final chapter on a ferry crossing between the Indonesian islands of Bali and Lombok. In Greek mythology, Charon (or Kharon), the Ferryman of Hades, would take the newly deceased across the River Acheron (later known as the River Styx), dividing the worlds of the living and dead. As the spiritual legend goes, if you could not pay the Ferryman, you'd be left behind to exist as a floating spirit for all eternity. Unsurprisingly, this supernatural fear porn had people going for the idea in a big way.

Short-change the Ferryman and wind up a floating ghost for all eternity? No, thank you very much!

So the dead were sent to rest with coins placed over their eyelids or mouths to ensure the Ferryman would carry them to the afterlife. The tradition was adopted by the Greeks, Romans, Celts, and Western Europeans. The Christians then carried it on into the 19th and 20th centuries. Is it still happening now? Imagine an ethereal entity requiring payment in fiat currency today.

They'd be the first to point out its lack of worth. In the 21st century, ensure you're buried with a portable crypto wallet to avoid becoming a lost ghost for all eternity. The Ferryman prefers Bitcoin.

With today's distractions, we conveniently worry less about living and dying. Work, endless streaming TV, computer games, online courses, pornography, alcohol, drugs, and gambling. Sports and reality TV, social media, and dating profiles. Most of which are available through devices that rarely leave our side. It's all out there for us. And what's around the corner? The Metaverse! An illusion within an illusion, where your avatar creates an avatar to explore a sprawling digital world and its inhabitants. Further separation. A dream inside a dream. How to wake up from that? One can only hope that the brands and participants planning to play in this virtual world have a mindful eye on mental health. Though, I won't be surprised if there's a meditation centre or two. The irony.

The branches of distraction continue to grow, offering boundless opportunities for mental clutter. We create, and we consume, ever hungry for more. Some assert that this life is fulfilling; I respect that truth. Others yearn for a deeper understanding of *why* we are here. They realise that simplicity is necessary to create space for self-discovery. This is my truth.

Spirituality

Phrases like "spiritual awakening" cause many to run a mile because they're not yet connected to their spiritual nature. That's okay. Where you are on your journey is where you are. You're where you need to be. My question is: what does "spiritual" mean to you? Many of us see it specifically as religious, which is a turn-off for folks with zero interest in dogma. But you don't need to be interested in religion to be highly attuned to your spirituality if you can see there's truth in all religions, but no religion is the absolute truth. And if we strip away the unnecessary rules and regulations set forth by man, at the very heart of spirituality lies love.

Spirituality speaks to that which is connected to the human spirit or soul. We are more than our minds since the mind is a practical tool. Therefore mindfulness philosophies and practices are also spiritual. Metaphysics and spirituality are one since neither relies on the five senses. My ethereal affinity has dramatically enhanced my happiness, and I am not alone in this understanding. My exploration inward — into meditation, yoga, and psychedelic use — has shown me that death is nothing more than another transitional stage of an infinite process. However, embracing the practice of acceptance, I have no desire to convince you of your spiritual nature, thus such inward inquiry is yours and yours alone. I support those who seek help, equally accepting those who do not. Ultimately, my only wish is that all people realise their connection with themselves and others. All this book was ever meant to be was a collection of the teachings of others, personal stories highlighting our shared experience, and transformative practical utilities for living and dying well. Therefore, I hope that you've found something amidst these pages. A seed of inspiration, a tool or two, or an alternative truth that resonated either subtly or profoundly. If these pages helped on any level, I have done what I set out to do.

Choosing to Change

Choosing change might require a significant wake-up for some. You don't have to wake up to your god-state nature or the existence of infinite dimensions, of which yours is just one. Nor is there a need to wake up to the notion that you're pure awareness reincarnating to experience myriad facets of yourself inside a giant hologram just for shits and giggles before returning home. I am, however, suggesting that to advance as a species, we must wake up to the dualistic dream spell into which we were born. To radiate and thrive, we must overcome our illusory separateness and learn to embrace oneness in our branches and roots.

Let Go of Fear

Live in the now. Be mindful of all that you consume. Fill your heart, every moment, and every day, with gratitude for the simple things you love — right down to the breath in your lungs. Meditate, breathe, move, and sing. Learn to accept that which you cannot change. Reclaim your sovereignty. *Be.* Then, at the very least, you'll take control of your life. Learning how to live well, your heart will show you how to die happy.

Notice when you judge yourself. Notice yourself noticing yourself judging yourself. Remember what the Buddhists call *Right Thinking*, a deep understanding of which will change your life forever. And if you fall, don't worry. Don't kick yourself when you're down because the magical getting-up part comes next. Mistakes are lessons in disguise, wearing the coat of impermanence. Look for the alchemy.

We can create change by working on ourselves, so our pasts and futures no longer control us. We can make great strides towards a life brimming with growth, peace, community, and love. The more we heal together, the more beauty and wonder we see every day. And the more we witness, the more enriched we shall be by our experience of Heaven on Earth. And it's in this place that I aspire to dwell.

Becoming Nothing

As for me? I'm just a man on the mend who learned something through the realisation that I knew nothing, which is exciting. But I have transitioned from being utterly deaf to my words and blind to my deeds to now being able to witness the voice in my head and Monkey, constantly trying to joyride my Earth Rover to undesirable neighbourhoods. I now carry a little shopper bag containing healthy and practical tools to lighten my mood and energise my mind and body. I avoid words that are untrue, unkind, and unnecessary. And if and when I do slip, I've learned to exercise the grace and humility to accept responsibility for my mistakes; to admit when I am wrong. It's taken me 47 years to realise all of this, and choose the path of becoming nothing, thus deconstructing the illusion that was me.

To die before one dies — what a glorious gift indeed.

What twists or turns await the remainder of the Martin Story? Perhaps you and a few other folks will enjoy this book, and the winds of change will blow once again. Or not. Such a transition would make me very happy, but I'll do well to avoid attachment to such an outcome. Honestly, it doesn't matter. What counts is where I am right now — beyond grateful for this life and its great experiential lessons. Despite the curveballs and catastrophes, I've had an absolute blast. And I am equally thankful for you and the magic you offer this world.

If ever (whenever) you feel lost at sea, focus on the basics: the Zen Venn. Make regular observational checks on whether any remnants of conditioning are at play in your thoughts or behaviour. Monkey is cunning like that. *Am I being kind to myself? Am I letting go? Am I allowing and encouraging a deep connection with those around me, cultivating further growth and opportunity?* Simple.

Okay, so it's *not* simple. You get that I know that, right? But then, as previously asserted, there is no silver bullet or magic pill. If it were simple, we'd all be fixed in a jiffy, and Earth School would have nothing to teach. Follow the process and experience less friction. The journey is worth every step, along which you'll discover incredible experiences you previously thought impossible. Growth requires hard work, practice, patience, and surrender. And above all, you have to want it. Don't be scared to let go of thoughts, emotions, and traits that no longer serve you. While it's perfectly normal to fear the unknown, remember that all endings make room for new beginnings.

The Gift of Happiness

Speaking of surrender, do you recall my friend Sarah from Chapter 14? During her visit to Bali, we discussed my chequered history with female partners. So she took me through a *perfect partner* manifestation exercise which included considering how I should like to feel in this imaginary woman's presence. It was a fun and heart-opening exercise, quickly forgotten after Sarah left and life moved on. Besides, after my previously prolific mistreatment of women, I wondered if mine might be a future of solitude.

A few months later, I met Jules and experienced all those feelings and more. This cool, laid-back, blue-eyed yogi embodied everything from the exercise. She had travelled the world and was profoundly spiritual yet equally unaffected. She was beautiful and humble. *She was love.* Jules cultivated a newfound peace in me; I was excited to learn from her while overwhelmingly contented by her presence. Covering her left shoulder and arm is an exquisite tattoo of a peacock. On the inside of her right forearm is a tattoo of a Sanskrit mantra:

Lokah samastah sukhino bhavantu.

Well, now, serendipitously, I was familiar with this prayer, as you may recall. Revealed as it was to me during a silent retreat, where I learned to love. What a wonderfully cosmic coincidence that this mantra should return to me in such a synchronicitous way.

It is a gift to be shared. Words that embody a new life, having shed the old. And thus, with sincere wishes of love, I now offer this prayer from my heart to yours:

लोका: समस्ता: सुखिनो भवन्तु
Lokah samastah sukhino bhavantu.

May all beings everywhere be happy and free, and may the thoughts, words, and actions of my own life contribute in some way to that happiness and to that freedom for all.

May *you* be happy, friend. And through all your endeavours, may you be free.

A Sidenote About Appreciation

With all my heart, I hope that you enjoyed this book. If so, please spread word of its existence. It may not seem so important, but rest assured that independent authors can crash and burn or soar to dizzying new heights, all thanks to reader reviews. So if you want to give *this* author a virtual hug, please go onto Amazon or GoodReads, and rave about How To Die Happy. And perhaps recommend it to a friend or two.

If you'd like to read more of my work, my newsletter shares essays and articles designed to improve one's experience of the Samsaric game of life. Subscribe via howtodiehappybook.com.

If you want to discuss specific themes from the book, send me an email or DM. I love talking about this stuff.

Now then, appreciation goes both ways, so it's my turn. *Thank you* for reading this book and for walking this incredible path of self-discovery. Healing creates a ripple like a pebble in a pond; the many benefits from the one. And so there is no act more heroic than to heal oneself.

May all beings be happy.

Made in United States
Orlando, FL
07 March 2024